Russia as I know it - Primary Source Edition

Harry De Windt

RUSSIA AS I KNOW IT

RUSSIA
AS I KNOW IT

BY

HARRY DE WINDT, F.R.G.S.

AUTHOR OF

"SIBERIA AS IT IS," "FINLAND AS IT IS," "THE NEW
SIBERIA," "PARIS TO NEW YORK BY LAND," ETC.

WITH NUMEROUS ILLUSTRATIONS

PHILADELPHIA
J. B. LIPPINCOTT COMPANY
LONDON: CHAPMAN & HALL, LTD.
1917

PRINTED IN GREAT BRITAIN BY
RICHARD CLAY & SONS, LIMITED,
BRUNSWICK ST., STAMFORD ST., S.E.,
AND BUNGAY SUFFOLK.

TO

MY FRIEND

GERARD WARRINER

FOREWORD

This work is not to be regarded as an authority on political, military or social questions connected with that vast empire, which, to most Englishmen, is a sealed book, for it has been chiefly compiled from rough, and hitherto unpublished notes, casually jotted down during my travels throughout European and Asiatic Russia. These wanderings amount in the aggregate to over 50,000 miles, and I may therefore, perhaps, claim to speak with some authority on the conditions of life in a country where I have passed, with intervals, nearly four years of my life.

Thus, I have travelled, on various occasions, from Pekin to Moscow (before the construction of the Trans-Siberian Railway), from Petersburg to Bombay (via Little Russia, the Caucasus, Persia, and Baluchistan), and from Paris to New York "*by land*," which latter journey (hitherto unaccomplished) took me from Moscow to the Béring Straits. I have also (by special desire of the Imperial Government) twice visited Siberia in order to investigate its penal methods, these tours of inspection including the famous silver mines of Nertchinsk, and prisons on the island of Sakhalin. Previously to this, Mr. George Kennan, the American traveller, had horrified the civilized world with his account of the sufferings of Siberian exiles, and my journeys of inspection were undertaken with the sole object of verifying this gentleman's statements, which, however, I was unable to do, the result of my inquiries being as favourable as Mr. Kennan's were the reverse. I may add that my views on the Siberian Exile system have since been endorsed by English travellers of repute who have followed in my footsteps, although during my prolonged Press controversy with Mr. Kennan I was accused, by more than one English newspaper, of having received a large sum

vii

of money from the Russian Government in order to
" whitewash " its prisons ! [1]

I shall now, however, deal chiefly with European
Russia, without omitting those minor details of town and
provincial life which, for obvious reasons, are not to be
found in more serious works on the subject. Wherefore
the average Englishman has, at present, the vaguest
notions about everyday life in the Tsar's great empire,
and this I frequently find when on returning therefrom,
I am invariably asked : " What sort of a place is it ? "
and pestered with questions on subjects so trivial, that
only one intimately acquainted with the country could
furnish the desired information. My present object,
therefore, is to present a bird's-eye view, so to speak, of
the cities, towns, and villages of Russia, and to describe
people of all classes, showing not only how they toil and
take their pleasure, but also how the stranger may best
conform to their occasionally curious manners and
customs. For I anticipate that, when this war is over,
thousands of my countrymen will visit Russia not only
on business, but pleasure bent, and it is for their benefit
that I shall now relate everyday experiences which,
although they would be out of place in an ordinary book
of travel, may prove useful to those in quest of a new
playground. And if the information thus gleaned
affords these tourists of the future any assistance in their
wanderings through the most mysterious, and therefore
most fascinating, country in Europe, *Russia as I know It*
will not have been written in vain. It is necessary to
state, however, that the earlier portions of this work
were compiled before the recent political crisis.

In conclusion I must express my thanks to Sir George
Newnes, Mr. John Murray, Messrs. Chapman & Hall,
and Messrs. Nelson & Sons, for kindly permitting me
to quote a few extracts from previous works of mine on
Russia and Siberia which these firms have, from time to
time, published.

HARRY DE WINDT.

Garrick Club, London,
   April 1917

---

[1] See *Siberia as It is* and *The New Siberia*, by the author.

CONTENTS

LIST OF ILLUSTRATIONS

RUSSIA AS I KNOW IT

CHAPTER I

PETROGRAD—FIRST IMPRESSIONS

I SHALL never forget the first time I crossed the German frontier into Russia, chiefly because the fact of my so doing changed the whole current of a life which had hitherto been devoted to anything but geographical or penal research. This was at Eydtkunen, one day in early autumn, when although the sun blazed from a cloudless sky, there was a chilly nip in the air, which, oddly enough, had been unnoticeable, an hour before, in Germany. Also, on alighting from the train, I became aware of a strange and subtle odour (the characteristic "Russian smell"), of which the chief ingredient is apparently smoked leather, and which, as I have since discovered, permeates the empire from the Baltic Sea to its Arctic confines at Yakutsk.

I stood, for a while, on the platform, noting the striking contrast between desolate, grey-green plains, rolling northwards to the horizon, and the wooded hills, red-roofed villages and yellow cornfields which now lay behind me to the south. Two great empires are here divided by a narrow, sluggish stream, where ducks disported themselves, and on the further side of which a dapper little Prussian sentry in "Pickelhaube" and sky-blue tunic aggressively strutted to and fro; while, on the nearer bank, a gigantic Russian linesman, in long drab overcoat, leant on his rifle and stared at him, much as a surly mastiff might view the antics of a performing poodle. For there was no love lost between Ivan and Fritz, even in those days, and on this lonely frontier, where mutual boredom might well have fostered temporary good fellowship, although I was assured that

B

anything of this nature between the confronting outposts was unknown.

My passport had been taken from me, before leaving the train, by a stalwart policeman who now approached and politely invited me to accompany him to the " passport room " in order to obtain permission to enter Russia. I could not, at that time, speak a word of the language, being under the impression that to master it must involve months of close and constant study. But this is a fallacy; for Russian is just as easily acquired as any other foreign tongue provided you merely wish· to express your needs, and this any ordinary intelligence should be able to accomplish in a couple of months. The chief difficulty is to master the letters and sounds, and the rest is then plain sailing. To become really proficient is, of course, another matter; yet there is no country in Europe (except perhaps France) where people are more anxious to assist you in this respect, or display more tolerance when you make ridiculous mistakes.

I found my fellow-travellers herded like sheep in a pen, in a spacious whitewashed hall, where nearly an hour elapsed before documents were returned to owners entitled to proceed on their journey. A flashily-dressed German Jew was alone detained for further inquiries, and while this solitary victim was imploring the police to permit him to return to Berlin, double doors at the end of the room were thrown open to disclose a handsomely-furnished dining apartment with snowy tables glittering with glass and silver, and swallow-tailed, white-tied waiters in attendance. I had yet to learn that Russian railway restaurants are the best in Europe, and this sudden change from the sanded floors and greasy viands of German refreshment-rooms, where I had been compelled to swallow disgusting food in equally offensive company, was only one of many pleasant surprises which I was afterwards destined to experience, both in European and Asiatic Russia. My lunch that day would have satisfied an epicure, for it consisted of green caviar, Volga sterlet, a " rabchik " (Russian partridge), and cheese *soufflé* which, with a pint of Crimean claret and coffee cost only four roubles, or about six shillings.

Here also I enjoyed, for the first time, a real Russian "papirosh," as superior to the spurious "Russian cigarette" generally sold in London (and formerly made in Hamburg), as a delicate "Corona" to a cheap cigar.[1]

The so-called "Express" which brought me from Berlin had crawled with exasperating slowness, but its speed was meteoric compared to the "Rapide" in which I completed the journey to Petrograd. Russian railways are, however, the most luxurious (and also the cheapest) in the world—provided you are not in a hurry. The heat was stifling, for although the Russians are proverbially a hardy race, they have a strong aversion to fresh air, so the windows were kept hermetically sealed, while, at night-time, a double one was raised to further exclude draughts. But then even Siberians seldom venture out in the height of summer without an overcoat!

My first impressions of Petrograd were distinctly unfavourable, although I arrived, on this occasion, during the dead season. Yet the very name of "Petersburg" was, in those days, suggestive of an atmosphere of boundless wealth and luxury, surrounding the most brilliant and exclusive Court in Europe, and I had therefore pictured a city of glittering uniforms, beautiful women, dashing equipages and priceless jewels, where the highest in the land revelled in riotous pleasures, heedless of the silent and sinister workings of Nihilism and the secret police! The place was also usually depicted by the English novelist (probably because, in most cases, he had never been there) as being strikingly imposing, and to drive from the station to my hotel through dusty, straggling thoroughfares formed by low, whitewashed buildings, was a sad disillusion! Yet had I but known it, this feeling of disappointment was largely due to the vague sense of depression which most Englishmen experience when they enter Russia for the first time. It is also disquieting, on arrival at an hotel, to have your passport taken away by the police, who inform you that, until it is returned, you must not,

---

[1] I have of late years procured excellent and *genuine* Russian cigarettes (imported from Moscow) from Kincaid & Co., 8, Norris Street, Haymarket, S.W.

under any circumstances, leave the city. And this applies to every town, however small, throughout Russia.[1]

I have never, since that day, visited Petrograd save in winter time (when it is much less depressing), for if Russia owes her limitless wealth and prosperity to Peter the Great, she has little cause to be grateful to that illustrious monarch for his selection of a swamp as a suitable building-site. Moscow with its "Kremlin" and exquisite Byzantine architecture, is a delightful city, purely typical of the great Slav empire which it represents, whereas Petrograd [2] is merely a bad imitation of other European capitals. But its illustrious founder probably designed the place less as an imperial residence than a commercial port, the establishment of which entailed almost as great a loss of human life as the erection of the Egyptian pyramids.[3] And, during this colossal enterprise, another evil arose, for the Tsar, although an ardent patriot, was hoodwinked by unscrupulous German adventurers, who rapidly acquired a political and commercial influence which, handed down to their descendants, has only been finally eradicated by the present war.

Petrograd has a population of about two millions and, with the exception of Constantinople, the highest death-rate of any capital in Europe. This is partly owing to the scarcity of pure water, wherefore the upper classes drink only from imported mineral springs, although the poor are compelled to fill their barrels from the Neva, with occasionally disastrous results. A portion of the city is built on piles, and ominous cracks and fissures in some of the public buildings testify to the silting, unstable nature of the soil, while the cemeteries are so frequently flooded that wealthy people are often interred in southern Europe, where they may rest in peace beyond the reach of inundations.

[1] Or did, under the Empire.

[2] Peter the Great's proclivities are clearly shown by the semi-German name he originally bestowed on his capital, "Peter's 'burg." The word "grad" is the old Russian name for "town" (from which the more modern "gorod" is derived), and its adoption has, therefore, given universal satisfaction throughout Russia.

[3] Most of the quarter of a million workmen imported by the Tsar perished from epidemics and starvation.

Russians take every precaution to ward off the cold, but no one seems to provide against heat, which is therefore intolerable in summer, especially in conjunction with the stench from the numberless canals, which, in spring-time, release tons of vegetable refuse which the ice, in winter, has collected and congealed. From November until May there is rarely a blue sky and bracing frost, but piercing winds, chilly mists and a leaden sky necessitating electric light throughout the day. Petrograd is, in winter, as dark and depressing as London, while it has no *matinées*, concerts or other amusements with which more fortunate dwellers on the Thames may dispel the gloom of a foggy afternoon. And talking of winter, the Russians are just as unreasonable as the English with regard to climatic changes and adaptable habits and costume. In October (however warm and muggy it may be), they get into furs which are not discarded until late in the following spring. Their houses are also heated on a certain date for a certain period, merely because it is the custom, although I have occasionally, even in the month of November, emerged from the suffocating heat of a crowded drawing-room to walk home without an overcoat. And just in the same manner, it is assumed that the season for sledging lasts five months : accordingly, wheeled vehicles are laid up in October, and nothing but sledges are used, whether the snow lies or whether it melts, in which case you are jolted to death over cobbled streets. Winter is, however, the pleasantest season here, although a summer night, with congenial companions, may be passed agreeably enough, beginning the evening, say, with dinner at that world-renowned restaurant " The Medved " (or " Bear "), and afterwards driving out in open " droshkis," to one of the many islands on the Neva— most of which, however, are connected by wooden bridges with the mainland. Here you may sup at the open-air restaurants of " Samarkand," or " Villa Rodét," listen to really good music performed by " tsiganes," and also witness the ease with which these wandering minstrels accumulate riches at the hands of the pleasure-loving, reckless Russian " millionaire," or you may enter the " Variety " Theatre, where most of the performers are French, occasionally mingled with third-rate English, artists. Women in the audience are chiefly of the *demi-monde* type (mostly Parisian), but there is generally a sprinkling of quietly dressed ladies of society, who are escorted here for a glimpse of so-called gay life, much as they are in Paris to the *cabarets* of Montmartre. Here you may stop till early next morning or even later, if so inclined, and find when you get home that (if not a guest) your expenses have run into two figures sterling—or more—as champagne, in these places, has to be freely distributed amongst importunate females who would never dare to accost you in the street. And I may add that although Petrograd has, in this respect, not always borne the best reputation, many undesirable establishments, which used to exist in the form of assignation houses and the like have now been as severely prohibited as the sale of alcohol. But social vice, even on the islands, was never aggressively apparent, although one visit to the latter was generally sufficient. For there is no real darkness here from June until the end of August, and scenes of revelry and dissipation which may occasionally be amusing under the glare of electricity become sordid and repellent in the cold grey light of day.

Lack of exercise is probably responsible for the pallid appearance of most people of the upper class who reside here. No one ever dreams of walking for health's sake (even a servant sent on an errand takes a " droshki "), so that the women have a pallid, washed-out look, while the men (I allude to civilians), though generally tall and sturdily built, are rarely physically powerful. Both sexes spend most of their time indoors, especially in winter-time, and consume tea and numberless cigarettes in stuffy, overheated apartments, the only ventilation being from one small aperture let into a window pane and rarely opened. On the other hand, the lower orders look aggressively healthy and robust, and although few of them can afford to eat meat, they appear to thrive, even in this land of climatic severity, on a diet solely composed of " shtchi " (or cabbage soup) and black bread.

You see fewer pretty faces in Petrograd than in any

other European capital, although *quand elle s'y met,* the Russian woman of gentle birth is incomparably beautiful. Nor do you often meet a really well-dressed woman walking in the streets, for even in summer they generally wear heavy material of some sombre shade, devoid of style or smartness, while every third man appears to be in civil or military uniform, the rest affecting broadcloth or dark tweeds with a straw hat, bowler or fur cap, according to the season. In winter, every one wears goloshes, which, when entering a house, are deposited in the entrance hall. But all this, of course, applies only to the towns, the peasants of almost every Russian province wearing its typical costume, as in the cantons of Switzerland.

CHAPTER II

PETROGRAD—AN EASTER DAY

THE " Nevsky Prospekt " is one of three main arteries
which traverse Petrograd, and contains its most imposing buildings and finest shops, being also, on a fine
day, a fashionable promenade, like Bond Street or
Piccadilly.   But it is a dreary, colourless thoroughfare,
and, notwithstanding its great length and incessant traffic,
there is a provincial air about this endless avenue of
red-brick and whitewashed houses, some of which have
green iron porticoes, as tawdry-looking as the buildings
of which they form part.   The aristocracy mostly reside
in flats, and there are, therefore, but few of the imposing
private mansions which in London and Paris convey an
impression of dignity and wealth.   For even the most
expensive flats here are outwardly mean, comfortless-
looking structures, occupied by both rich and poor, and
generally surrounding a cobbled, untidy courtyard,
littered with firewood stacked for the winter.   Each
group of flats has its " dvornik " or porter, who is as
inquisitive and as great a gossip as the Parisian *concierge.*

The best and poorest shops in the Nevsky are intermingled with startling incongruity, for here you may see
a jeweller's windows blazing with diamonds, and next
to them a grimy little alcove for the sale of old clothes,
while a few yards further on a fishmonger dispenses his
wares under the nose of a fashionable florist !   Large
ironmongery, drapery, boot and fur stores abound, also
dainty sweet and cigarette shops, but there are no
furnishing emporiums of the " Waring," and " Maple "
class, London or Paris generally providing this class of
goods.   Fortnum and Mason, however, have in Petrograd worthy rivals, who provide not only ordinary
groceries and preserves, but also the special Russian

delicacies known as " zakouski," on which many people here seem to subsist to the exclusion of more substantial food, fifteen to twenty kinds being usually served before every meal. A few of these shops have little private rooms at the back, open day and night, where you can order champagne and the finest oysters, caviar, or sterlet on the market, for the fair one of your choice. Kousnetzof and Románof (on the Nevsky) also provide a daintily cooked repast to follow, or used to do so, for these customs may have changed since the war.

Personally, I do not (as the reader may have inferred) care about Petrograd, for it lacks the typical beauty of Moscow, the sylvan charms of Kieff, and Parisian aspect of Odessa. But although I prefer the aforementioned cities, the capital certainly possesses many unique objects of interest, amongst them one of the finest cathedrals in the world : St. Isaac's. And, by the way, I passed on my way thither (during a short walk from my hotel), a Catholic, Dutch, and Lutheran place of worship, besides a Jewish synagogue, thereby realizing that the stories which I had heard in England anent religious persecution in this country were about on a par with the falsehoods which, at one time, were freely disseminated about the inhuman treatment of Russian exiles.

The glittering dome of St. Isaac's is a familiar landmark visible for many miles, and its golden cross (thirty-three feet higher than that of St. Paul's) surmounts one of the most beautiful and costly churches in the world, the foundations of which alone cost £200,000 ! Enormous sums were contributed towards its erection by Catherine of Russia, and donations have poured in ever since from all classes of people, from the reigning Tsar to the humblest " moujik." St. Isaac's, therefore, now possesses a prodigious amount of treasure, of which the gold and silver articles alone weigh over two tons, while its jewelled " ikons " and sacred vessels, old and modern paintings, and marvellous mosaics must be worth many millions of roubles.

I first went there on an Easter Sunday when the building was crowded with worshippers, for this is, in Russia, the principal festival of the year. And having

just left a bright, sunlit street I stood, for a moment,
half dazed by the gloom of that vast, domed structure
faintly illuminated by flickering tapers, as I listened, spell-
bound, to the chanting of a wondrously trained choir.
Never, even at St. Peter's in Rome, have I listened to
such exquisite sacred music, and although there was no
organ (it is forbidden in the Greek Church), the extra-
ordinary depth and volume of bass voices amply atoned
for any lack of instrumental accompaniment. Some of
the Gregorian hymns I heard that day were many
centuries old,[1] and I was destined, in after years, to hear
those plaintive melodies sung by unhappy beings with
even more sadness and pathos than by the choristers of
St. Isaac's—in the prisons of Siberia.

A sudden air of life and gaiety pervades Petrograd
on Easter Day, when the long Lenten fast comes to an
end, for the greeting " Cristos Voskress "[2] has a more
significant meaning here than among less devout nations
who do not practise the same amount of religious self-
denial. Easter eggs are purchased all over the city, from
those taken from the hen-roost and stained in bright
colours, to others, delicately wrought in gold and set
with jewels, in the jewellers' shops of the Nevsky.

On this occasion the streets were packed with dense
crowds, every restaurant was crowded, and I passed an
enjoyable day with a party of Russians than whom there
are no more hospitable and charming people in the
world. Lunch at the " Medved " was followed by a
drive out to the islands in " droshkis," a diminutive
victoria to seat two persons, and so narrow that the
latter hold on to each other; an act of apparent famil-
iarity which occasionally startles a stranger, especially
when the occupants are of opposite sex. I remember,
one summer evening, dining with an officer in the
" Chevaliérs Gardes," when an English friend of mine
and his wife, who had just arrived from London, were
the only other guests. Our bachelor host was rather
notorious as a " Don Juan," and his marked attentions
to the lady throughout the meal were greatly resented
by her husband, who was of a jealous disposition. After

[1] Some are said to date from the fourth century.
[2] " Christ is risen ! "

dinner a drive was suggested, and we set out in two
"droshkis," the Russian and the lady leading the way,
but when, having taken his seat, my military friend
calmly encircled his fair companion's waist, her husband
fairly exploded with amazement and wrath. "Why,
d——n the fellow's impudence!" he cried; "he's got
his arm round her now!" And it took me all my time
to explain that this was only an ordinary Russian
custom. But my friend was, I think, the most insular
Briton I ever came across, who, upon another occasion,
in midwinter, insisted upon wearing a tall silk hat on the
Nevsky, although no one ever dreams of doing so at
that season of the year, and very rarely at any other!

But to return to Easter Day, during which, by the
way, our afternoon excursion was nearly brought to a
tragic termination by an "isvostchik," who, having
partaken too freely of "vodka," collided with another
"droshki" and deposited the writer and another passenger—fortunately without injury—in the middle of
the road. These "cabmen of the North" are a strange
race, many of whom in summer work in the fields
and only become "isvostchiks" in winter-time. Their
costume is the same in every town throughout the
empire: a low-crowned cloth or beaver hat and loose,
dark coat, which reaching nearly to the feet, is gathered,
at the waist, into a voluminous pleated petticoat. The
dress worn by private coachmen is similar, but, in their
case, the head-dress and clothing are of finer material,
trimmed with fur, and in some cases richly embroidered
with gold lace. Private "isvostchiks" are generally of
huge proportions, for a fat coachman is regarded as a
sign of wealth and prosperity, while he is also preferably
selected of enormous girth to act as a wind-screen.

The "isvostchik" is a bearded, jovial fellow, but
nevertheless is full of guile and should never receive
more than a third of the sum he claims as legal fare, a
reduction which, to do him justice, he generally accepts
with cheerful resignation. These men always drive at
a furious rate (they are the only people in Russia who
ever appear to be in a hurry!), but their kindness to
animals is proverbial. I have driven thousands of miles
in "droshki," "tarantass," and sleigh, and have never

once seen a driver touch his horses with a whip, merely using the voice and reins, to which animals here seem to respond quicker than to the lash in other countries.

We also went, that afternoon, to one of the many public gardens around Petrograd, most of which, even in summer, are desolate-looking places hardly worthy of the name. In this instance, the dull frame-windows of a weather-bleached, wooden " restaurant " seemed to stare reproachfully at a vista of trampled lawns, weedy pathways, and beds of scentless flowers, while both trees and shrubs displayed the absence of verdure with which nearly every so-called " Garden " in northern Russia seems to be stricken. But there were crowds of holiday-makers (especially young officers and the Petrograd type of *midinette*), plenty of music, and refreshments galore, and although barely two hours had elapsed since lunch, my host now insisted on ordering " zakouski," cakes, and sweetmeats which were served in the verandah around a hissing " samovar." Some people are under the impression that the latter has cryptic powers of producing super-excellent tea, whereas it is merely a gigantic kettle, of complicated shape, filled with hot water, which is kept at boiling point by a metal tube running down the centre, and filled with live charcoal. The ordinary " samovar " (a Tartar invention) is made of brass or copper, but I have occasionally seen some exquisitely chased and engraved, and made of silver—or even gold.

The fashionable world in Petrograd dines early, seven o'clock being the usual hour, but this evening I returned to my friend's house for another elaborate meal which was served even earlier, and left me wondering how any human frame could possibly assimilate such an abundance of food in such a limited space of time ! We then adjourned to the opera to hear Glinka's *La Vie pour le Tsar*, the work of one of Russia's greatest composers, and it has always struck me as strange that although Tchaikovsky, Moskovsky, and others of their class, are deservedly popular in England, yet Glinka (whom some Russians deem superior to them all) is seldom heard of.

The Opera House here is as large as Covent Garden, but it is a barn-like place, and the audience seemed to lack distinction, for evening dress was only compulsory on "gala" nights, when the performance was attended by the Tsar and Tsaritza and a gorgeously-apparelled Court. The scene was then one of unrivalled splendour, in which priceless jewels, dazzling uniforms, and costly flowers were confusedly blended, although the unattractive appearance of the "proscenium" rather marred the effect of an otherwise brilliant spectacle. It seemed strange that a State which annually lavished millions of roubles on the finest operatic artists, should not have expended a comparatively unimportant sum to provide them with a more suitable setting.

The Russian ballét is, of course, the finest in Europe, as all those must be aware who, in England, have witnessed the inimitable grace of Pavlova and Kyasht. Catherine of Russia was the first to introduce professional dancing from France and Italy, since which period all the principals engaged in these performances receive a fixed salary from the Government, and, at the end of fifteen years, a substantial pension. But every first-class theatre in Petrograd is subsidized by the State, and English plays, translated into Russian, are very popular; their répertoire ranging from *Romeo and Juliet* to *Charley's Aunt!* Shakespeare is also idolized, and it is said that the Empress Catherine was so inspired by his works that she once essayed to write a tragedy, on the literary merits of which, however, historians are ominously silent.

The opera was over early, and having thanked my host for his kindness and hospitality, I was about to return to my hotel, which, however, Madame would not hear of, urging as an additional inducement, that supper was awaiting us at their house. So we sat down to yet another meal of several courses, which was gaily and indefinitely prolonged, for wit and champagne flowed freely. Only country people retire here at anything like a normal hour; and two or three a.m. (in the towns) is regarded as rather early for bed than otherwise! And the supper was as enjoyable as such gatherings generally are in Russia, where the men are always friendly towards an Englishman, and the women, as a rule, amusing and well read. London and its doings were the chief topic of conversation, for of recent years interest in Paris has somewhat declined in favour of the former, probably by reason of the friendly relations which, even before the war, existed between the two nations and which have since been cemented into a staunch and, let us hope, permanent alliance.

Supper was followed by music and cards, and while I was being initiated into the mysteries of " vindt," or Russian whist, Madame and her friends retired, leaving the men to their game. At its conclusion my inde-fatigable host suggested a last " snack " of sandwiches and pale ale, but I, this time, firmly resisted all remonstrances, and finally took my leave, at six o'clock in the morning! So ended my first experience of a Russian Easter Day!

The palaces in and around Petrograd are worth seeing, although only a few could formerly be visited without a special order. It was once my privilege to be received at Gatchina on an occasion when the Ex-Tsar (then Tsarévitch) was graciously pleased to accept one of my works on the Russian penal system; but with the exception of the Anitchkoff within the city, and Pavlosk on its outskirts (where I visited General Kireéf—a brother of the famous " O. K.," [1]), I have entered no other imperial residence. The Winter Palace, on the banks of the Neva, is perhaps the most interesting, not only by reason of its imposing exterior, but also the air of silence and mystery with which it is (or used to be) eternally enveloped. For the " Little Father " was here as well and secretly guarded as the Grand Lama of Thibet, and thousands of troops were employed for this purpose. I remember standing, one winter's night, in the square in front of the palace, and watching squadron after squadron of mounted Cossacks defile, like moonlit spectres, around the great building, the tramp of their horses muffled by deep snow—for this was one of the precautions then taken every night, from sunset until dawn, and throughout the year. And this ghostly patrol was typical of the powerful but secret machinery which was formerly kept perpetually in motion to ensure the personal safety of the sovereign. The Winter Palace has only of late years been used for important Govern-

[1] Madame Olga Novikoff.

ment functions, *levees* and Court balls. There were three
of the latter during the winter season; one attended
by about 3000 guests, and one to which only about a
third of that number were invited. The third was
limited to the most exalted members of the aristocracy, officials of the highest rank, and representatives
of the Powers, and took place at the "Hermitage,"
a continuation of the Winter Palace. Fabulous sums
were expended by the State upon this ultra-exclusive
entertainment, which, from all accounts, was so artistic-
ally conceived and lavishly organized that it resembled
a scene from fairyland.

The Tsar drove out in public less than any other
European sovereign, and, when in the streets of Petrograd, I never saw the Empress, who, by the way, was
generally called the "Tsarina" in other countries,
although such a title did not exist! "Tsaritza"
is the nearest approach to it, but Russians always
alluded to their Majesties as the "Emperor" and
"Empress" when speaking to a foreigner, and as the
"Gosudar" and "Gosudarinya" amongst themselves,
the Tsar, at Court, being invariably styled "Imperator."
"Tsarévitch" was another title which was rarely heard
in Russia, "Naslyednik" or "the heir" being generally
used.

I shall not attempt to describe the famous "Hermitage" with its valuable paintings by Vandyck, Rubens,
and other great masters, exquisite art-treasures, and
perhaps richest museum in Europe; nor the Imperial
Treasury and its crown jewels, the Admiralty, or "Corps
des Mines," in which latter one can faintly realize the
inexhaustible mineral resources of this great empire, for
details of these may be found in any guide-book. I may
mention, however, one object which attracted my
attention : the colossal bronze statue of Peter the Great,
and especially its pedestal, an enormous block of granite
which, weighing over 15,000 tons, was dragged from the
marsh where it was unearthed, five miles away, by
primitive machinery and 80,000 horses.

Every Russian town has its public market, which is
extremely convenient, for a stranger has no occasion to
inquire : "Where is this or that to be bought?" or

wander through a town in quest of a particular object when he is perfectly sure of finding it in the "Gostinnoi Dvor." The latter at Petrograd stands just off the Nevsky, and occupies many acres of ground. The outer buildings are two-storied and enclose a maze of streets, courts and alleys—resembling a huge human bee-hive—in which, as in the bazaars of the East, every quarter has a special article for sale. Here you may stroll for days through endless avenues of stores containing every imaginable class of goods from diamond tiaras to a coil of rope, and purchase almost anything in creation. Bargain-hunters will be most attracted towards the quarter where wonderful old "ikons," antique gold and silver, and modern second-hand jewellery are sold. It was once my good fortune to secure from the latter a tiny gold watch, of exquisite workmanship, and set with brilliants, for about one-fifth of the price it would have cost near by in the Nevsky Prospekt, whence, I believe, it originally came !

Every precaution is taken, in the Petrograd Market, against fire, the whole place being exclusively built of brick and iron, for precisely at sunset all business ceases for the night. Every shop is then shuttered and barred, and its owner returns home, while watchmen and their dogs keep guard over his property until his return early on the following morning.

CHAPTER III

HOLY MOSCOW

Moscow is about as far from Petrograd as London from Dundee, and you generally travel by the night mail, which is immaterial so far as passing objects of interest are concerned. For the tortuous line originally designed to accommodate commercial and social centres was ruthlessly condemned by Nicholas I., who, with the sole object of shortening the journey for his own convenience, called for the plans, and with pencil and ruler drew a straight line between the two cities. The stations are therefore often a considerable distance from the adjoining town, to the serious inconvenience of its inhabitants.

The ancient Muscovite city covers an enormous extent of ground—less by reason of its population (about one and a half millions) than owing to the fact that its squares, streets, parks and gardens are on such a vast scale, while the town stretches over a series of undulating hills, which render it a pleasing contrast to flat, monotonous Petrograd. My first impressions of the place were rather vague, for it would need at least a month to fully appreciate the features of historical and artistic interest which, at every turn, confront a stranger. There is, at first, a sense of incongruity, for modern thoroughfares and handsome buildings are promiscuously mingled with wooden shanties and mean-looking alleys, while portions of the city present more the appearance of a provincial town, or even village, than that of a great national centre. Only the principal streets are asphalted, others are of cobbles, with plank side-walks; some not paved at all, for even Moscow presents in places the untidy, unfinished appearance of all other Russian towns, with the exception of Odessa. Yet nowhere else

C   17

in the world will you find such a bewildering array of constructive beauty as in the Kremlin,[1] with its cluster of beautiful churches, some with golden domes, others with towers and cupolas of every imaginable hue, from maize or apple-green to the darkest shades of purple, which somehow always harmonize with the bright or sombre red-brick walls beneath them. This gorgeous carnival of colour might, elsewhere, seem tawdry and discordant, but in this atmosphere of barbaric associations it is always in keeping with the picture.

"Moskva-Matushka" (or "Little Mother Moscow") is not, as many people imagine, a very ancient city, for, with the exception' of the "Kremlin" and its churches, it does not contain a single edifice over three hundred years old, having been for centuries entirely constructed of wood,[2] and therefore constantly been burnt down. The first settlement was founded as far back as 1147, since which period this has been the scene of the most tragic events in Russian history, from wholesale massacres, in the dark ages, by Tartar hordes, to the assassination, only a few years ago, of the Grand Duke Serge. No city in creation was ever afflicted by such an appalling series of sieges, plagues, and conflagrations, or, on the other hand, ever rejoiced in a more joyful and decisive victory than when Napoleon's legions were decisively routed by those overwhelming forces, fire and cold.

The River Moskva is about the same width as the Seine, without the latter's picturesque quays, although a stone embankment has now been built along the stream, which used, in olden days, to reach the walls of the Kremlin. The latter has five entrances, through massive square towers, and near one of these, the "Nicholas Gate," is a cross commemorating the assassination of the Grand Duke, while over another (the "Spaski," or "Gate of the Redeemer") is a gold ikon representing the Saviour of Smolensk,[3] an object of such veneration that all passers-by are compelled by an armed sentry to uncover. There is a legend that

---

[1] Derived from the Tartar word, "kreml," a fortress.
[2] Wooden buildings are now prohibited.
[3] Pronounced "Smaleeonsk."

Napoleon, when riding through its portals, haughtily refused to remove his cocked hat, but that, by divine intervention, a gust of wind blew it off ! Near this spot are numberless rows of cannon captured from the French during their famous retreat, the former being embossed with the imperial crown, and bearing names like ships, such as " Immortalité " and " Sans Peur," on their breaches.

The Kremlin is not only a citadel, for its walls, which are over two miles in circumference, also enclose a palace, cathedrals and monasteries, streets and squares. It is therefore practically a town within a city, from which former rises, in solitary grandeur, the Tower of Ivan Veliki, which contains the largest (suspended) bell in the world,[1] while, in the square beneath it, mounted on a granite pedestal, is the broken " Tsar-Kolokol," in which a score of people could dine with ease. This " king of bells " (cast in the reign of the Empress Anne) weighs nearly two hundred tons, which was the primary cause of its downfall and destruction, although it always had a dull, unmusical tone, imparted by jewels recklessly cast by the reigning Tsaritza and her ladies of the Court into the melting-pot.

Russian bells are the finest in the world (from the one just described to the jangling *grelots* which have often lightened my Siberian journeys), and in Moscow there must be many thousands of all sorts and sizes, with tones varying from the deep bass of some metal monster to shrill and silvery chimes. And night or day they are never silent, for you may wake at four in the morning and hear them tolling for some monastic service or the repose of a soul, while when all are simultaneously set in motion on Easter Morn the clamour, in conjunction with salvoes of artillery, is almost intolerable. Tchaikovsky is said to have conceived his famous symphony " 1812 " on a similar occasion.

The historical and artistic treasures stored within the Kremlin are probably worth millions sterling, for the Palace alone contains a throne of solid gold set with two thousand precious stones, and the diamond crown of the Empress Anna Ivanovna, surmounted by

---

[1] It weighs sixty tons.

a ruby worth sixty thousand roubles. One may wander here for days through dimly lit churches, with altars of silver, pillars and pavements of agate and malachite, priceless vestments and tapestries, rotting with age, and exquisitely painted ikons, so encrusted with gems that the image itself is often concealed. The Cathedral of the Assumption is, if not the most beautiful, perhaps the most interesting building here, for its relics include one of the nails used at the Crucifixion, a portion of the garment then worn by our Saviour, and a painting of the Holy Virgin, with jewels attached to it worth thirty million roubles. Here you stand in the very heart of Holy Russia, for in this sacred edifice all her Tsars are crowned, which reminds me that the last coronation has, for the writer, pathetic memories by reason of its association with an unhappy woman who, shortly after the ceremony, was banished for life to Arctic Siberia. She was exiled to a place [1] which, when I reached it, had only once been visited, during the past thirty years, by beings from the civilized world, save those who had been sent there " by administrative process." The former were two sailors, whose ship (the Arctic exploring vessel *Rodgers*) was burnt in the Béring Straits, and who eventually contrived to reach this ghastly haven, after enduring, for over two months, unspeakable privations and suffering. And it was only after four months of incessant travel from Moscow, chiefly in horse and reindeer sleds, that I contrived to find this abiding-place of fourteen miserable captives, one of whom was Theisa Akimova, who had attempted to assassinate Nicholas II. during his coronation in Moscow. Akimova was well-born and still young in years, spoke several languages fluently, and had taken high honours at the Paris " Conservatoire of Music." And I learnt, from this wretched exile's own lips, how her plans had been thwarted only just in time by the secret police, and how she had nearly succeeded in killing the now Ex-Emperor by means of a bomb which, had it exploded, must also have caused serious loss of

---

[1] It is marked as " Sredni-Kolymsk " on the map, but merely consists of a few log-huts. A detailed account of the place appears in *From Paris to New York by Land*, by the author.

life in that crowded assembly. For this Theisa was condemned to death, the sentence being commuted to imprisonment for life in the God-forsaken settlement where she has probably, by this time, ceased to exist. This was the only information I could glean, on that occasion, regarding the affair, but a year or two ago I chanced to read the following account of the outrage in a work written by a friend, which, although details of the crime were carefully concealed at the time, describes how he probably witnessed the unhappy girl's arrest.[1]

" I met Harry de Windt " (he writes) " on his return from his terrible journey overland from Paris to New York, a journey that took him into that fierce district in Arctic Siberia when the temperature was fifty-one degrees below zero and occasionally fell to eighty. It was somewhere up in these latitudes that he came across a little unknown settlement of political prisoners. One was a woman who had attempted to assassinate the Tsar, Nicholas II., on his coronation. A thrill went through me as he told me how she had a bomb concealed in a glass receptacle in the form of a prayer book, for did her seizure account for an incident which sent our hearts into our throats whilst we, at the coronation of Moscow, were waiting for the Tsar to come out of the Cathedral of the Assumption and cross the Square to the Cathedral of St. Michael?

" He did not come, and suddenly in the vast crowd there was a thud and a moving struggle. The dust went up, and then all was quiet. Still the Tsar did not come, but when he did come, it was not from the appointed door, but from an unexpected opening between the Tribunes; and when he stepped out from beneath the canopy near where I was placed he looked deadly blue-white. It was at that moment that I was able to take a photograph of the scene, afterwards enlarged by Russell our Court photographer for His Majesty and the Grand Dukes. Was this thud and scuffle, about which we never heard a word, the seizure of this woman who told her story to my friend de Windt in the icy North? "

[1] See *Reminiscences and Gossip of Men and Matters*, by James Baker (Chapman & Hall, London).

Nor was this the only tragedy on that eventful day, for, during the would-be regicide's arrest, several thousand men and women were being crushed to death on a plain outside the city while wildly surging forward to secure the enamelled tea-mugs [1] which were presented by the Tsar to his poorer subjects as *souvenirs* of the ceremony.

Most of the churches in the Kremlin were built by famous Italian architects, but the Florentine and Venetian schools of art are occasionally quaintly blended with Byzantine work. Every church is surmounted, not by one, but a number of domes, of various sizes, connected with the walls beneath them by dangling golden chains, which appear to be restraining the balloon-like spheres from soaring into space. The Cathedral of St. Michael is a contrast to the floridly decorated Assumption, having a more sombre aspect in keeping with the fact that it contains the remains of the Tsars who reigned from the fourteenth to the seventeenth century. These illustrious dead are laid to rest in coffins draped with purple velvet, and one contained the corpse of little Prince Dmitri (murdered by order of the Tsar Boris), whose embalmed features were exposed, through a sheet of plate glass, to the public gaze. Near the bier was a side chapel, brightly illumined by wax tapers, where a Mass was being said, and that solitary patch of light vividly contrasted with the surrounding gloom and stillness.

"St. Basil the Blest," which was erected in the sixteenth century by order of "Ivan the Terrible," is certainly the most curious building here, being less suggestive of human construction than of some architectural freak in a nightmare. For there is no attempt at either form or symmetry about the exterior, which is composed of crudely coloured or whitewashed walls supporting a cluster of domes, cupolas and spires of the most grotesque shapes, some inlaid with glazed tiles of great age and such brilliant hue that they resemble chips of coloured glass in a kaleidoscope. The great Napoleon must have had peculiar notions of art, for he greatly admired this atrocity (which did

[1] One is in the author's possession.

not prevent his using it as a stable for his dragoons !); while Ivan the Terrible was so favourably impressed when the building was completed, that he is said to have put the architect's eyes out in order that the latter should never build another like it ! But this is a favourite story anent despotic monarchs, and its authenticity may, in this case, be questioned, for although Ivan's insensate cruelty was sometimes that of a maniac, he could also on occasion prove himself a wise and powerful ruler, by whose strenuous efforts Siberia was annexed, and trade originally established with England. Nevertheless the Tsar's sudden demise before his eighth marriage, to an Englishwoman, Lady Mary Hastings,[1] was for the latter probably a fortunate occurrence, in view of the mysterious and probably unpleasant fate of some of the former's previous consorts.

The Palace of the Kremlin [2] rather detracts from the picturesque buildings around it, being a modern, commonplace edifice, with an exterior solely embellished by the golden spread-eagles which so freely adorn everything in Russia, from house-fronts to cigarette-boxes. It is, however, an enormous structure, accommodating over two thousand people, and some of the reception halls are very beautiful, notably those draped with the colours of various military and civil orders : black and yellow for that of St. George, crimson for St. Alexander Nevsky, and the turquoise blue of St. Andrew. The throne room is upholstered in white satin, with gilt furniture, crystal candelabra, and massive pillars of malachite, and is separated by a covered garden of tropical vegetation from the State dining-hall, the marble walls and ceiling of which are supported by columns of lapis lazuli, and where everything, including chairs and tables, is of solid silver. The suite occupied by the Tsaritza was furnished in the Louis XV. period, while the Tsar's private study was suggestive of an English gentleman's library, with its writing-table and easy-chairs, well-filled bookshelves, and modest air of comfort and seclusion. A private

[1] Daughter of the second Earl of Huntingdon.
[2] It was built in 1849 under Nicholas I.

passage leads from the Palace into the Cathedral of the Assumption, where their Majesties, when residing at Moscow, always attended Mass.

Towards sunset, one fine summer's day, I ascended the Tower of Ivan Veliky,[1] from which, by the way, on a grey wintry afternoon, Napoleon watched the fire break out which proved the forerunner of his defeat. The " Man of Destiny " must have retained unpleasant recollections of this famous belfry, for previously to this he had ordered the massive cross above it to be dismantled and sold, assuming it to be of pure gold, only to find that it was composed of gilt iron. Seen from this eminence, Russia's Holy City presented a map-like panorama of crowded white buildings, red roofs, and green gardens, from which arose the glittering domes and crosses of the greatest number of sacred buildings to be found in such a limited area throughout the world. At my feet the little River Moskva, spanned by innumerable bridges, flowed lazily through the city and out on to fertile plains, where it was lost, in a silver thread, on the horizon, while I could faintly distinguish the Sparrow Hills, whence Napoleon first beheld the promised land so soon to be torn from his grasp. White-winged pigeons circled incessantly around the tower, and one perched on a buttress close to my hand, as if conscious that no man could harm him, for here this bird is symbolical of the Holy Spirit, and therefore sacred, and legally protected. And as dusk crept over the world, and lights began to twinkle, like glowworms, about the darkening city, the bells of the Kremlin pealed out, as if at a given signal, producing such a wild and exquisite wave of melody that for many days after it lingered in my memory.

[1] Erected by the Tsar Boris Godunoff, in order to provide work for the starving population of Moscow during the great famine of 1601.

CHAPTER IV

MODERN MOSCOW

AN Englishman arriving in Moscow for the first time in summer would probably be unfavourably impressed, for it is then very hot and oppressive, while the slightest breeze raises clouds of dust. The streets are therefore uninviting on dry, sultry days, being seldom watered, while in wet weather they become seas of mud, which clings to everything, especially public conveyances, from which it is seldom removed. Closer attention to sanitation would certainly render the place healthier, although if the millions of money which have been lavished on Petrograd had been expended here, Moscow would now be one of the most attractive and salubrious cities in Europe.

Many hotels have sprung up here since the completion of the Trans-Siberian Railway, but before its construction the "Slavianski-Bazar" was the best, and superior to anything of the kind in the capital. This old-established house was so essentially Russian as to be almost a national institution, even the waiters being sallow, flat-faced "Buriats" from the Russo-Chinese frontier. The "restaurant" was decorated in the Byzantine style, and of such palatial dimensions that the numberless tables beneath its lofty dome looked like toys in a doll's house. At one end of the hall a long sideboard groaned under every imaginable kind of "zakouski," and in the centre a marble fountain plashed into a miniature lake, where sterlet disported themselves beneath a floating carpet of water-lilies. Here you could pick out your own fish, secure him with a miniature landing-net, and, a few minutes later, see him served up at table, boiled, fried, or *à la Tartare*, as the case might be. But this alluring pastime becomes expensive when this delicacy is out of season, for the diminutive sterlet which I then ingenuously landed figured on my bill at £2 ! !

The term " Holy "_is aptly applied to even modern Moscow, where you see in every street saintly images before which people invariably uncover and even occasionally prostrate themselves. This outdoor worship is not confined to the lower orders, and (with deepest respect to the Greek Church) I could not help reflecting how strange it would seem if, in the height of the season, fashionable London thus practised its devotions, say in Piccadilly or Pall Mall ! For these shrines abound even on the " Pont des Maréchaux," the principal promenade, which on a fine afternoon is crowded with private carriages, motor-cars, and fashionably dressed women, though the latter would not have dared, even seventy years ago, to walk alone in the streets, or even, a century earlier, to be seen anywhere in public. The women of Muscovy were then as jealously guarded as their Mahometan sisters of to-day, and in the older portion of the Kremlin Palace you may still see the " terem " which, in mediæval days, was solely occupied by the fair sex, and the latticed windows whence they could furtively peep at men. Peter the Great was the first to introduce free social intercourse between the sexes, and there is a drill-ground near Petrograd where its imperial founder made women march unveiled before a regiment of soldiers in order to inure them to open male scrutiny.

The best shops here have outwardly vastly improved, even during the past decade, for plate-glass fronts now replace the dingy frame-windows which formerly disclosed shabby specimens of the goods sold within. But the " Pont des Maréchaux " is now an avenue of modern and extensive establishments for the sale of jewellery, furs, and other luxuries of the rich, who may here also purchase the latest Parisian " creations " in feminine apparel and dainty underwear. The women dress better here than in other Russian towns—at any rate in the streets; while nearly everything exposed for sale in the shape of men's clothing is advertised as coming from London, but nevertheless was (before the war)

generally " made in Berlin "! For in those days
thousands of German merchants and tradesmen resided
here, and on the outbreak of hostilities public feeling
against them rose to such a pitch that within two days
all had fled or been safely interned by the authorities.
Many were, however, maltreated, and some even killed,
before they could escape the fury of the mob, which
wrecked their business premises and set fire to princely
mansions which some had erected from their ill-gotten
gains. The riots were eventually quelled by military
intervention, but not before every alien store in the
place had been looted and then burnt down, nearly
involving the whole city in a general conflagration.
The anti-German " demonstrations " in London were,
therefore, nothing compared to those which took place
in Moscow, and all Russians whom I have recently met
are amazed at the laxity of the British Government in
permitting Germans (even when naturalized) to swagger
about at liberty, while our prisoners are so barbarously
treated in their own country.

One great charm about Moscow is its undercurrent
of Oriental life, which, however, you must visit the
slums to observe and appreciate. I first came here
direct from Persia, and was therefore doubly impressed
by the aspect of some of the dingy courts and alleys
frequented by the Tsar's Eastern subjects. And one
day, while standing in a narrow, crowded passage,
where light filtered through a smoke-begrimed roof on
ragged Kirghiz, wild-eyed Circassians, and even white-
robed merchants from Merv, I could scarcely realize
that I was again in Europe. The familiar odour of
spices and roasting " kabobs," clink of water-sellers'
cymbals, and snarling of mangy curs, were much more
suggestive of some remote bazaar in the Far East.

My friend the late French author, Aurelien Scholl,
once remarked to me that a lovely city without greenery
resembled a pretty woman shorn of her locks. " For
what," urged this charming writer, " would even my
beloved Paris look like without trees and verdure? "
And additional charm is lent to even beautiful Moscow
by the now drained and cultivated moat around the
Kremlin, and the many public and private gardens

which here present a less neglected appearance than usual. Nevertheless the only real gardens in Northern Russia (according to our English ideas) are those which cost large sums of money, and are composed of tropical and hot-house plants kept under glass. I saw one of these at a house in Moscow owned by a rich manufacturer who, although his name is Scotch, could not speak a word of English. And I have since met many descendants of canny Scots who sought employment under Peter the Great, and also Russianized Frenchmen whose forefathers fought under Napoleon, and who, after his retreat, remained in the country and became loyal subjects of the Tsar. Even General Skobeleff, of Central Asian fame, was of British extraction, his family having changed their name from Scobell.

Before the war German was more widely spoken in Russia than French, but now the former language is strictly prohibited and every one is learning English, especially in the mercantile world, for after peace has been declared an enormous increase of trade with Great Britain is anticipated. Up till now the English in Russia have been commercially overwhelmed by the wily Teuton, who, as he was frequently a native of the Baltic provinces, and therefore practically half Russian, possessed an enormous advantage over the Britisher with his insular customs and ignorance of the language. The latter has always been the chief stumbling-block to Britain's commercial relations here, and as our language is now being so eagerly acquired in Russian schools, a similar movement in England would surely prove useful in view of our approaching struggle to capture Russian trade from Germany, which the Huns, when the war is over, will surely make desperate efforts to re-establish.

These were the views of my Russo-Scotch host, who also imparted the fact that no two places could be more socially dissimilar than Petrograd and Moscow, the former being a city of pleasure and reckless extravagance, and the latter solely a metropolis of trade and commerce, where people were too busily engaged in making money to worry about Court or Society functions. Only the most ancient members of the nobility resided in Moscow, to whom the latter was a kind of

Quartier Saint-Germain, whence they regarded frivolous Petrograd much as the old French *noblesse* looks askance at less aristocratic dwellers across the Seine. But Society in Moscow is chiefly composed of mercantile people, who have amassed fortunes in the iron trade and in the manufacture of textile fabrics. The yearly products from the latter alone amount to something like £25,000,000, and I met on this occasion a wealthy cotton-spinner who employed over 80,000 workmen in his various mills.

There were present that day several leading lights of the commercial world and their families who hoped I preferred their city to Petrograd, to which I could truthfully reply in the affirmative. This seemed to please the ladies, who referred to the latter with an air of assumed indifference which scarcely tallied with their eagerness to hear the latest news about the Court, or any recent titbit of scandal concerning less exalted beings. And while guests at similar gatherings in Petrograd had lightly discussed events in foreign social centres or matters connected with their own sporting and dramatic world, the chief topic of conversation amongst the men here was the acquisition of wealth, while their wives seemed to be engrossed in their children's ailments and the latest fashions from Paris. There was as great a contrast between the cultured refinement of the one city and the provincial tone of the other as that which characterizes the upper social circles of, say, London and Liverpool; although all here seemed convinced that Moscow must eventually supersede its neighbour as chief city of the empire, a prophecy which, however, I have never heard elsewhere expressed.

My host invited me to his charming villa near Moscow, and nearly every wealthy Russian possesses one of these " datchas " in which, as there are here so few mountain or seaside watering-places available, he generally spends the summer months. I found my friend and his family attired in peasant costume, and outwardly affecting an ultra-simple life which was hardly compatible with gambling, late hours, and the ministrations of a French *chef*. Fresh-water bathing and fishing enter largely into this rural life, and there is little else to do in the shape of amusement but to walk to the railway station and see trains arrive and depart. Meals are taken in the garden even although the weather is frequently chilly, and as these cottages are built solely for hot weather, a lengthened stay in a "datchas" under these conditions becomes a dubious pleasure. The lower classes here have a poor time of it in summer, for there are no cheap pleasure resorts and excursion trains, as in England, and their holiday trips, therefore, seldom extend beyond the precincts of their native town.

My host was, as I have said, of Scotch origin, and therefore of less erratic temperament than a thorough-bred Russian, but it has always been a mystery to me how the latter ever make money by their own exertions, for, judged by ordinary standards, they are the worst business men in the world. And if "mañana"[1] characterizes indolent Spain, the word "zavtré" (which means the same thing) is equally applicable to Russian commercial methods, for every one here has a dilatory way of transacting the most important affairs, which to a stranger is incomprehensible. Having once been interested in a Siberian gold proposition, I travelled expressly to Petrograd in order to confer with the holder of the concession, whom I found a charming man, and so hospitably inclined that three days elapsed before I could persuade him even to listen to a scheme by which we both might, if successful, have made a considerable sum of money. But nothing would induce my casual friend to stick to business, the discussion of which he invariably postponed, even on the most trivial pretext, until a fortnight had elapsed, when, having lost all patience and accomplished nothing, I returned to England! This procrastination seemed to permeate the empire; and once, in Arctic Siberia, it nearly cost me my life, when the owner of a reindeer "stancia" refused, out of sheer laziness, to furnish me for several days with deer which he could have easily obtained in as many hours. He thus caused an unnecessary delay, by which my sled was nearly submerged through the rapidly melting surface of a frozen river.

[1] To-morrow.

Both indoor and outdoor places of amusement abound in Moscow, and the principal theatres are conveniently situated in the centre of the town. Here also is the " Hermitage," one of the finest restaurants in Europe, and famous for its *cuisine*, rare old vintages and wonderful gold plate, where you are served by picturesque Tartars in snow-white garb and Russian embroidery, who wear list shoes so that silent waiting may enhance the enjoyment of a generally perfect meal. In Petrograd dress clothes (or at any rate a dinner jacket) are worn at such places, but in Moscow men of the upper class rarely dress for dinner, although their ladies appear in the most elaborate *toilettes*, in striking contrast to the broadcloth and tweeds of their male companions. But most men in Russia wear a uniform of some sort, or even the opera here would present a very dull appearance.

The Hermitage is an enormous building, with vast public dining-halls and a perfect rabbit-warren of *cabinets particuliers*, which, discreetly concealed, have been the scene of many a secret love meeting, and even once of a tragedy, resulting in a fatal duel and the social downfall of a fair but frail one who had hitherto graced the most exclusive circles. And while on this delicate subject I may mention that I am frequently asked which, in my opinion, is the most immoral city in Europe—a riddle easily solved, for the Eulenburg scandals and other revelations have conclusively proved that Berlin is unequalled for every form of social depravity and sordid vice. Paris, on the other hand, has always, to my mind, been greatly maligned in this respect, for London is probably much more wicked in a dull, depressing way. On the whole, I think the most dissolute European city I have known of recent years is the Rumanian capital—while Buda-Pest is a good second, or was, for the latter was morally purified (some years since) by order of the late Emperor of Austria, who from all accounts was scarcely himself a paragon of virtue ! Moscow itself was, twenty years ago, by no means a school of morals, although the hotel porter did not, it is true (like his Hungarian colleagues in the past), welcome male guests with a book containing photographs of attractive ladies willing (for a consideration) to dine, sup, and otherwise entertain the lonely stranger. Nevertheless even here the latter would (in those days) be quietly given to understand that he need never suffer, during his sojourn at the hotel, from a lack of pleasurable female companionship!

Moscow was once the chief point of departure for criminal and political offenders sentenced to imprisonment or exile in Siberia, and both men and women were formerly dispatched from its great forwarding prison on a journey which might, according to circumstances, terminate just over the Asiatic border or be prolonged as far as the Polar Sea.[1] It was in this gloomy building that I first made acquaintance with the inside of a Russian prison, a preliminary experience which led to my inspection of every penal establishment and house of detention throughout Siberia. But that is another story, and I merely mention the Moscow gaol with reference to a curious incident which occurred there during my first semi-official visit, and which tends to show that "All is not gold that glitters," especially with regard to the "distinguished foreigner" who occasionally honours England with his presence. I was accompanied by the Governor, a stern, punctilious personage who, when we had traversed numerous wards and courtyards crowded with convicts, led me to a secluded portion of the building reserved for prisoners awaiting trial. Each one occupied a separate cell, and enjoyed certain privileges which enabled him to retain his own clothes and purchase other comforts suited to his means.

"We have here a sad but interesting case," said my guide, pausing in front of a low, iron-studded door; "for this man is very highly connected, was an officer in the 'Chevaliérs-Gardes,' and speaks about a dozen languages like a native. Yet this is his third offence in Russia alone, for which he will certainly be sent to penal servitude in Siberia. It is always the same story: swindling and embezzlement. A charming and popular member of society with the instincts of a thief! Very

---

[1] Most prisoners have of recent years been deported by sea from Odessa to the island of Sakhalin.

sad ! " he added, as a gaoler drew back bolts and bars to admit us into the cell, the occupant of which rose from a table at which he had been seated. And I stared in amazement as the subdued light from a small, barred window fell upon a tall, slender figure wearing well-cut blue serge and smoking a cigarette. In a moment I had recognized those handsome features (although the latter were now partly concealed by a long, fair beard), and as our eyes met in mutual recognition, its owner sprang forward and, joyfully seizing my hands, addressed me by my Christian name ! The Governor said nothing, but fairly gaped with astonishment, which, under the circumstances, was not surprising !

Yet the explanation was simple, for this was an individual with whom only a few months before I had freely associated, and almost regarded as a friend ! When Count Tchertoff (as he then called himself) came to London he was almost unknown, but adroitly contrived to obtain admission to the best town and country houses, where he was soon regarded as a favoured guest ; indeed, he even once attended a garden-party at Marlborough House ! As the Count was apparently possessed of ample means and a guileless nature, he became immensely popular, especially amongst the members of one of my clubs, to which he was temporarily elected, and where he lost heavily at cards. Tchertoff was, in short, such a cheery and amusing companion that I felt really sorry when he left England. An unfortunate love affair was, he explained, the cause of his departure, although it is now significant that, just before the latter, a diamond tiara was stolen from a ducal country mansion in which the Count was staying at the time. But Tchertoff had, in those days, only just embarked on the criminal career which has since rendered him notorious throughout the world, for there is probably not a detective in Europe or America who has not heard, at some time or another, of that audacious prince of thieves and swindlers, Nikolai Savine.

The Count, on this occasion, blandly informed me that debt was the cause of his detention, whereas it was a jewel robbery at Warsaw which, a month later, sent him for five years to the silver mines of Nertchinsk.

D

From these, however, this daring rascal managed to escape and make his way on a small sealing vessel, via Vladivostok, to America, where, as luck would have it, I met the fugitive face to face in the Palace Hotel in San Francisco. Here Savine was posing as a wealthy French nobleman (under the name of "Count de Toulouse Lautrec"), but this time there was, on his part, no effusive greeting, for on seeing me my old friend hurriedly turned away, left the hotel, and never returned for his luggage !

Savine must now be nearly sixty years of age, and, notwithstanding all the efforts of his titled relatives to reform him, has passed quite a third of his life in prison. Only a year ago I read that he had again been convicted for a fraud committed at Pau, in France. But all efforts to explain my former and innocent association with this arch-crook failed to convince the Governor of Moscow prison, who, although I had the highest official credentials, regarded me for ever after with ill-concealed distrust !

CHAPTER V

MY FRIEND THE MOUJIK

I CALL him my friend as he has so often proved one when I have urgently needed his assistance. Many a time, when paralyzed with cold, have I been carried from a sleigh into his stuffy, but welcome, " izba," there to be gradually restored to life by scalding brick-tea and other comforts which even the poorest Russian peasant is ever ready to lavish upon the homeless wanderer. For hospitality is here regarded less as a virtue than as a matter of course, and the money which I have tendered on such occasions has generally been refused, even by those who could ill afford to lose a " kopek," much less entertain a hungry guest.

The Russian language is universal throughout the empire, and never varies, whether it be spoken in the *salons* of Petrograd or icebound Arctic regions. There are, moreover, no dialects, for the plebeian talks with as pure an accent as the patrician, and a man's station in life is more readily detected by his manners than by his mode of speech. This national unity also applies to Russian villages, which, although they naturally differ as to prosperity, size, and neatness, present a uniform appearance, whether they be situated in Europe or the wildest parts of Siberia. All are built of wood (for the Moujik regards stone or bricks as unhealthy to live in), and have one straggling street formed by detached cottages of various sizes, which are either thatched, or roofed with wooden slats or sheet-iron, according to the means or taste of the owner. One or two may have a second storey, and these are generally occupied by the " starosta," [1] local " tchinovnik," [2] or village priest, while even

---

[1] Head man of the village.   [2] Government official.

the squalid hovel has an enclosed space for stables, outhouses and cattle byres, where fruit and vegetables are also grown. The post-road (which is also the main street) is usually a rough, uneven, and occasionally grass-grown highway, worn into deep ruts and holes by constant traffic which in wet weather renders it a quagmire, converted in winter into a smooth sleigh track of frozen snow. Two prominent objects are the wooden church with its sky-blue or apple-green domes, and the other the granary, a spacious black barn where grain is stored for public use in case of a lean harvest. The wells are also a distinctive feature, each having two lofty poles (like the Egyptian *shadoof*), for drawing purposes, which impart a quaint Oriental touch to the landscape, while at the entrance to each village is a wooden sign-post bearing the name of the place, the number of men, horses, and cattle which it contains, and in some instances the number of versts separating it from the capital.

The Moujik generally builds his house himself, end on to the street, and although his tools are very primitive, he uses them with wonderful dexterity. Thus, an ordinary axe is made to serve as plane, saw, chisel, and mallet, and is also occasionally employed as a weapon of self-defence, or to cut a track, in winter, through the snow. Indeed, there is very little which a Moujik cannot accomplish with this instrument, which in the hands of even a skilled British workman would probably be useless. Peasant courage and ingenuity were strikingly demonstrated some years ago by one Telushkin, who, for the sum of eighty roubles, undertook to regild single-handed the spire and cross of the Cathedral of St. Peter and St. Paul in Petrograd. And this herculean task was accomplished without the aid of scaffolding, Telushkin sitting astride a little wooden saddle which he had himself suspended by cords, although the spire, from its base to the summit of the cross, is four hundred and fifty-five feet high !

There is little variety in the architecture of a Russian village, where the smallest and poorest hut is but a replica of the most imposing building; while rustic decoration, in the shape of trellised porches, summer-houses, or the like is unknown. The few shops are indicated by rough fir boards, displaying crude paintings of wearing apparel, joints of meat, or loaves of bread to indicate that the occupier is either a tailor, butcher, or baker; and there is always a forge, which, in posting districts, is of course a necessity. Horses and cattle roam about at liberty, to the danger at night-time of vehicles on the post-road; while, when their parents are at work in the fields, little children are sometimes attacked by gaunt, grey hogs, which boldly enter even the houses in search of food. Most Russian villages have a cheerless, squalid aspect, even in brilliant sunshine, for they are generally surrounded by monotonous plains or gloomy pine forests, which add to their air of solitude and dejection.

Let us assume that we have reached one at dusk after a long day's journey in dirty weather, and over atrocious roads. The first thing is to find a night's lodging, which, if there be a post-house, is always obtainable, although the latter is usually dirty and comfortless, and you are kept awake all night by the arrival and departure of travellers, even if you can sleep at all, devoured by vermin, on a hard wooden bench. The best plan, therefore, is to knock up the " starosta," who, if you have a Government permit, is bound to receive you, but who, in any case, will probably offer you hospitality. Let us, then, enter this village magnate's house, where I first enjoyed peasant hospitality, and where my first impression was one of intolerable heat and stuffiness, for although it was a sultry autumn evening, the double windows were tightly closed. These are common throughout Russia. In October, no sooner has the first sharp frost set in, than the smallest crevices are stopped, the double sashes which have been removed are replaced—only a small air-hole being left here and there. In the intermediate space between the double windows, salt, sand, or cotton wool, are placed to absorb the damp collecting there. The salt is heaped up in all sorts of fanciful forms, which stand untouched till spring; and the layer of sand is planted with artificial flowers and other ornaments. Every house has its own devices, and it is amusing to make a tour of the streets on a bright winter day and observe the different ways in which the double windows are decorated. This was on this occasion the sole attempt at adornment, with the exception of two large oleographs of the Tsar and Tsarina, and the " ikon " suspended in a corner with its little silver lamp which is lit on feast-days. When in Russia, you must always uncover upon entering a room, whether it be in palace or hovel, for it invariably contained this sacred emblem, and, as a rule, also a portrait of the reigning sovereign. I once had my hat knocked off by an irate stranger in a Siberian *café*, when, being ignorant of this custom, I had not at once removed it on entering the place.

The starosta's house consisted of one large apartment, about forty feet by twenty-five, with walls and ceiling of rough-hewn logs caulked with tarred felt, and uncarpeted deal planks for a flooring. It contained a circular deal table, three or four horsehair chairs, and wooden benches around the walls, which latter, at night-time, formed a resting-place. One end of the room, screened off by a thick curtain, was used as the women's chamber, in which there was presumably a bed, although the men seldom use one. There were also in this superior dwelling a few books—cheap editions of Tolstoy, Pushkin, and a translation of one of Dickens's works, but in most peasant households the library consists solely of a Bible and other sacred volumes.

My venerable host introduced me to his numerous family, who were drinking tea around a " samovar," and whom I joined, while noting that nearly a third of the room was occupied by an enormous stove, the top of which is used, in winter, by the men and boys of the household as a sleeping-place. These stoves generally indicate their owner's condition in life, those of the better class being made of glazed porcelain, while inferior beings have to be content with clay; and the ovens which they contain are used, not only for cooking, but also to subject clothing to great heat in order to destroy parasites. For nearly all these dwellings are infested with vermin—especially the " tarakan," a kind of small cockroach, thousands of which swarm on the walls and ceiling of even the cleanest houses, and which are derisively called " Prussak " or Prussians. Nothing is therefore more essential, when travelling through Russia, than a supply of strong insecticide, for although the Moujik's person is cleanly his clothes and surroundings are generally very much the reverse. Occasionally fowls are kept indoors, bringing with them legions of fleas, and the living-room is littered with rubbish and thick with dust, while the floor is engrained with the dirt of years. But these are minor discomforts to a tired and hungry man, so I thoroughly enjoyed that first supper under a Moujik's roof, the meal consisting of white bread (a rare delicacy), cold pork, " agourtsi," [1] wild berries and cream. But the starosta was a rich man, and the fare, therefore, sumptuous compared with that which I have shared, on similar occasions, some hundreds of times since.

My experience of Russian village life during the past thirty years has led me to the conclusion that the Moujik is, generally speaking, one of the best fellows in the world, which fact is greatly to his credit, seeing that, up to the time of his emancipation, he was practically regarded as an animal, unworthy of the treatment or ordinary privileges of a human being. He was in those days badly housed and habitually ill-treated, his women, if young and attractive, were outraged, and his children neglected and starved, for the serfs were regarded as mere beasts of burthen, and their condition was almost as abject as that of an African slave. Yet, notwithstanding that long period of oppression and degradation, the Moujik has contrived in less than sixty years [2] to become a decent member of society, [3] and if this social improvement has been partly due to legislation, some credit is due to the peasants themselves for suggesting the organization of their now existing " mirs," or village communes. The

---

[1] Pickled cucumbers.

[2] The emancipation of the serfs was decreed in 1861.

[3] In 1868 only eight per cent. of them could read and write, whereas now nearly half of them can do so.

latter were instituted for the purpose of local self-government, and are now empowered by the State to settle economical matters, revise and equalize village taxes, and elect an executive administration under the presidency of a " starosta," or local chief, justice being thus administered according to the laws and traditions of each district. Every village is authorized to select this official, who may be its wealthiest or poorest inhabitant, provided that he is the person best qualified for the work. Sometimes every member of the " mir " is appointed by turns, for the office is not popular, as it involves frequent and often heated discussions with the " tchinovnik," who is not always a man of integrity or honesty of purpose. There is also the " zemtsvo," a higher provincial council to which every litigant before the " mir " has the right of appeal.

A Russian village has nothing in common with ours in England, where the name is generally suggestive of rural peace and sylvan scenery, for here there is no squire's mansion, ivy-grown rectory, or old-fashioned inn which, surrounded by snug homesteads, render its English prototype so homely and attractive. The landowners here generally reside for only a few weeks on their estates, in the summer-time, their winters being passed in Petrograd or Southern Europe, and there is therefore no one to take a kindly interest in the peasant or to lighten his lot in health or sickness. Moreover, the local priest or pope [1] cannot be compared to an English parson, being generally an illiterate individual with a partiality for vodka, which he is fortunately no longer able to gratify. He receives, as a rule, no stipend from the State, but merely a small piece of land for farming purposes, and as he is otherwise dependent on the private fees received for baptisms, marriages and burials, his flock is generally made to pay their pastor through the nose. Most of the rural popes I met were unctuous, crafty individuals, who looked like birds of prey in their long, dark robes, with greasy ringlets streaming down their shoulders.

[1] " To put it in the most charitable way, the Popes are not respected by the ' Moujiks ' " (Stepniak's *Russian Peasantry*).

The local "tchinovnik" was equally objectionable, and only associated with the peasants when compelled or when he could secretly extort a few roubles, for most of these rural officials are out to make money, and generally succeed.

The Moujik is the soul of hospitality and generous to a fault, but economical, not to say stingy, where his own wants are concerned, for, even when wealthy enough to obtain them, he will not only deprive himself of the ordinary comforts of life, but undergo severe privations in order to save money. I have thus often found a man living in a hovel which contained enough cash to buy up half his village, this anomalous condition arising from a desire to leave his heirs well provided for, and not with any miserly notion of hoarding wealth. On the other hand, even the most careful will financially cripple themselves in order to purchase good agricultural machinery. For the Moujik's sole object in life is the improvement of his land, to which he is so devotedly attached, by tradition and lifelong association, and if this strange being were offered a life of luxury and an inexhaustible banking account in Petrograd, he would probably refuse them.

The "traktir" [1] is now no longer a favourite resort after working hours, but it is only fair to add that drunkenness has never been so prevalent here as is generally supposed in England. The habitual intemperance once ascribed to the Russian peasantry is on a par with other exploded insular myths, such as, for instance, the bearded Cossack, who, in my early youth, was depicted as devouring tallow candles by the score! Every Moujik was also supposed to beat his wife, and no doubt, in former days, chastisement was occasionally administered by a husband to his lazy or erring spouse; indeed, I once saw a birch suspended on the wall over a conjugal couch, but it was jokingly alluded to by the owner as a relic of a barbarous and bygone age. In any case, the cheerful readiness with which these people have given up "vodka" in favour of "kvas" is ample proof that they were never more than occasional

---

[1] Public-house.

inebriates, who would make up for a week's abstention by getting gloriously drunk on the seventh day and, throughout the rest of the week, keep strictly sober.[1] And I can safely say that I have never, in all my experience, seen their womenkind the worse for liquor. Nevertheless one must have seen (as I have) one-third of a small village composed of " traktirs " to thoroughly appreciate the benefits conferred upon the nation by the recent restrictions on the sale of alcohol. Those have also greatly hampered the operations of Jewish usurers, formerly the curse of every village, for when things went wrong, owing to sickness or drought, the Moujiks were often compelled to raise money, and this was the village Shylock's opportunity to advance it at a ruinous interest, obtaining the borrower's house and land as security. When a number of plots had thus become mortgaged, the Jew would refuse further credit, and having appropriated the various properties, become a landed proprietor at his clients' expense. This evil was obviously at its worst when the grog-shops drove a roaring trade, and financial transactions were conducted by victims excited or fuddled by drink, a condition quickly taken advantage of by the sober and crafty Israelite.

Nearly every Russian province has its typical costume, but this is only assumed on State occasions, the ordinary summer dress being a shirt of red flannel or chintz material, and black velvet or linen trousers tucked into high boots, worn, as a rule, by stalwart, bearded fellows of magnificent " physique," although they subsist almost solely on fish (fresh or salted according to circumstances), " kasha," eggs and black bread. Only the wealthier peasants partake of meat (which is boiled in "shtchi" or cabbage soup before being eaten) and then only rarely, for the Moujik dislikes anything in the shape of food which is not of his own production, and he is not often a large cattle-owner. Nor will he ever touch bears' flesh, believing that the latter was originally a human being who was punished for his sins by being transformed into a beast; whilst hares he

---

[1] "The suppression of the sale of Vodka has lessened the Imperial Revenue by one-fourth" (*Europe's Debt to Russia*, by Sarolea).

regards as vermin, and, in some districts, pork as unclean and therefore uneatable. The Moujik is also
very particular as to the way in which his food is prepared, and although the table may be swarming with
" tarakans," the fare, however humble, is always
served with scrupulously clean plates and glasses.
They are not great smokers in the rural districts (except
in the south), and rarely smoke cigarettes, but prefer
a cheap Bessarabian tobacco called " mahorka," which
is used, not only for smoking, but to keep the moth
out of clothing. For its fumes will instantly kill any
insect, and although I am used to strong mixtures, a
few whiffs of it made me violently sick !

In winter-time both men and women wear sheepskins, and high felt boots, which are only removed for
bathing purposes. Some cottages are provided with a
steam-bath, where the whole family assemble on Sundays
and feast-days, which, as there are about one hundred
and seventy of the latter in the yearly calendar, main-
tains at any rate their bodies in a state of cleanliness.
Every village also has a public bath-house, which is
paved with bricks so heated as to emit dense clouds of
steam when water is poured on them. Profuse perspiration is induced by birching with twigs, and this
operation is followed by a cold water douche, or in
winter by a roll in the snow or immersion in the ice-hole
of the neighbouring river or stream, which is always
kept open throughout the winter in order to draw
water.

Russian peasant women are rarely attractive (except
in the southern districts), and this is partly because they
work hard in the fields as well as the household, while
their everyday costume consists of an ill-fitting cotton
bodice and voluminous skirt of the same material.
It is only on Sundays and holidays that the younger
ones are attired in spotless white, occasionally trimmed
with delicate Russian embroidery, and also wear the
" kakoshnik," a kind of tiara of ruby or turquoise velvet
adorned with tiny seeds-pearls. Those worn by the
upper classes are set with priceless gems, and this
head-dress is so becoming that one wonders it has not
been more widely adopted in England.

A Russian village looks its best on a fine summer's evening, especially if it be on a high-day or festival, when every one wears the national costume, and there are athletic sports, perhaps a travelling shooting gallery or merry-go-round, and much singing and dancing to the accompaniment of the accordion and " balalaïka." The Moujik is passionately fond of music, especially of a mournful description, for even his merriest choruses have a strain of sadness, and the famous peasant song " Matushka-Volga," which is sung from the Baltic to the Polar Sea, is as melancholy as a funeral dirge. Many of the women have clear, musical voices, and in the " khorovod," or " dancing choir," form a ring around the prettiest girl in the village, and dance around her while each one sings an impromptu verse generally descriptive of marital infidelity, illicit love, or that universal object of fun and derision : The Mother-in-Law ! But gaiety never lingers long in either the Moujik's mind or melodies, and when sunset has deepened into dusk the villagers, young and old, always assemble before retiring, to join in some simple hymn of the Greek Church, or one of the old Russian folk-songs so typical of the great and gloomy land which gave them birth. And when night has fallen, and lights begin to glimmer from cottage casements, the watchman goes his round, beating, at brief intervals, a wooden clapper (which has often kept me awake all night), to recall belated lovers to their homes and warn evil-doers of his presence. But there is little need for this precaution, for crime is very rare in Russian rural districts, which in this respect compare very favourably with some of our Welsh counties. Conjugal murder by poisoning, generally by the wife, is the most frequent penal offence (because divorce is almost unattainable), and also arson, which when committed out of revenge, is known as " letting loose the Red Cock." But forgery, theft, and embezzlement are very uncommon, for the Moujik has a rigid code of honour regarding his neighbour's property, which he generally regards as sacred.

On the other hand, morality in most Russian villages is rather lax, a fact which must be partly ascribed to cramped and insanitary housing conditions, where men, women and children are so promiscuously herded together that it is impossible to conform to even the common decencies of life. For instance, the writer once stayed in a cottage in Little Russia where sixteen people of both sexes, whose ages ranged from eight years to threescore, nightly occupied a space measuring only eighteen feet by fifteen, and where five women and four of the men were between twenty and thirty years of age, and not even relatives. This was, of course, an exceptional case, as in most districts men and women sleep apart, although even this restriction is comparatively useless in places where the sexes constantly bathe together in a state of nudity. But the Moujik has only a vague notion of right and wrong regarding sex relations, and so long as his wife remains faithful, is generally indifferent as to the doings of his other female relatives. This state of immorality probably arises less from vicious inclinations than ignorance, while at present the Russian peasants' mode of life is certainly not calculated to engender either delicacy of feeling or purity of mind. Both men and women marry very young, but generally less from love than mercenary motives, and large families are the rule, although more than a third of the children die under five years old.

These people have one remarkable characteristic which is perhaps chiefly due to severe physical training and a simple life: indifference to physical pain. I have seen them submit to the extraction of several teeth at a sitting without wincing, and their aversion to a surgical operation is caused less by fear of the knife than superstition, for amputation, they aver, would entail their entering Paradise in a mutilated condition! I recollect on one occasion cutting my hand rather severely, and my village host at once attempted to apply boiling tar to the wound, which, he informed me, was his usual custom! The Russian peasant, moreover, regards death almost as callously as the Chinaman, an indifference which is shared by most of the Russian lower orders. Thus Mr. G. Brandés relates that during the Crimean War a wounded Cossack was dragging himself painfully along after his " sotnia," [1] and his comrades, seeing there was no hope of his recovery, offered to bury him and so put an end to his sufferings. The wounded man at once agreed, and a grave was hastily dug, in which he calmly laid himself down to be buried alive. His colonel, on hearing of the incident, was naturally horrified, remarking : " But the poor fellow must have suffered intolerable torture ! " " Nitchevo ! " (" Never mind ! ") was the reply; " we stamped the earth down quickly with our feet ! " Yet these men had acted solely out of kindness and sympathy, and were so eager to release their friend from further pain that they entirely overlooked the mental and physical agony which must have preceded his end.[2]

Although death has generally no terrors for the Moujik, he is morbidly superstitious, and delights in legends concerning ghosts and fairies, which are generally of a blood-curdling description. Even babies chuckle when told of a gigantic witch with nose and teeth of iron, whose forest dwelling is fenced in with human skulls, and whose powers of working evil are unbounded. The peasants are also great believers in spirits and spells, and when sick will often place more faith in witch-doctors than medical practitioners. Many of these village sorcerers make a good income out of herbal treatment and incantations, though the penalty for such unorthodox practices is a long term of imprisonment.

In summer the Moujik works sixteen hours of the twenty-four, and will often prefer to sleep in the open all night rather than lose an hour of daylight during haymaking or the harvest. In winter, when no work can be done on the land, he hibernates like a dormouse, although neither he nor his women are idle during those dreary months of semi-darkness. For Russian village industries in winter-time are now yearly growing in importance, every district manufacturing its special class of goods. The villages along the Volga river turn out sheepskin coats and Oriental slippers, those of Central

[1] A military Cossack term signifying 125 men.
[2] *Impressions of Russia*, by G. Brandés.

Russia dainty embroideries, silver ornaments and cutlery, and so on. Of late years special attention has been devoted to the construction of wooden toys, such as were made in Germany, and the war will surely stimulate keener competition in this branch of industry. The "koustar" (as these winter workers are called) are encouraged by the State not only because the villagers are thus usefully engaged when the devil might otherwise find them employment, but also because their labours are a yearly increasing source of profit to the Government. Some of the work is really beautiful, notably lacquer, lace, and the exquisite Russian embroideries, which may now be purchased in England; while agricultural implements, watches, silver ornaments, samovars, "ikons" and innumerable other useful and ornamental articles are also manufactured to find a ready sale in the towns, partly because of their admirable workmanship, and partly because purchasers feel that they are assisting in a useful and philanthropic scheme. "Koustar" work is, of course, strictly restricted to the winter-time, for in summer there is too much to be done on the land.

As an impartial observer, for some years past, of the Moujik and his methods, I can only liken him to a giant with a baby's brain (the pathetic result of ages of mental stagnation) who is only just beginning to realize his national importance, which is, to say the least, considerable, seeing that he represents ninety per cent. of the entire population. And as time goes on, and the peasant becomes imbued, by better education, with more progressive views, he will certainly no longer recognize the counsel and authority of those ubiquitous tyrants, the village "pope" and rapacious "tchinovnik." The change may be gradual, although it is now clearly realized that the day is not far distant when the country will have to rely mainly upon the loyalty and support of the agricultural classes. And a prominent Russian official whom I recently met declared that in his opinion (which was shared by many of his distinguished colleagues) the trade, industries, and international commerce of Russia would, after this war, attain such vast proportions that one result of the

increase would be the formation of a powerful middle
class, for the first time in the history of the nation.
But any revolutionary element (my friend added)
introduced by these altered conditions would in no
way affect autocratic rule, for the backbone of the
Russian nation (as he styled the "Moujiks") would
certainly never tolerate any other form of Government,
as has been clearly shown, of recent years, by a persistent but generally fruitless Socialist "propaganda."
I heav frequently heard in village traktirs the Moujik
express political views in an open and aggressive manner
which would have ensured arrest in any town, but the
"tchinovnik," when present, never interfered, being
too well aware that the Tsar's most staunch and devoted subjects are numbered amongst these sons of
the soil.   For if it is now common knowledge that,
just before the outbreak of hostilities, Russia was on
the point of a revolutionary outbreak, it is equally
certain that all classes are now firmly united against
the common foe, even political terrorists in the depths
of Siberia having petitioned the Emperor to be allowed
to return to Europe and fight for him.

Dr. Charles Sarolea, in his recent work, *Europe's
Debt to Russia,* thus testifies to the Moujik's unswerving
allegiance to the crown : " Loyalty," he writes, " has
been for generations a religious tradition, and almost
an instinct with the Russian peasantry, and such instincts have a very tough life in them, especially in a
slow, patient, passive being like the Moujik.   After the
disaster to the Russian fleet in 1905, I visited many
villages in every part of the empire.   The image of the
Tsar was still hanging in every ' izba ' with the ikons
of the saints.   The peasants remember the broad fact
that Tsardom has ever been on their side, and
that they are indebted for their freedom to the Tsar
Liberator."

When peace is declared, the peasantry will probably
enjoy even greater prosperity than before the war,
for years must elapse before Russia can sufficiently
develop her mineral resources to compete with other
nations as a manufacturing centre.   Meanwhile, she
will have to rely chiefly upon agriculture, which has

already rendered her a formidable rival as a grain-producing country to Canada and the United States.[1]

I have endeavoured in this chapter to show that the Moujiks are a simple and lovable people, destined by their already overwhelming, yet yearly increasing, numbers to play in the near future an important part not only in the agricultural, but also political development of, Russia. For although the peasant was, but a few years' ago, compelled to cringe before his superior, he has now acquired a sense of personal dignity which would certainly resent any infringement of his recently acquired rights; while, like most growing children, he now despises conditions of life with which he was formerly quite content. The Moujik is no longer, so to speak, satisfied with an accordion but must now possess a gramophone—indeed, may soon require an electric pianola; and these growing needs (which arise from a clearer perception of his growing importance) now apply to every phase of his daily existence.

And if in England one result of this titanic struggle may be to promote closer relations between the upper and lower classes, in Russia the steadily increasing political and social influence of the peasantry will as surely impel the latter to exact greater privileges from the State, by which, only sixty years ago, they were regarded as mere machines, whose sole mission in life was to accomplish a certain amount of manual labour. Everything now indicates that, when Russia has recovered from the effects of this disastrous war, she will, with the other Allied nations, go ahead in every respect with lightning rapidity, and there are also unmistakable signs that the Moujik will keep pace with her.

[1] " Were the Russian fields cultivated as are those of Great Britain, Russia could produce enough corn to feed a populace of 500,000,000 souls. In European Russia the cultivated land is only 21 per cent. of the whole area, while in France it is 83 per cent." (Stepniak's *Russian Peasantry*).

E

CHAPTER VI

THE COSSACK—IN PEACE AND WAR

THE Cossack is usually depicted, in England, as a picturesque blackguard of predatory instincts whose sole mission in life is to harass a retreating foe, or to convoy and occasionally massacre Siberian exiles. An English novelist's conception of this type is therefore generally a pitiless ruffian, bestriding a rat-like pony, which gallops like the wind while its rider performs prodigies of skill with a slender but deadly lance and his terrible " nagaika." [1]   Indeed, according to British ideas the Cossack apparently does nothing else, although I have found him (when not engaged in warfare) a homely, placid individual, as devoted to home life and rural pursuits as honest John Hodge of Wilts or Sussex. That his existence, however, has two distinct phases is indicated by the fact that I once stayed, in a remote village, with a hospitable peasant who wore the red shirt and " caftan," was idolized by his family, tilled the land by day, and romped with the children at night; and a few months later met the same man in Warsaw during a political disturbance in which many people were slain by the military patrols.   And at first I entirely failed to recognize my once domesticated friend in the wild-eyed, yelling fiend who was savagely hacking his way through a crowd of helpless men and women. Anyway, this sudden and evil transformation convinced me that Stevenson's Dr. Jekyll and Mr. Hyde present no greater contrast than this strange and complex Russian character in peace and war.

The Cossacks (the word was formerly Turkish) have a somewhat mysterious origin, but they probably date from the fifteenth century, when in the vicinity of the

---

[1] A short-handled whip, with a heavy, tapering lash, somewhat resembling the " knout," which is carried by every Cossack.

River Dnieper a number of settlements were formed by Russian refugees driven out of their homes in more southern regions by Turkish and Tartar hordes. Thousands of the former therefore took refuge in the " Zaporosjie-Setch," [1] as the place was called, and amongst them many renegades and vagrants who gradually established powerful robber communities. And the district became, in time, so thickly populated that a kind of republic was founded composed not only of industrious labourers and workmen, but also of men skilled in the use of arms, the latter being so numerous that the Governors of southern Russian provinces eagerly sought their services, in case of need. Thus it came to pass that all men of a fighting age in the " zaporosjie " were finally enrolled as soldiers of the Tsar, whom their descendants are serving at the present day. It is interesting to note that, even in those mediæval times, these people could be, one day, peaceful husbandmen, and bloodthirsty warriors the next.

A Cossack is, while on active service, subject to the same military rules and penalties as an ordinary soldier, he swears allegiance to only one supreme leader, the Tsarévitch, who from time immemorial has been his " ataman " or chief, and he therefore cherishes feelings not only of loyalty and devotion, but also of warm personal affection for the heir apparent whom in most cases he has never even beheld in the flesh ! and his dwelling is therefore easily recognized, for it invariably contains a portrait of His Imperial Highness, as well as those of the Tsar and Tsarina, and generally also one of the late General Skobeleff, who was a staunch friend of the Cossacks, for whose fighting capabilities he had a profound admiration. Had the " White General " [2] lived (he is said to have been poisoned by an attractive Berlin adventuress in the Moscow " Hermitage ") he would certainly have figured as a prominent leader in the present war, and Russia undoubtedly sustained an irreparable loss by his untimely end.

The Cossacks now number over three millions in

[1] " Setch " signifies a fortified settlement.
[2] General Skobeleff was so called as he invariably rode a white horse in action—in order to render himself more conspicuous to the enemy.

all, and they are known throughout the empire as
" Otchainy," a term signifying one of reckless or " dare-
devil " qualities. Military service is in their case
compulsory for a period of twenty years from the age of
eighteen, twelve years of which are passed with the
colours, and the rest in the reserve. And this is probably the cheapest force in the world to maintain, for
a man provides his own horse and everything in the shape
of uniform and equipment, only receiving a rifle from the
Government. But they are thrifty, industrious people,
many of whom grow wealthy, and are well able to afford
the outlay, which in any case would be cheerfully expended; while the State grants them certain special
privileges in return for their military services. The
officers are not all of Cossack birth, for many are transferred from the regular army, the colonel of some crack
cavalry corps being generally appointed to command the
Cossacks of the Guard—who always accompany the
Emperor on State occasions. And a most impressive
sight is that of His Majesty driving through the streets
of the capital surrounded by an escort of this famous
regiment, clattering by on their compact, blood-like horses
under a moving forest of spears. The uniform is a dark
single-breasted garment reaching to the ankles, tightly
secured at the waist, and adorned across the chest with
a row of silver cartridge-belts, with olive-green or crimson breeches and a tall sheepskin bonnet. The officers
wear side-arms adorned with valuable jewels, while
every man carries a cavalry sabre and brace of pistols,
a lance, and the formidable " nagaika."

The Cossacks differ essentially from the ordinary
Russian peasantry, to whom they regard themselves
as greatly superior not only by reason of their ancient
and distinguished lineage, but also of the valuable services
which they have, for many centuries, rendered to the
State. For although those who, in olden days, were
first employed by Russia in the Turkish and Polish wars,
were lawless marauders, yet even they possessed a
strain of chivalry which raised them far above the level
of sordid thieves and cut-throats. Yermak, the conqueror of Siberia,[1] was a case in point—and the granting

---

[1] See chap. xi.

to his tribesmen of special favours was only one result of his glorious achievements. Thus, the Cossacks are the only people in Russia permitted to observe certain laws of their own, which are framed by the chiefs of the various " voiskos " (or Cossack districts), of which the most important are those of the Don, Astrakhan, Ural and Amur in Eastern Siberia. They have also a central administrative department at the Ministry of War in Petrograd, to which a delegate [1] is appointed by each " voisko," which is also responsible for the proper maintenance of education. And the latter is so well conducted that, at the present day, there are very few Cossack children of either sex who cannot read and write. Cossack women are also superior to those of the moujik class, not only as regards intelligence and morals, but also in their personal appearance, indeed I have seen some who were strikingly beautiful. Their chief failing is incorrigible laziness, wherefore a Cossack home is never as clean or comfortable as a moujik's dwelling, which is itself seldom a model in this respect !

Although I have met Cossacks in all parts of Russia, I am best acquainted with those of the Amur (in Siberia), who have specially distinguished themselves in the present war, and with whom I have occasionally stayed in peaceful villages situated on the banks of the great river which flows from Lake Baikal to the North Pacific Ocean. And I found them excellent farmers, although less concerned about the care and cultivation of their land than the condition of their horses, which, in Siberia, are of a peculiarly hardy and useful stamp.[2]

A Cossack village (which is called a " stanitza ") has a characteristic military air which renders it unlike any other, for even when in the bosom of his family the Cossack calls it " being on leave," and never entirely neglects his military duties, or even regimental

[1] " In the autumn of 1914 Russia had 328,705 Cossacks mobilized, and seven-tenths of them were concentrated on the German and Austro-Hungarian frontiers and met the first columns of the hostile force. Together with all the 1st, 2nd and 3rd Reserves Russia is able to put in the field not less than about 1,000,000 Cossacks" (*Russia in Arms*, by Lieut.-Col. Roustam-Bek).

[2] A Cossack officer, Nikolai Pieskoff, once rode the entire distance from Manchuria to the Baltic (6000 miles) on a small Siberian pony.

dress, generally wearing a pair of striped overalls. Both uniform and accoutrements are kept ready to put on at a moment's notice, which accounts for the marvellous rapidity with which this force was mobilized in the autumn of 1914. Even little children in a " stanitza " wear old striped breeches discarded by their parents, and are put on a horse and left to their own devices almost before they can walk !

A Cossack generally owns two or three horses, which are kept in the pink of condition, and have as much attention lavished upon their feeds, grooming and exercise as though they were in the ranks; while as they seldom exceed fifteen hands, they are better adapted for getting over rough and difficult ground than animals of larger build. The Cossack loves his horse as dearly as his wife and children; in fact, it is practically regarded as a member of the family, which perhaps accounts for its marvellous sagacity when on campaign. I once stayed in the Ukraine with a farmer who remained all night in his stable to tend a mare with the gripes, while his child lay dying indoors; yet this was not from any lack of fatherly affection, but merely because the horse is the one object on earth which inspires these people (like the Arabs) with an intense and absorbing passion, indeed it is part and parcel of their very existence. And I could cite many instances of when, in the deserts of Central Asia, Cossacks have given their last drop of water and mouthful of bread to sustain the life of an equine friend while they themselves have perished.

Colonel Roustam-Bek (who formerly commanded a Cossack regiment) relates the following anecdote,[1] which proves that the Cossack is not only a lover of animals, but, when occasion demands, an accomplished thief ! " I remember once," he writes, " during the Pamir Expedition, our ' sotnia ' penetrated into a valley of the Trans-Alai Mountains through the Ak-Baital Pass. There was no grass at all, and we were short of barley, which was the only food for our horses. The officers had succeeded in keeping some sacks of this precious grain, and, in order that it should not vanish, we put these sacks at night under our pillows. The men were

---

[1] *Russia in Arms*, by Lieut.-Col. Roustam-Bek.

very grieved that their horses were in a state of semi-starvation, and how they managed it I have never understood; but a great part of the barley belonging to their officers disappeared every night, and it was impossible to find the thief!"

When a Cossack is mobilized his mount is put through the severest physical tests before being finally passed for service. It must, for instance, be able to cover fifty miles a day—for a month on end—without showing signs of distress, and when its owner is called up is often ridden an enormous distance, to join its unit at the nearest railway station. It must also be able to swim like a duck, having on several occasions had to cross broad, rapid rivers like the Pruth and Dniester during the present war.

Although well acquainted with the wild American West, I have never in my life seen such horsemen as the Amur Cossacks, although I believe the latter are even considered inferior in this respect to those of the Don and Ukraine. And their horses are equally wonderful, for the two ponies belonging to Ivan, my host on the Amur, would lie down, rear up on end, or go down on their knees at word of command like trained "artistes" in a circus. They would also stop at full gallop (with a suddenness that would have sent an unskilled rider flying), and lie down motionless as if shot, for the Cossack, in action, takes cover behind his mount. My friend's work on horseback with the lance was marvellous to behold, for, while going at full speed, he would impale a chicken or pig with equal dexterity, pick up a bit of paper, or lie under his horse's belly at full gallop— a favourite device, so that the enemy may think that only riderless steeds are stampeding towards them. Ivan would also drop the reins, and his pony would turn to the right hand or left, or even turn completely round by word of mouth. I never witnessed the "Djigitovka" in which even these clever feats would be regarded as child's play, and which so excited the Kaiser's admiration that he endeavoured to introduce it in the German Army, with lamentably futile results! My host, in addition to his equestrian skill was also a marvellous marksman, as are most of the Cossacks, whose ranks contain some of the best shots in the army, and he was also as quick as a Mexican cowboy with the lassoo, which is used when pursuing an enemy.

The Cossacks have many peculiar and unique methods of warfare, which although handed down from their ancestors, are no less startling and successful when practised against modern troops. One of these is the mode of attack known as the " Lava," which Colonel Roustam-Bek so graphically describes in his interesting work, *Russia in Arms*, that I may perhaps venture to retail, for the second time, this distinguished Cossack officer's remarks for the benefit of the reader.

" The most interesting tactical exercise of the Cossacks " (writes the Colonel) " is their celebrated ' Lava.' Everybody knows the word ' lava ' as applied to the liquid products of volcanic activity, but I think it is not known in England that the same word has been applied for centuries to a special form of attack employed by the Russian Cossacks. I have not been able to find any description of this use of the word in English. Germans and Austrians, however, know it, and have many times tried to introduce it in their army, but without success, their men and horses lacking the necessary smartness. Cossack horses are specially trained for this attack and do not need to be guided by hand or knee; they know what they have to do after the leader has cried ' Lava ! ' so both hands of the Cossack are free for fighting.

" When news is received that a detachment of cavalry is approaching or ready to attack, an order to be ready for ' lava ' is given by the commander. The leading ' sotnia ' (squadron) spreads out to right and left, and the others at full speed form up on either side of it in a semicircle or half-moon. Every man with a lance is attended by a man wearing a ' shashka '—the Cossack sword—and all the officers, with the colonel at the head, are in front of the men of each ' sotnia.'

" The other ' sotnias ' in the neighbourhood do not wait for a special order, and at once take up the same formation, endeavouring to surround the attacking force from another side. With loud shouts and cries the Cossacks rush down on their enemies, and even if this first assault is repulsed, another ' lava ' pours

down on the shaken enemy, and very often surprises
them in the rear. In the present day the Cossacks,
besides lances and swords, also use hand-grenades, which,
if they do not cause very serious injuries, serve to
demoralize both horses and men. A special reserve
of 'lavas' follows the attacking force of 'sotnias'
and picks up the wounded, and usually collects the
ammunition and horses of the beaten enemy.

"The Japanese faced this terrible attack only once,
and after that never stopped to meet it. In the present
war the 'lava' has been used very often and with the
greatest success, especially in Poland, for the heavy
German cavalry was never able to open its front quickly
enough to meet the sudden 'lava' of the Cossacks."

I may add that the author of the above (one of the
ablest military critics in Europe) is of opinion that the
Russian cavalry is far superior to the German, and even
better than the Austrian, which is more efficient than
that of its ally. Colonel Roustam-Bek does not, however, compare the Cossacks with any of these, for they,
he declares, are matchless !

I was once the guest of a Cossack regiment quartered
in a small town in the Caucasus, my host being
Prince Z., whom I had met in Paris, where he always
spent his leave, and with which he was as well acquainted
as with his native Circassian mountains. The regiment
was in barracks, which enabled me the more closely to
observe the men while on service, and I noted that,
although their officers treated them on friendly, and
occasionally even familiar terms, this in no way appeared to detract from the severe discipline which
prevailed. But, as my friend Z. remarked, " Make pals
of your men and they will follow you to the Devil ! "

I never met a pleasanter set of fellows than the officers
at T., for most of them had visited Europe and even
America, either to study various military methods
or on pleasure bent, and they had in either case apparently lost no time ! Champagne flowed like water
every evening (this was ten years ago), and one night
a concert and dance were organized in the barrack-yard
with a score of privates as performers. Every Cossack
is a born dancer, and the merry tinkle of a " balalaïka "

band eventually proved too much for the colonel (a grey-haired veteran of over six feet), who suddenly rose from his seat, hurriedly left the messroom, and the next moment was wildly "pirouetting" amongst his men with, notwithstanding a flowing robe and spurs, the grace and agility of a ballet-girl. Imagine a staid British field-officer under similar circumstances! yet this and other outward signs of equality only serve to cement good feeling between all ranks here, although such laxity could scarcely exist elsewhere without deleterious effects. Anyhow I left T. less under the impression that I had been entertained by a cavalry regiment than by a happy and united family! And, by the way, my hosts had a curious custom which was then new to me, but which I have since observed amongst Russians of the upper class. Nearly every man's gold cigarette-case had various little ornaments sunk into its surface in the shape of a crest or monogram, single sleeve-link, stud, coin, or other object which had been presented to the owner by intimate friends, and as these *souvenirs* were mostly composed of diamonds and other jewels, the effect was rather novel and attractive.

I have never been fortunate enough to witness Cossacks engaged in actual warfare (for the Warsaw episode was merely a street-riot), but I had reason, on one memorable occasion, to appreciate the courage and resource which they invariably display at times of imminent peril. This occurred during my land-voyage from Paris to New York, when Stepán Rastorguyéff (a Siberian Cossack) was lent to me by the Russian Government at Yakutsk to accompany me for the remainder of that hazardous and hitherto unattempted journey.[1]

I will not weary the reader with a description of the difficulties overcome before a serious disaster overtook us in the neighbourhood of Tchaun Bay, on the frozen shores of the Arctic Ocean. To reach this we had travelled for over three weeks from the Kolyma river, and had here hoped to find natives and some food, for we were by this time reduced to fourteen frozen fish for nine men and sixty ravenous dogs. But we vainly

[1] See *Paris to New York by Land*, by the author.

THE COSSACK: "STEPÁN"

searched that pitiless waste of ice for any signs of human life, well knowing that to stop meant death from cold and starvation, so we struggled slowly and painfully onwards, growing weaker hour by hour. And, during that long day of agony, I and the others, overpowered by drowsiness and despair, lay down more than once in the snow, from which we might never have risen had it not been for Stepán, whose spirits never flagged for a moment as he trudged doggedly on with the indomitable pluck and tenacity of his warlike race. And it was solely owing to this brave fellow that on that very night, when things appeared to be on the verge of a fatal crisis, we sighted our longed-for goal—two miserable walrus-hide huts—which, however, meant deliverance from a lingering and painful death. And I can safely assert, as leader of the Expedition, that I and every member of it must that day have perished had it not been for my Cossack friend's invaluable encouragement and aid.

However inhuman and rapacious the Cossacks may have been in the past, they have in the present war not only fought with even more than traditional bravery, but have shown a tolerance and kindness towards their prisoners which the latter would certainly not have displayed under reversed conditions.[1] And more than once, when Russia's legions have, from lack of munitions, been pressed back by overwhelming forces, the Cossacks have saved the situation, not only as skilful scouts, but resolute opponents, as the Austrians, especially, know to their cost. I recently met an English newspaper correspondent, just returned to London from the Russian front, who told me that he had one day conversed in Galicia with an Austrian Colonel of the " Radetsky Hussars." And the latter, who had been taken prisoner,

---

[1] " Sworn evidence of the cruelties practised by German prison guards upon Russian prisoners is contained in the latest report of the Russian Commission of Inquiry.

" Torture by the drawing of nails, cutting of tongues, and tearing of ears has been inflicted upon Russians unwilling to betray their comrades. Men have been burned alive for the sheer amusement of their captors.

" This has been sworn to by many prisoners and by a Russian sister of mercy " (*Daily Mail*, September 22, 1916).

declared to my friend that he had hitherto been under the impression that his men would face anything in existence, but that he had been sadly disillusioned when (as the Austrian pathetically explained) " they met those damned Cossacks ! "

CHAPTER VII

SPORT, AMUSEMENTS AND FOOD

VERY few Russians care for sport in our English sense of the word, although their country is so well adapted for its enjoyment, which is practically within reach of all. Yet only members of the highest aristocracy regard it as seriously as the average Briton, having probably acquired a taste for its various branches in other countries but their own. A love of the chase and manly games is innate in every Briton, rich or poor, but even the young and stalwart Russian of independent means is generally an " indoor man," who only braves the elements when compelled to do so in order to transact public or private business, his leisure hours being generally spent at the club or card-table. Horse-racing has become popular of recent years (there is now a Russian " Derby " run at Moscow), but the public attend meetings more with the object of gambling than from any interest in the breeding or performances of the animals engaged. The Russian is also as a rule an indifferent horseman, who does not care to ride, but only drives, for pleasure, and then seldom handles the ribbons himself. I only once went out partridge-shooting with a Russian friend, who was got up for the occasion in a Mexican *sombrero*, long green coat, linen knickerbockers and side-spring boots, and spent most of the time crawling about on his stomach in order to shoot the birds before they could rise ! Yet my friend was a crack shot with a rifle, and could plug the ace of spades three times out of five with a duelling pistol at twelve paces.

Big-game shooting in Russia is therefore restricted to the nobility, amongst whom bear-hunting is the most popular form of amusement, and also an expensive one; for it entails many preliminaries and innumerable attendants and beaters, as I saw when once attending a battue on Prince V.'s estate not far from Petrograd. The best time for bear-shooting is in the early autumn when the first snow falls, and the quarry selects a secluded spot in the forest in which to hibernate. Many peasants make a living at this season by " ringing in " the beast, which is done by first finding its track and then starting at right angles from the latter and making a large circle around it in the snow. No further traces outside this boundary show that the bear has been successfully " ringed," but if any marks are visible beyond the first circle, another is made, this operation being repeated until an unbroken snowy surface denotes that the quarry has been roughly located. When, say, half a dozen bears have been thus traced to their lairs some wealthy sportsman in the nearest town is informed of the fact; and the animals are purchased by him for a good round sum (whether they are eventually killed or not) and a hunt organized. Meanwhile the various rings are continually watched daily to make sure that the bears have not escaped.

We left Petrograd by train on a clear, calm November evening, arriving about eleven o'clock at night at a small railway station, where a number of sledges were awaiting us. We numbered a dozen guns, and on arrival at the appointed spot, fifty or sixty beaters surrounded the first ring and moved slowly forward with flaming torches, their advance being preceded by the discharge of two or three rifles to stir up Bruin. Fox terriers were also employed to indicate the latter's whereabouts, and we had not long to wait before a crashing of branches was heard, as the brute broke from his hiding-place and emerged into the open, where, as it was bright moon-light, he was plainly visible. Each man had a couple of rifles, a revolver, and hunting-knife, and every beater also carried a spear in case of a scrap at close quarters. In this case a cool head and steady nerves are essential, for in the event of a miss, it is useless to try and escape over deep snow, gnarled roots, and other obstacles. Indeed, this sport seemed so risky, that I was surprised to hear that accidents rarely occur. Only one bear fell to our guns that night, but he was a splendid fellow, brought down by a lucky shot from my nearest neighbour, about a hundred yards from where I was standing. The sport was therefore rather poor, although we did not return to the village until late the next morning, to do ample justice to an excellent breakfast which had been specially prepared by our host's *chef* in a beater's cottage.

The nearest approach in Russia to fox-hunting is chasing wolves on horseback, with hounds, now well known in England as " borzois." Covers are drawn by sending mounted men through a wood with a number of dogs of any sort of breed—mongrels for choice, for they make the most noise ! Other horsemen select a spot in the open where the wolf is likely to break, each holding a " borzoi " (or perhaps a couple) which, as soon as the wolf dashes into the open, are slipped in pursuit, when horsemen, hounds, and yelping curs gallop madly in pursuit. When the wolf is pulled down the foremost rider dismounts and dispatches him with a hunting-knife—a ticklish operation which needs considerable skill and experience. In winter a different method is pursued, for it is then impossible, owing to deep snow, to follow on horseback, and wolves generally prowl about the country in packs. When one of them is located, a dead horse is placed near the spot to keep them from straying until the guns can reach the spot.

Hawking is a favourite sport amongst the Tartars in the south, and in the northern provinces capercailzie and black-game shooting are popular amongst the upper classes. But game of all sorts abounds in European Russia and Siberia, especially the latter, where in various districts wild geese, partridge, teal, widgeon, wild duck and snipe are found in unlimited quantities, for they are rarely shot at, but merely trapped for sale in the towns.

The youth of Russia seems as little attracted by manly exercises as their elders are by sport. I have visited colleges and schools in all parts of the country and have never yet seen young men or boys engaged in gymnastics or healthy outdoor games such as cricket, football or rackets. Although there is plenty of opportunity, they seldom skate, but in winter spend their leisure hours indoors, or in summer idling about the streets of a town or village, unless there be a river or stream handy, when fishing, being a lazy employment, is rather popular. Occasionally youths are seen playing at " ball," or battledore and shuttlecock, but they never seem to indulge in any pastime involving trouble or muscular exertion, which is probably why lawn tennis has never really caught on in Russia. Parallel bars, trapezes and swings are erected in the garden of nearly every country house, but are hardly ever used from one year's end to another. Russians, however, of every age and class, are fond of tobogganing, ski-ing, and (those who can afford it) ice-yachting—one of the most fascinating amusements which I have ever enjoyed. The aristocracy join in these winter sports with the lower orders, and otherwise amuse themselves very much as they do in any other country—racing, yachting or pigeon-shooting, for which in winter-time they generally visit the south of France. Nearly everything in the world of sport is copied from the English, for whom, notwithstanding a popular belief to the contrary, our allies have always, even long before the war, evinced a sincere regard and admiration.

The Russians are, like the French, great play-goers, but even the houses subsidized by the State lack the comfort of our English theatres, which in this respect are superior to those of Paris. Even the Opera House in Petrograd has a gloomy appearance, being less well lit and cared for than, say, Covent Garden, while although the former engages the finest operatic artists in the world, and its balléts are unrivalled, the scenery and mounting of the latter are generally inferior to those at the larger London music-halls. The best variety entertainments, even in the capital, are of a third-rate order, and it is perhaps because the Russians are such ardent lovers of their own classical music, that music-halls here are less extensively patronized than in other countries. On the other hand, the circus, which elsewhere in Europe appears to be dying out, is as popular here as ever.

Most Russians prefer tragedy to comedy, especially lurid dramas of the Transpontine order, but of late years musical comedy of the *Merry Widow* type has become increasingly popular, although Petrograd and

Moscow have up till now been spared the inane " Revue," which in England is such a misnomer, having nothing in common with the generally bright and clever satire on passing events which justifies its title in France. The Russian farce, like most Russian comic papers, is generally dull and lacking in humour; but the works of Tolstoi, Turgénieff and other Russian authors are of course masterpieces which should only be portrayed by Russian artists, for when they are translated and played in English, the local atmosphere entirely disappears.

The real Russian *cuisine* (although generally confined in England to " bortsch " and " caviare ") is, to my mind, the best in Europe. I do not here refer to wealthy private establishments where the *chef* is generally a Parisian, but to the style of cooking which corresponds to the French *Cuisine Bourgeoise*. The national dish, which appears in varying degrees of culinary excellence before both the millionaire and the " moujik," is " schtchi," which, although its chief component is the humble cabbage, is the most delicious soup in the world, there being an old proverb which avers that " Schtchi, Tchai, and the Tchin, are the Muscovite's three divinities ! "[1] For as roast beef, macaroni and " pumpernickel "[2] are respectively suggestive of a British, Italian and Teutonic appetite, so is " schtchi " inseparably linked with that of the Russian, whose first care on settling in a wild and lonely district is to sow cabbages, in order that this essential article of diet may be quickly forthcoming. There are, however, many varieties of " schtchi "; the one which I preferred being that which is found in every humble household and made of shredded white cabbage, half a pound of pearl-barley, a quarter of a pound of butter, and mutton cut into small pieces, with two quarts of " kvas," although broth may be used instead of the latter. This may seem a very ordinary " recipe " but, even when I have specially ordered it in the best London and Paris restaurants, it has never tasted so good as in the poorest peasant's

---

[1] " Cabbage soup, tea, and the official world."

[2] This word is said to be derived from the fact that when Napoleon I. was offered one, he ate a mouthful and then gave it in disgust to his charger, remarking: " C'est seulement *bon pour* ' Nicki.' "

F

" izba " in Russia. " Bortsch " is very much the same as " schtchi," only here cream is a necessary adjunct, and beetroot replaces cabbage as the chief ingredient.

Nearly every winter dish here has, in summer, its cold counterpart, and " batvinia " is generally served in very hot weather instead of " schtchi," the former also being composed of " kvas " with various herbs, cucumber, cranberries, small slices of salmon and sturgeon, and plenty of ice. Another cold soup is " akroshka," which is almost similar but contains sliced apple and rissoles of " caviare." Both are excellent and would probably be much appreciated if introduced into England.

Russians rarely roast their meat but prefer it boiled, and seldom eat bacon, sausages and similar dishes; and I have never tasted, in any country, such delicious bread, or seen it baked in such innumerable forms, several varieties always accompanying early breakfast. Moscow is famous for its " kalatchi," which are eaten throughout the length and breadth of the empire, and " blinis " (a kind of pancake, eaten with fresh "caviare ") are almost as popular and may now be had at the best London restaurants. Siberia is productive of thousands of edible wild berries, of which delicious preserves are made, for the jam here, like the bread, is the best I ever tasted. All kinds of pickles made in the country are served at every meal, also salads, not only of lettuce, but cherries, grapes and other fruits preserved in vinegar.

The national beverage of Russia is " kvas,"[1] which, as I have already remarked, is used not only as a drink, but also in cooking. It is a kind of small beer, which is generally seen at table instead of water, and is easily prepared by adding two pounds of barley meal, half a pound of salt, and a pound and a half of honey to a quart of water. The mixture is put in an oven overnight with a slow fire and left till next morning, when the fluid is strained off and kept till fit to drink in about a week. The cranberry grows here like a weed, and a syrup made from it is largely consumed now that " vodka " is no longer obtainable.

[1] According to the Chronicle of Nestor "kvas" was in use among the Sclavonians in the first century of our era.

Most of the hotels and " restaurants " in Petrograd and Moscow have now adopted French culinary methods, but many places still exist in both cities where only Russian fare is provided, and these may easily be found on inquiry at any hotel. A Russian eating-house generally supplies soup, a rissole of minced meat, an *entrée*, joint and sweet for a rouble. Russian cooking therefore possesses one advantage to the traveller not possessed of unlimited means: it is cheaper than any other, but it must be eaten in Russia, and nowhere else, to be fully appreciated.

CHAPTER VIII

FINLAND—IN TOWN

I MET him one evening in the bar of the " Hôtel de France " at Petrograd, a genial person with flaxen beard and steely-blue eyes, who wore an ill-fitting, shiny black suit, vaguely suggestive of commercial travel or the mercantile marine. The stranger, to judge from his political opinions, was evidently not a Russian, although he spoke that language, French and English with equal facility. I was feeling depressed, having just been compelled to postpone an expedition to Arctic Siberia on which I had set my heart, and which was to have started within a month. So I accepted my new acquaintance's proffered cocktail as an anti-dote to gloomy thoughts, while the former condoled with me over the failure of plans which would, I ex-plained, keep me at a loose end throughout the approach-ing autumn. My companion's rejoinder then solved all my doubts as to his nationality. " You have time on your hands? " said he. " Why, then, not visit *my* country—Finland? "

Finland! I had always associated the name with desolate forests and stagnant lakes, where a few poverty-stricken natives on the coast subsisted by occasionally trading in fish, tar and timber. The only Finn I had hitherto met was an intemperate mariner on an American whaler, who had not inspired me with any desire to extend my acquaintance to his country or compatriots. Why, then, should I go to Finland?

Simply because my conception of the country had been absurdly incorrect, according to this informant, whose glowing accounts of culture and progressive people, wonderful cities and boundless natural re-sources, I naturally received with some mistrust.

The Finnish capital, Helsingfors, he described as a miniature Paris, from which railways radiated to various places equally attractive from an historical, commercial and sporting point of view, while I was assured that a tour through the entire country need only occupy six weeks, which, as it was now early in August, would enable me to inspect it in warmth and comfort. And so easy and alluring was the plan of travel sketched out by my friend (who also promised me letters of introduction), that I resolved to take his advice and visit this remarkable land of which I had apparently formed such erroneous ideas. So it came to pass that, within twenty-four hours of coming to a decision, I found myself in Helsingfors, which, by the way, was reached, after a night's journey, in a comfortable sleeping-car.

Here let me briefly explain that Finland [1] (in Finnish, " Suomi ") is about the size of Great Britain, Holland and Belgium combined, with a population of about 2,500,000,[2] which includes a large number of Swedes. The country is flat and marshy from end to end, covered with dense forests, and honeycombed with the sheets of water known as the " Thousand Lakes," which vary from small ponds to an inland sea three times the size of the Lake of Geneva, and which with connecting canals form useful waterways. There is no river of any importance through the country, but rapids and falls abound, which are utilized not only for motive power, but for the floating of thousands of tons of lumber yearly from inland forests to the sea.

Finland has endured many struggles and vicissitudes, for she has always been a bone of contention, and wars have been constantly waged between Russia and Sweden for the possession of this wild, but coveted, strip of territory. The Finns always fought as Swedish allies until the early part of the nineteenth century, when Russian rule was finally established over a race which, although at the outset was bitterly opposed to it, has

[1] The name Finland is derived from the old word, "finn," which signifies a wizard, or witch.

[2] Fifty years ago the Finns numbered about 1,500,000, and the latest census shows nearly double these figures.

gradually learnt to appreciate the benefits to be derived from a wise and tolerant Government, to say nothing of a more powerful protectorate' than that which it formerly enjoyed. German agents have in recent years (and in view of the present conflict) attempted to sow seeds of revolution throughout the country, and even at the present time there exists a certain section of malcontents (my Petrograd friend was one) who would welcome a Swedish restoration, especially as these people are so closely allied in every way with their Scandinavian neighbours. But the majority of the Finns are now content to remain Russian subjects, provided they are granted conditional Home Rule, and this they have now practically obtained. Countries annexed by Russia have generally been, so to speak, Russianized in a comparatively short space of time, such as, for instance, Poland, and more recently Central Asia, where, in Merv and Bokhara, the golden domes of the Greek Church now largely outnumber Mahometan minarets. But in Finland Swedish is the language of civilization, especially in the towns, Finnish being only spoken in the provinces, for this country, like France, has an irrepressible nationality which only centuries will finally eradicate.

Helsingfors is not a very large place (it contains 100,000 souls), but I was certainly surprised to find a town which, anywhere in Europe, would be considered imposing and well planned. Even the outlying districts are laid out with such care and cleanliness that this may be described as a "slumless" city, within the walls of which I never saw a beggar. The Finnish capital rather resembles Stockholm with a bit of Paris (in the shape of leafy boulevards) thrown in; but even Paris lacks the pine-clad hills and breezy roadstead which render this place so attractive in summer-time, when I could not picture it under snow and swept by Arctic blizzards. One might be a thousand miles from Russia, for everything except the climate is different, from the neatness of towns and villages to the coinage, which here consists, not of "roubles" and "kopeks," but "pennis" and "marks." It was also a relief to escape the official supervision so prevalent over the border.

A policeman at the railway station stopped me, as I thought, to examine my papers, which, however, he politely declined, while handing me a small brass disc with the number of my conveyance in case of overcharge or loss of property. And in most of the towns I was never even asked for my passport!

Finland has one peculiarity—the best hotel in every town is always named the " Societetshuset," which certainly saves unpleasant mistakes. The one at Helsingfors was a plain, unpretentious building, but very comfortable and up to date, every bedroom being provided with a telephone. The charges were most moderate, but this advantage I enjoyed (and not only as regards hotels) throughout the country. My windows at Helsingfors overlooked the blue harbour and busy quay, while inland a handsome cathedral dome towered over the fair white city, with roads winding from it into an endless panorama of pine forest, in which lakes shone here and there, like bits of crystal set in dark enamel. At right angles to the quays was the " Esplanade Gatan,"[1] or chief thoroughfare, lined on one side by gardens, and the other by excellent shops, where I was able to purchase a good cigar which cost fourpence, and which I should have paid at least two shillings for in any Russian town, where cigars are seldom smoked, and are therefore generally bad and atrociously dear. There were also good libraries and bookshops, with all the latest English and French publications, but scarcely any Russian literature. The chemists alone were inferior, and I may add that the sale of the most innocuous patent medicine is strictly prohibited throughout Russia, where even a grain of calomel cannot be obtained without an order from a medical man.

My letters of introduction included one to a distinguished Professor at the University, who was justly proud of its college library, which contained 200,000 volumes. Degrees are taken here in science, medicine and art by both sexes, and the girl graduates affect masculine tailor-made costumes and little velvet caps of various colours, such as are worn by Swiss students. For women here take a very prominent position in life,

---

[1] " Gatan," a street.

being not only admitted as Members of Parliament, but employed as clerks in railways, banks and counting-houses, while in the country they work on the land and attend to horses and cattle.   Yet I never met a militant suffragette in Finland, probably because equality of the scxcs is regarded as a matter of course, and women are never compelled to sacrifice domesticity and refinement in order to uphold their " rights."

As a rule Finnish women are flaxen-haired and blue-eyed, with well-developed figures, and generally incline to stoutness before middle age.   They usually marry young, and anything like conjugal infidelity is, on either side, regarded as an unpardonable sin, for which the offender is eternally ostracized, although a divorce can be obtained on such trivial grounds as incompatibility of temper.   Moreover, a husband need only be absent for a year, and if at the end of that time he does not reply to his wife's advertisement in the local newspapers, she is free to marry again.   I have already referred to the immorality existing in certain capitals in Europe, of which, judging from what I saw of it, Helsingfors is certainly the most virtuous.   There is not a music or dancing hall here which a lady may not visit alone without fear of annoyance, which is strange, seeing that Petrograd and Stockholm are within such easy distance.

I met few Russians in Helsingfors, for they generally hold official appointments and do not associate much with Finns; but wherever I went throughout the country the Emperor of Russia and his consort were regarded by all classes with loyalty and respect, and I heard many instances of the kindness shown by members of the Imperial Family while in Finland, notably of one which is related of the late Alexander III.—when His Majesty was fishing one day, attended only by an equerry.   Lunch was served in a woodcutter's hut on the banks of a trout stream which had been the scene of sport, and the Emperor was struck not only by the beauty of his humble hosts' daughter, but also by her dejected appearance, of which His Majesty inquired the cause.   " Her betrothed is going away to-morrow to join the army," explained her father, " and she can't marry him, poor soul. The Tsar will want him too long for a soldier ! "

"Indeed ? " said the Emperor, much amused. "Where is this unhappy lover ? Bring him to me."

A good-looking lad was summoned, and shyly confronted the stalwart stranger, who had now risen from the table, and was lighting a cigarette.

"So you want to marry your pretty little sweetheart, eh ? "

The boy awkwardly nodded assent.

"Well, give her a kiss, and tell her you are not going away. General, see that this man is permanently exempted from military service." And the Emperor turned to leave the place.

"But, Excellency," cried the old woodcutter, trembling with amazement, "what will the Tsar——"

"I *am* the Tsar, my friend," said Alexander III., glancing back from the threshold; "Tsar of Russia in Petersburg, but here only Grand Duke of Finland ! "

This anecdote is authentic, for it was told me by one who afterwards employed the youth in whom the Emperor had taken such a kindly interest.

My friend the Professor was a character, and also a pleasant companion, and we made together many excursions around Helsingfors, one to the quaint old town of Borga to admire its cathedral, a wonderful specimen of early Finnish architecture, and visit the house of Runeberg, the poet-patriot, which remains as it was in his lifetime. Of pleasure resorts there was the island of Hogholm with its pretty park and restaurant; for the Finns, like the French, delight in open-air meals, and here, on a fine evening, crowds of people would assemble to dine under the trees, to the music of a fine orchestra. The gardens of Brunnsparken are reached in a few minutes by little steamers plying around the harbour, and this was a favourite resort of the Professor's, with whom I dined there, to find that Finnish " smorgasbord " was an even more formidable prelude to meals than " Zakuski," and I could scarcely face dinner after smoked and raw salmon, pink and grey caviare, many kinds of fish, smoked reindeer-tongues and potted meats. Then came " soupe à la bisque " (a

speciality), followed by " flundra "—a delicious blend
of the sole and sterlet, which only a Finnish cook can
properly prepare. Roast partridge was the only *pièce
de résistance,* for in northern *menus* fish always predominates, and, if you don't happen to care for it, to
a rather superfluous extent.

On the way home we landed at a little island occupied
by the " Nyland Yacht Club," which, as usual on a
summer night, was crowded with members. Here the
Professor was joyfully welcomed, and, the evening being
sultry, I was initiated into the mysteries of " miod,"
an amber-coloured beverage, composed of cider, many
liqueurs, wild strawberries and chunks of ice, an apparently insidious but extremely potent beverage. Yet
my companion and his friends drank it like water, but
experience has shown me that, the further you go north,
the more can man dispose of large quantities of alcoholic
refreshment without apparent ill effects. Many members of the Nyland Yacht Club owned racing craft built
in England, and their home resembled an English
country house, with its oak-panelled rooms and cosy
furniture. The theatre wound up an enjoyable evening, for although the piece was played in Swedish, I
gradually realized that it was the *Private Secretary,*
which was so well acted that its performance might
have earned even the appreciation of its original pro-
ducer in England—my old friend Charles Hawtrey.

The fortress of Sveaborg, within easy distance of
Helsingfors, is, under present conditions, of considerable interest, and the steamer by which I journeyed to
it across the harbour was crowded with Russian officers
returning from leave, for this Gibraltar of the North is
as jealously guarded as its Mediterranean prototype.
From the moment I landed, shifty-eyed, plain-clothes
men strolled after me, while sentries waved me sternly
away from the more important works. Sveaborg is
now practically impregnable, having been greatly
strengthened since Crimean days, and even then the
allied French and English bombardment had as little
effect upon it as a fly buzzing against a battleship.
Previously to this the fortress (or rather succession of
forts) capitulated to Russia in 1808, but only under

similar conditions to those by which Metz was treacherously ceded to the Germans in 1870, for the Swedish commander, Admiral Cronstedt, surrendered with 6000 men and two ships of the line without firing a shot. Sveaborg has now a garrison of 10,000 men, the heaviest and most modern type of guns, and is provisioned to sustain a siege of five years. The Kaiser's fleet will therefore find it a very hard nut to crack—if they ever attempt to crack it!

As I have previously said, summer here is very delightful, although not so gay as the winter season, with its sledging parties, ski matches and skating, which latter is here a national pastime, although in Russia you seldom see a pair of skates. Helsingfors has a huge open-air rink where thousands of people congregate at night in the glare of electric light, and there are also trotting races on the ice, for which horses are sent from long distances to compete, and ice-boat contests over the mirror-like surface of the frozen lakes; so that, what with outdoor sports by day, and dinner-parties, theatres and dancing at night, there are many duller places in winter than this. Even in wet weather one need never feel bored, for there are spacious arcades which, though perhaps not so gay as the Palais Royal, afford amusement and a comfortable shelter on a rainy afternoon.

I stayed for a couple of days at Viborg (where only a ruined citadel now remains of the first settlement built in Finland by the Swedes), and having an introduction to its owner, called one day at a pretty villa embowered in creepers and honeysuckle, overlooking a picturesque lake. Surrounding the latter were similar dwellings, each with its tiny landing-place, trim garden, and smooth lawn sloping down to the water, from a background of pine forest, cleared, here and there, into meadowland flecked with yellow gorse. My host and his wife received me on their little private jetty, to which was attached a flotilla of pleasure-boats brought by friends, for I arrived on the joyful occasion of a golden wedding, then being celebrated by a dance which, commencing in the afternoon, did not terminate until the next day! But everything was admirably done—although some of the male guests wore rather fanciful evening dress, which started well with a swallow-tail coat, but lapsed into lavender-coloured pants and canvas shoes !

There were no seats and therefore no " wall-flowers " in the ball-room, where even aged couples circled gravely around to the strains of the latest valse or polka. The younger women wore white, and might have passed for English country girls, though the latter would hardly have moved with such grace through the mazes of the Russian " mazurka," which is an intricate gavotte-like measure, unlike the one which was formerly danced in England. And there was a charming informality about the proceedings, where every one seemed gay, good-humoured, and polite, that recalled similar entertainments in far-away France.

Coffee was served as the departing guests assembled on the landing-stage, and our host's white steam-launch then bore us swiftly back to Viborg, which, as we neared it, was emerging into sunshine from the chilly mists of dawn. And I went sleepily to bed, scarcely able to realize that this was the Finland which I had pictured so differently only one short week ago !

CHAPTER IX

FINLAND—IN THE COUNTRY

My friend the Professor was portly, well on in the sixties, and had lived every day of his life, yet, like most hardy Northerners, he had contrived to retain the mental and physical vigour of a middle-aged man. Also, being a naturalist, various travels in the wilds had imbued him with the contempt for time and mileage which I have often noticed amongst Russians, especially in that land of stupendous distances, Siberia. For instance, this light-hearted scientist one morning suggested a visit to an adjacent island by penny steamer, and the next moment exclaimed, as if struck by a bright idea: "No! We will go to our seaside resort, Hango," which was as if a short trip to, say, Richmond, had been suddenly abandoned in favour of a journey to York! For Hango meant at least six hours by rail, which my companion would cheerfully have undertaken without luggage and the vaguest idea as to our return! But I have known aged Siberians, whose English prototypes would need a Bath chair, think nothing of several days in an open sleigh, with 40° below zero, and only frozen fish to subsist on!

Anyway, we did not go to Hangö, and the next day found me on a train bound for the famous falls of Imatrá, the Professor accompanying me to the station, where he stacked up the carriage-rack with Finnish newspapers, probably to impress me with their number and importance (for he must have known I could not read them!), of which the Finns have reason to be proud. For there is now no town of any importance in the country without its newspaper, while Helsingfors publishes half a dozen in the Finnish and Swedish languages. Some of them were nearly twice the dimensions of a London daily (for advertisement is the rage here), and contained reviews of tales and articles in several weekly and monthly magazines also published in the capital. I had already been shown in Helsingfors some exquisite specimens of local printing and engraving, notably a wonderful atlas [1] containing thirty-odd maps of Finland, and giving, by means of coloured plans, every interesting detail connected with the latter concerning education, meteorology, agriculture, communications, industries and mines. Even the innumerable lighthouses and beacons on and off the coast were classified with a care and precision which must have entailed years of research.

Railway fares in Finland are so cheap that you may cover nearly the entire railway system for the price of a first-class return ticket between London and Eastbourne! I travelled second-class, and my fellow-passengers displayed, like all Finns, a curiosity which in any other country would have savoured of impertinence. " Where are you going? " " Are you married? " " What is your income? " were some of the questions to which I replied, for they were put in a childish way that disarmed resentment, and the cross-examination was generally followed by unsolicited details concerning the questioner's own private affairs! The latter was on this occasion a brewer, with whom I shared a pint of his own excellent " pilsener " (brewed in Helsingfors [2]), and who voluntarily informed me that he suffered severely from gout, was a widower with an income of £500 a year, and had seven children. This communicative companion was the essence of good-humour until a well-dressed Russian woman entered the compartment and proceeded to light a cigarette, when he could hardly conceal his indignation and disgust, for smoking in Finland amongst women is unknown.

· I was disappointed in the Imatrá Falls, probably because they had been described to me in Helsingfors as the finest in the world, with the tiresome reiteration

---

[1] *Atlas de Finlande.* Helsingfors, 1899. Société Anonyme. F. Tilgmann.

[2] There are fifty breweries in operation throughout Finland.

that I have had to undergo in Japan and Australia
anent the beauties of Fujiyama or Sydney harbour!·
The Finnish falls are, however, picturesque, and rush
down a defile of precipitous cliffs with such a deafening
roar that, although you could pitch a biscuit from shore
to shore, the report of a gun at your elbow would be
almost inaudible; and they were most impressive at
night, when their foaming waters resembled a cascade
of molten silver under the rays of electric light.   The
River Vuoksi, of which they form part, is a fisherman's
paradise, and portions of it are reserved by an English
Club at Petrograd, the members of which have erected
a residential clubhouse on the spot.   Trout run up to
twenty-five pounds (the best months are from June to
September), and you fish from a boat which is provided at the hotel, with an experienced man, for five
marks a day.   Local fishermen use a light salmon-rod
with a fine, strong line terminating with a salmon
collar, which should have a trace of fine, single grey gut
attached to it.   Two or three yards of collar with swivels
should be used, and the finer the gut the better.   The
brown palmer is the best fly, the best minnows " Totnes "
and " Phantom," and early morning and sundown the
best time of day.   In July the grayling are plentiful,
and salmon are also caught near the Vallenkoski Rapids,
a few miles down stream, but the northern lakes and
rivers are best for these.   An Englishman can always
obtain a free permit to fish from the Petrograd Club,
and also use its quarters if he prefers them to the hotel,
which is also very comfortable.

One great charm of Finland in summer is that you
can generally get from one place to another by steamer,
for lakes and canals are interwoven into the most
perfect system of inland water communication in the
world.   Even the smallest sheet of water has its service
of steamers with every comfort on board, for the Finnish
waterways cost 25,000,000 marks, and a yearly expenditure of 250,000 marks, the Saima Canal, which unites
Lake Ladoga with the Gulf of Bothnia, being forty
miles long.   A cheap and enjoyable trip was made by
a friend of the writer, who travelled in a " Rob Roy "
canoe for over a month through the country, without

once revisiting the same spot, and getting excellent fishing every day, with nothing to pay for it.

So, the weather being fine, I travelled as far as I could from Imatrá by steamer to Tammerfors, passing by Keparasen, a lovely spot, where Satan is said to have tempted our Saviour. The country looked fresh and green, and they were getting in the hay, much later than we do in England and on a different system, by laying it on horizontal poles a few feet from the ground, where it dries more rapidly. Meadows in Finland are, as in Russia, enclosed by only wooden palisades, which lack the homely look of our English leafy hedges and grassy banks.

Tammerfors, the "Manchester of Finland," is more like a pleasure resort than an important commercial centre, this being due to the fact that fuel is rarely used here, only water being employed for motive power. The latter is lavishly supplied by a narrow but turbulent river connecting two great lakes, which enables manufacturers to run their machinery at an almost nominal cost, while in England it would entail an enormous expenditure. This once small and unimportant place owes its wealth and prosperity to Alexander I. of Russia, who, while on a visit here, conceived the idea of developing the latent resources of the district by utilizing its water-power, which was then being wasted. And the Tsar's ingenious idea was quickly adopted by the Finns, with the result that Tammerfors is now the third largest town in the country.

I arrived here early on a Sunday to find the streets deserted, for the Finns are strict Lutherans, and throughout the morning every one was in church! But during the afternoon the park and a military band attracted crowds of people, where artisans, workmen and factory girls sat under the trees, eating ices and enjoying the music, in close association with their wealthy employers, for in Finland there is little or no class distinction. And as I strolled about I heard English frequently spoken, for many of the mills and foundries here employ overseers and occasionally skilled mill-hands from England; indeed, I conversed with a Lancashire lad who seemed quite unimpressed by his picturesque surroundings, preferring Manchester, with all its darkness and perpetual rain. There were no amusements, he complained, no music-halls or pictures; and this was true, for by 11 p.m. the moonlit streets were cleared of every living being save policemen. So I also retired early, to fall asleep to that eternal Finnish lullaby, the sound of falling water.

Even the busiest quarters of Tammerfors are attractive, for the mighty river which brought the latter prosperity rushes through them, the torrent being spanned by a granite bridge from which one can watch the waters foaming through an avenue of mills and manufactories, to mingle with the placid blue waters of Lake Nasijarvi, a few miles away. Just below the bridge is a tiny island, and on it the " Stromparterren " Restaurant (noted for a local delicacy, fried sprats), and on the left bank the mansion and beautiful gardens of Mr. Notbeck—a wealthy millowner whose fortune was derived from the manufacture of paper, the chief article of export here. A few years ago only the coarsest stuff was turned out for local use, but since the adoption of modern machinery this town provides the leading capitals of Europe with the most expensive qualities, extracted from pine and poplar pulp. Celluloid is also produced in large quantities, and both these articles are put on the market at a much lower price than if steam were employed. In 1874 only 1,000,000 kilograms of paper were exported yearly, and now over thirty times that amount is sent out of the country—chiefly to Great Britain.

The output of cloth has increased here during the last twenty years in the same proportion, and this is of the finest (and also shoddiest) description, the former being almost equal to English make. I visited a factory where over 1600 hands were employed, and where tweeds, especially, were turned out with special regard to durability and good taste. My English friend in the park was receiving three times the wages he received at home, and although Tammerfors employs over 10,000 workpeople a strike has never been known there, and probably never will, so long as the cordiality which now exists between capital and labour continues. For " sweating " in Finland is unknown.

G

But the industries of this prosperous little town are not limited to cloth and paper, for it has also iron-foundries, besides factories producing furniture, glass, china, matches, and even aerated waters; and this reminds me that when, at the local " Societetshuset," I ordered Vichy water, it was brought in a transparent bottle with a red label inscribed " Made in Helsingfors " !. I then called for Apollinaris, and in this case the bottle, although genuine, bore a notice stating that its contents had been " Manufactured in Vasa " !

The roads in Finland are good, and I motored from here to the rapids of Nokia, ten miles distant, a charming drive through fragrant pine woods carpeted with wild flowers. We passed on the way a timber shoot, where lumber is hauled from the head of the lake system, north of Tammerfors, about a mile over a steep hill, and floated down stream to Lake Nasijarvi. Over a million logs are thus transported yearly from this place alone to the steam saw-mills of Bjorneborg on the sea-coast.[1] Returning home we passed some grimy tents by the roadside, where a group of swarthy, ragged men and olive-skinned, dark-eyed women, in gaudy robes and cheap jewellery, sat round a camp-fire. They waved a welcome, and informed me that they were Rumanian gipsies, who had taken over two years to travel here from the plains of Hungary.

If Tammerfors is wealthy, so are its outskirts, as I soon discovered at a large dairy farm not far from the town, where I learnt that a large proportion of the butter consumed in England as " Danish " really comes from here. The farm which I visited might have been in England, with its old-fashioned garden, ivy-clad walls, and lattice windows overlooking grazing grounds thousands of acres in extent. Their owner informed me that the number of cattle in his possession ran into four figures, and that of late years the breed had been greatly improved by the importation of foreign stock, chiefly from Holland and Ayrshire. There are hundreds of these large steam dairies in the southern districts, where almost every town has its school of instruction

---

[1] The export for 1897 was £1,137,121, but this has now been considerably increased.

in farm and dairy work—for the Government encourages this branch of industry, the State railways providing specially constructed milk and butter cars, heated or cooled according to the season.

Finland is an idyllic place for dairy-farming, and only a small capital is needed to make a start, for grazing is cheap, and water and ice cost nothing. Only the winter cold and swarms of mosquitoes in summer present any serious difficulties, especially the latter, which often render it impossible to milk in the open, so that in the evening fires are lit in the fields, and the cows stand in their smoke until the operation is over. The dairies, long, low buildings with numerous ice chambers, were admirably contrived, and looked deliciously cool with their marble flooring, blue-tiled walls, and endless rows of shelves supporting great earthenware dishes of milk, cream and butter. In another building a number of women were putting up the latter for export, and most of it was going to England, of course via Denmark, where it was, so to speak, to be naturalized and re-christened. This trade, I may add, has largely increased since ice-breakers at Hango have opened up navigation throughout the winter.

My host was also a breeder of horses, and I inspected his extensive paddocks, which contained several useful-looking brood mares of foreign importation. The Finnish horse is of Tartar breed, a tough, wiry little beast, well adapted for ploughing, but very rough for riding purposes. A young, sound horse fetched from ten to twelve pounds, but these prices have probably increased since the war. Even before it, from eight to ten thousand Finnish horses were annually sent to Russia and Sweden, where they made a good profit.

I supped with my host and his charming wife, who in the evening entertained us with Finnish folk-songs [1] on the " kantélé," a kind of zither—and the national instrument. Madame was a Karelian, who are all born artists and musicians, and who, although Finlanders, entirely differ in customs, and even appearance, from the Tavastlanders, who occupy the south-western parts

[1] A volume of these, entitled the *Kanteletar*, may be had at any music-shop in Helsingfors.

of the country, while the Karelians live in its northern and eastern districts. The greatest poets and composers are of the Karelian stock, whose women are famed for their beauty, while the men are as Bohemian and indolent in their mode of life as the Tavastlander is plodding and industrious. An old Finnish proverb, " Karelia for pleasure, Tavastland for work," aptly describes the marked difference between these two Finnish races, a mixture of which is found in the " Savolax " (between Karelia and Tavastland), which has also produced many distinguished literary men.

At least one-third of the towns and villages in Finland have names ending in " joki " or " jarvi," [1] which is not surprising seeing that the former signifies a river. and the latter a lake, while " koski " (or rapids) is also a common termination. And it is as well to know, before visiting this country, that nearly every town in it has a double name : Helsingfors (Helmski), Tampere (Tammerfors), and a host of others. Fortunately, the second appellation generally has a slight resemblance to the first, although the town I now visited is called Vasa—Nikolaistad; the first being Finnish, and derived from the great Gustavus, while the second was bestowed in honour of Nicholas II., Tsar of Russia. Russians therefore call the place " Nikolaistad," while Finns know it as " Vasa," which occasionally leads to awkward mistakes in the postal department.

Vasa lacks the commercial activity of other Finnish towns, as was shown by the fact that only two ramshackle vehicles awaited the arrival of the train, and, for once in a way, there was no " Societetshuset," the best hotel being called the " Central," this being a Swedish innovation. For in Vasa ultra-Swedish manners and customs prevailed, and portraits of the Tsar and Tsarina in public rooms were here replaced by those of King Oscar and his consort. No one, of course, spoke Russian, and in order to find my way about I drew my requirements on bits of paper—a method which I had found useful amongst the Tchuktchis on Béring Straits, but which here signally failed. For unless you speak his language without a trace of foreign accent no Swede

[1] The letter " J " is pronounced as " Y."

will understand you, and even the simple word *ägge*, which so closely resembles *egg* in English, and means the same thing, seemed beyond his powers of comprehension.

Vasa (which contains about 15,000 inhabitants) was the least attractive town that I visited, perhaps because the soil, owing to its rich and fertile nature, is so dark; for this is essentially a grain-producing district, oats, barley and rye being largely exported, and most of the atter finding its way to Russia. There were therefore large stores for the sale of the agricultural implements (the land here is now chiefly cultivated by steam), and although England formerly furnished the machinery employed, there are now excellent local manufactories of steel and iron work, so that in a few years' time there will probably be no market here for British goods of this description. It is, however, consoling to think that, before the war, Germany had started several foundries for their production, which have, of course, now been confiscated.

Brandö, about a mile distant, is the port of Vasa, a lovely spot, the beauty of which is rather marred by the cranes and grain elevators erected along its wharves. I strolled down here one evening when a glorious sunset was darkening the pine-clad shores of the fjord, which gleamed like burnished steel in the twilight. The quays were, at this hour, deserted, and silent save for the shrill notes of a concertina played by a solitary figure on the deck of a steamer alongside the pier. Swedish colours drooped over her stern, but the musician, quickly recognizing a compatriot, put down his instrument and invited me, in broad Scotch, to board the vessel and partake of a whisky-and-soda. My white-haired but sturdy host was now chief engineer of the *Karl XV.*, but had started life on an ocean tramp, managed an Alaskan saw-mill, and driven a steam whaler, before settling down in the Baltic timber trade, which, as pay was good and work easy, he had no intention of leaving.

This canny Scot was well posted in local maritime commerce, but I was chiefly interested in his personal experiences of the Baltic—that perilous northern sea which in summer swarms with shipping, but over which in winter you can almost walk dry-shod over

the ice from Brandö to Sweden.   Mr. Macfie cared little
for storms, but owned to a wholesome dread of fog on
this rocky coast which bristles with reefs and shoals,
while there are as many islands off it as lakes inland—
islands of all sizes, from that of the Isle of Wight to
small, jagged rocks just awash, that would not harbour
a dog.[1]   The shores of Finland, however, are as well
lit as those of Great Britain, the hydrographic survey
having been carried out solely by the Finns, a task
that entailed an enormous amount of expense and
labour.   Sixty years ago a ship had to grope her way
guided only by beacons and roughly constructed land-
marks, but the pilot and lighthouse service are now as
carefully organized as any in Europe; in fact (as my
Scotch friend put it), this coast is as well lit as Regent
Street, and in clear weather a vessel need never drop
one light without picking up another.   Survey work
alone costs Finland over 100,000 marks a year, while
there are no less than 182 lighthouses,[2] many of the
latter being stationed in the crowded archipelago off
the coast.   Of these the Bagskav Light (situated on a
lonely rock far out at sea) is the most modern, being
constructed of iron, with cemented foundation of great
depth.   This lighthouse cost over 500,000 marks to
erect, with, owing to its exposed position, the loss of
many lives.

Uleaborg (*alias* Oulu) was the terminus of my journey
and the last town I visited in Finland, for it is situated
only a few miles from the borders of Lapland.   A few
miles north of Vasa the line bisects great plains, with
sparse belts of woodland, and the cold, crisp air of the
Arctic, with its typical scent of coarse verdure and
lichens, stole in at the carriage windows.   Many tourists
would surely visit these parts were they better known;
for although other parts of the world may be attractive,
give me a summer in the Far North, with its bright,
sunlit days and calm grey nights which exhilarate like
champagne, and render the smoke of a camp-fire more
fragrant than the perfume of flowers.   Of course there

[1] At one spot there are over 600 crowded into a space of six square
miles.

[2] These entail a yearly expenditure of nearly 3,000,000 marks.

are mosquitoes, but they are a minor discomfort compared to the mental and physical benefits to be derived from such perfect climatic conditions. And winter up here is almost as enjoyable, notwithstanding unpleasantly low temperatures and occasional scarcity of food. To paraphrase a famous poet : " If you have heard the *North* a-calling you will never heed aught else ! " and although I have suffered more than once in frozen regions from the deadly grip of cold and hunger, it is there that I always wish to return.

Uleaborg is less modern than other Finnish cities, and its old-fashioned buildings and cobbled streets were more suggestive of some sleepy English seaport than an important foreign mercantile centre. The town, however, possessed a " Societetshuset " of such palatial exterior that it might have graced the shores of a Swiss lake, although only four of its hundred rooms were occupied. I partook of a meal (facetiously described as " dinner ") in a huge restaurant which, although deserted save for a solitary waiter and myself, contained an empty music gallery, which loomed sadly through the dusk. This leviathan building had been erected in anticipation of many guests, which the railway, then in course of construction to the Swedish frontier, has by now, let us hope, provided.

There was little to be seen here of interest with the exception of the tar stores at Toppila, which, although two miles away, wafted their clean, pungent odour into my bedroom at the hotel. Steamers of every nationality lay alongside the quay, loading the barrels which extended for half a mile along the waterside, for 70,000 to 80,000 of these are collected every summer for exportation. In fact, I was told that most of the tar used in Europe comes from here, although, like " Danish" butter, it is known as " Stockholm tar."

Captain Ekholm (who has resided here for many years and to whom I had an introduction) gave me some interesting facts concerning this product, the trade in which has declined of late years, owing to the increased value of timber and scarcity of labour. And I learnt that tar is now obtained in precisely the same manner as it has been for centuries : by piling timber

in a huge stack on an elevated platform, which is
bricked over, its interior sloping inwards from every
side to an aperture in the centre, which leads into a
vat below.   The wood is then covered with a thick
layer of earth and turf, and having been ignited from
below, combustion continues until the pile sinks in.
In about ten days the tar has flowed into barrels and is
ready for exportation.

The proprietor of the Toppila wharf also worked
lumber to the tune of about £70,000 a year, and I
noticed in his office an interesting plan showing the
various exports of Finland at a glance, by means of
numbered cubes.   Timber came first with 120, wood
pulp and cereals at 38 each, and finally, paper, butter
and tar at 28, 25 and 24 respectively.   Captain Ekholm's
distinguished career in the mercantile navy had led to
his appointment as Director of the Naval College here,
and he told me that even thirty years ago 25 per cent.
of the population was under experienced tuition.
Uleaborg boasted, when I was there, of seven schools
for the upper and middle classes, besides five for the
children of the poor.

My informant was a keen sportsman, in whose opinion
Uleaborg is the best place in Finland for all-round
sport, the Oulojoki, near by, being one of the finest
salmon rivers in the world, yearly producing 90,000
marks in the short netting season from June to the
end of August.   Kajana, on Lake Oulujarvi, is the
easiest place to fish from, and there is a comfortable
inn, where rough shooting may also be had.   The
Kajana river teems with trout and grayling, and here
the best flies are those used on Scotch rivers.   A permit
for the season may be obtained at the Kajana Hotel
for about sixteen shillings, wherefore English sportsmen have drifted up here of late, and their number is
yearly increasing.   Ekholm related an amusing anecdote anent one of these, a stout and choleric Londoner,
who bitterly complained of the snail-like pace at which
he was driven every morning to the place of sport.
He therefore begged the village pastor, with whom he
lodged, to acquaint him with some startling Finnish
oath in order to compel the shock-headed lout who

drove his " karra " to quicken the pace, and the required expletive was smilingly imparted. Nor was it long before the native swear-word was put into requisition, but for some time it had no effect whatever on the clodhopper's stolid brain. " Rakastansunia ! " repeatedly yelled the infuriated passenger, finally leaping to the ground and violently seizing the driver, who, with an expression of terror on his face, suddenly dropped the reins, jumped out of the vehicle, and ran for his life across country, while the horse galloped away down the road, leaving the discomfited sportsman stranded. An hour later an exhausted, but still enraged, Briton staggered into the nearest post-house (where his driver had taken refuge), and explained what had occurred to the postmaster, who spoke a few words of English. " Rakastansunia ! " repeated the latter, shaking with inward laughter. " No wonder the lad thought you had taken leave of your senses ! Why, it means, ' I love you ' ! "

CHAPTER X

THE ARMY

The Russian Army appears to be, generally speaking, an unknown quantity in England, where, at the present day, no two persons ever seem to agree regarding its numerical strength, or capacity of dealing a decisive blow in the allied cause. One man will declare that Russia must, sooner or later, annihilate our common foe, while another will assure you with equal confidence, that our ally's position was hopeless from the first, and that every third man in her ranks is now reduced to fighting with a scythe ! The truth here probably lies, as usual, between two extremes, and a brief statement of what I know, from personal experience, of Russia's military power, may perhaps enable the reader to form a clearer conception of its strength and organization than the vague assertions of those whose knowledge is chiefly derived from English newspapers.

Let us first clearly realize that the population of Russia is now 180,000,000, which outnumbers that of Germany by well over 100,000,000, and while the former is increased every year by 3,000,000, the latter only annually adds about 1,000,000 to her 70,000,000.[1] It may therefore not unreasonably be assumed that a nation, which even now contains 60,000,000 people more than Germany and Austria-Hungary combined, and must, at the present rate of progression, number within the next fifty years something like 300,000,000 souls, is not likely to experience a shortage of men for the purpose of carrying on the present campaign, even should the latter be indefinitely prolonged, and in this titanic struggle men,

[1] The British Empire has 435,000,000 to its credit, China comes second with 400,000,000 and Russia third with 180,000,000. Germany and the dual monarchy contain about 120,000,000 souls.

like money, must tell in the end. Russia's financial position is equally satisfactory, for her revenue amounted in 1914 to over £350,000,000 exclusive of the French loans obtained since the Japanese War, which were chiefly expended on the army and navy. Above all, Russia is entirely a self-supporting country, and as the billions of tons of grain which were formerly exported to all parts of the world now remain within the empire, the latter is, unlike other belligerent nations, suffering not from a scarcity, but a superabundance of food. For it is an undisputed fact that Siberia alone could feed the whole of Europe.[1]

Russian military service begins at the age of twenty and ends at forty-three. About 250,000 men annually come up for enrolment, and of these only undeniably strong and healthy recruits are chosen, many being rejected for trivial ailments or infirmities which in any other country would pass unnoticed by a Medical Board, although the standard of height is very low, being five feet for the line, and three inches higher for the cavalry. Russia has in peace-time not one, but three distinct armies : those of Europe, Asia and the Caucasus, which in the aggregate amount, on a war footing, to about 8,000,000 men, this number including the reserves, but not the Cossacks or " Opolchénié " (a kind of " Landsturm "), which may collectively be estimated at another 2,000,000. The latter is practically a territorial force, divided into two classes : the first including not only men who have served their time in the line and reserve, but also young recruits who have been rejected as being superfluous from the regulars ; and the second, the levy *en masse*, which is only raised in war-time, when those previously exempted for various reasons are called up to join the colours. Besides all these, about 50,000 men are permanently employed to guard the railways, and there are also about 30,000 " Gendarmerie," both these forces being composed of old soldiers drafted, on attaining a certain age, from more active branches of the service.

---

[1] It is estimated that Russia grows 51 per cent. of the rye, 25 per cent. of the oats, 33 per cent. of the barley, and 22 per cent. of the wheat harvested all over the world.

A Russian line regiment [1] numbers in peace-time 2000, and on campaign no less than 4000 men, and ordinary cavalry regiments have six squadrons of 1000 men, but Cossack units have only 600 troopers divided into "sotnias" of about 125 each. An army corps is composed of from 200,000 to 300,000 men (on a peace footing), and these are stationed at Petrograd, Moscow, Kiéff and other large cities. There are also one in Finland, one in the Caucasus, and two in Central Asia. A division is composed of two brigades of two regiments of four battalions, also an artillery brigade of field batteries with ammunition columns, engineer train and half a dozen "sotnias" of Cossacks.

An artillery brigade has six batteries and each of the latter eight three-inch field-guns, the horse artillery being provided with quick-firing Schneider-Creuzots of three-inch calibre. What Russia now chiefly lacks is heavy siege armament, most of that which she possesses having been made by Krupp of Essen, although the Russian arsenals at Obukoft and Sestoretsk are also providing a rapidly increasing supply in addition to that which is being obtained from Japan and has been captured from the enemy.

The Russian cavalry includes sixteen divisions, in addition to the two Life Guards divisions (sixteen regiments) and four brigades of two regiments each. Each division has two brigades, and each brigade has two regiments. Every division is composed of dragoons, uhlans, hussars, and Cossacks. The cavalry is now provided with machine-guns, and its training and equipment have frequently been admired at manœuvres by foreign military attachés, while London has also occasionally seen the first prize for horsemanship carried off by its officers at Olympia. For those in crack regiments pay enormous prices for their chargers, many of which are English or Irish thoroughbreds by the most fashionable sires.

The indigenous Siberian tribes are exempt from military service; but there are, of course, many alien

[1] A regiment is called, in Russian, a "polk," from which the word "polka," signifying a dance, was probably derived.

races fighting for the Tsar, such as Circassians, Turkomans, Kirghiz and others, while the Jews have done so well in this war that they are now (for the first time in history) allowed to rank as non-commissioned officers. The "moujik," however, as I have said, is the backbone of the nation, and he is also that of the army; which latter is almost entirely composed of the peasantry, who, even in time of peace, lead a life of privation and endurance which admirably fits them for the severer hardships and perils of a campaign. Besides, as I have already remarked, the moujik has little or no fear of death, which, after all, is a soldier's chief qualification.

"Ivan" (as the Russian linesman is nicknamed) is as brave as a lion, and generally sturdy and muscular, but he lacks the jovial, contented look of our English "Tommy," and is indeed of a rather surly demeanour, only enjoying a joke if it be of a very broad and obvious kind. Also, according to our ideas, he is anything but well fed, his diet chiefly consisting of "schtchi," fish and rye bread, yet he seems to thrive upon this meagre fare, which would certainly not satisfy the average Englishman. And "Ivan" must now sadly miss the "vodka" which formerly enlivened his rather colourless existence; although, on the other hand, he is passionately fond of music, and is seen at his best when, at the end of a day's march, the men gather around the camp-fire for the national and inspiriting songs and dances which they love so well. Many line regiments are preceded by a trained choir as well as a band, and the former is generally preferable, for Russian military music is, with few exceptions, brassy and inferior.

Yet "Ivan" takes even his pleasures sadly; not that they ever amount to much, for his daily pay is even less than that of the French *poilu* (who, in some cases, receives only a sou a day), and no games or recreations of any kind are provided for him when in barracks. In peace-time, however, he can in his leisure hours earn a few extra kopeks by working for private employers, and this is his sole privilege, with which, being ever stolid and uncomplaining, he appears to be quite content. But for all his rough and uncouth exterior, "Ivan" has a generous nature and warm heart, and is therefore seldom cruel or vindictive towards a fallen foe. An example of his unfailing good-nature even on the battlefield was only recently shown when, upon an order being given that all prisoners found with explosive bullets in their possession were to be shot forthwith, a Russian officer detected some of his men in the act of trying to conceal some of the latter which had been secretly handed to them by their Austrian captives.

There is a Russian expression which, when used in the army, has a totally different meaning to when it is spoken by civilians. This is the word " Tak " (the military significance of which is somewhat akin to that of our slang word " Righto "), the Russian soldier's invariable reply when instructed to carry out an order, whether it be to storm a citadel or bring some shaving water. And either command will be cheerfully obeyed; for whatever he is told to do, the Russian soldier will do it, even though it involve his own destruction, as is shown by the following incident which was related to me by an artillery colonel, who had himself seen it during the Russo-Turkish War. On a certain occasion, near Plevna, it became necessary, at a critical moment, to move some field-pieces across a deep swamp, where no wood or faggots were obtainable to make a passage for the guns. Volunteers were therefore called for from an infantry regiment to serve this purpose, and a number of men at once left the ranks and lay face downwards in the mud, while several batteries galloped over their prostrate bodies, the guns and horses crushing and trampling most of them to death ! And I could cite several other instances of heroic self-sacrifice, in the Russian ranks, which are certainly unsurpassed in the military annals of any other nation.

During the reign of Peter the Great the Russian Army was modelled upon German lines, a system which continued until the accession of Alexander II., who was such an ardent admirer of Germany that the latter provided him with military instructors, some of whom (notably Adlerberg and Todleben) became naturalized Russians, whose descendants are now fighting against their former compatriots. In former days, therefore, both drill and uniforms emanated from Berlin, and it was only after the Emperor's tragic death in 1878 that his successor introduced the plain but serviceable dress of to-day, which consists, in winter, of a loose drab overcoat (of the same material as that worn by Siberian prisoners) secured by a leathern belt, and a circular fur cap, bearing the regimental badge or number. In summer a flat, peakless cap and loose white linen blouse replace the thick winter tunic; stout high-boots, into which baggy breeches are stuffed, being worn throughout the year. This may not sound attractive, yet notwithstanding its sombre, drab appearance, and the rather slouching gait of the men, a Russian line regiment on the march has a tough-looking, workman-like aspect which amply atones for outward pomp and display. Some of the cavalry, of course, have brilliant tunics and facings, the olive-green and magenta of that crack regiment the Grodno Hussars being almost startling, while the "Chevaliérs Gardes" wear an even more dazzling and expensive uniform than that of the Kaiser's Imperial Guard.

The infantry is armed with a five-cartridge magazine rifle, with a range of 3000 yards, and although at first they were very short of quick-firing guns, this defect has, as in England, been remedied.[1] Russia also uses a field-gun closely resembling the famous "75," which is made at the Creuzot works in France, and is being supplied with a very similar, but even more modern, weapon by the Japanese. But the Russian prefers cold steel to the most costly and accurate rifle ever invented; and that he knows how to use the former was proved at Plevna, when that almost impregnable fortress was taken chiefly at the point of the bayonet.

I have many personal friends in the Russian Army, ranging from a smart and dapper captain in the "Chevaliérs-Gardes" to a rough and rugged Cossack colonel smothered in decorations, who before this war was stationed in the wilds of Central Asia, though Heaven only knows where he is now! And, having occasionally been entertained as a regimental guest, I have had

[1] Great Britain uses the "Lee-Enfield," Germany the "Mauser" rifle.

opportunities of closely studying Russian military life, both in the mess and barrack-room. My first experience of this kind was some years before, my latest five years after, the Japanese campaign, which terminated in such a disastrous Russian defeat, although the latter proved a blessing in disguise; for had it not occurred, the nation would probably have remained in ignorance of its urgent military needs, and certain reforms which have now evolved a more powerful and efficient army than the nation has ever possessed might never have taken place. For the Japanese War was lost, not from any lack of bravery or enterprise on the part of the troops, but from the sheer incapacity and indifference of most of their generals, some of whom were carousing with French *cocottes* in Mukden, while their presence was urgently needed at the front. Moreover, thousands of Russian soldiers in the Japanese campaign practically died of starvation owing to a deficient transport and commissariat, and the latter even now is far from being perfect, although the medical branches of the service have been thoroughly reformed and reorganized.[1]

The Russian officer is as brave as he is hospitable (which says a great deal), but it is only of recent years that his attention has been turned to serious professional studies which were formerly almost entirely neglected, even in such important branches as the artillery and engineers. But such a change has now taken place not only in the discharge of his professional duties, but also in his mode of life, that I was amazed, on the occasion of my last visit to a regiment which I had known in the old " happy-go-lucky " days, to behold such a complete transformation in such a short space of time. When I first went to Russia, thirty years ago, the higher branches of military science were studied only by a select and zealous few, who were generally laughed at by ribald companions for their pains. Drill occupied a few hours in the morning, after which the afternoon and evening were generally devoted to women, cards and champagne,

---

[1] So inefficient was the Russian Commissariat during the Crimean War that of 60,000 men who marched in winter from Moscow to Sebastopol, only 12,000 reached their destination.

not only by gay and giddy subalterns but also their grey-haired elders holding high commands, and I often wondered how even the latter could habitually indulge in such reckless extravagance, seeing that a general then received about the equivalent of a British major's pay.[1] In the old days, an adjournment was invariably made after dinner to a theatre, music-hall, or some less reputable resort of a garrison town; but during my last visit I was left to my own devices on the first evening after mess, my host and his brother officers having excused themselves on the plea of having to attend a lecture on tactics! And this occurred nearly every night, while most of the day was taken up with severe outdoor work, for the Russian officer of every rank is now as keen to acquire scientific and technical knowledge as he formerly was to indulge in frivolity and dissipation.

And this salutary condition of affairs is certainly partly due to the fact that champagne is now as rarely seen on a mess-table as " vodka " in the canteen. For even twenty years ago a man who could not freely dispose of alcohol was regarded as rather a milksop, and I retain a lively recollection of a certain dinner with the gallant —— Hussars in Warsaw when, being the only guest, I had to drink the health, separately, of every officer present. And when I had been compelled to partake of every sort of wine, followed by coffee and liqueurs, a huge silver bowl was borne in, into which all the fruit left at dessert was first placed, and the dregs of every decanter and wine-glass on the table emptied, together with a quart of cognac, which was then set on fire! Having rashly imbibed some of this mixture, I was suddenly tilted from my chair by several young officers, who then formed a ring, laid me on their clasped hands, and tossed me violently up and down on this substitute for a blanket! This, I was afterwards informed, was considered a great honour, but it was nevertheless one with which I could willingly have dispensed as a sequel to such a " wet " evening! But those nights of riotous revelry are now relegated to the past, for those who once indulged in them (and especially the new type of Russian

---

[1] The scale of officers' pay in the Russian Army has now been increased.

H

officer) are quite as deeply impressed with the vital importance of their mission in life as their comrades in the armies of Great Britain or France.

The friendly, not to say familiar, relations which here exist between officers and men could never exist elsewhere in Europe. Even a general coming on parade greets his men as " brothers," and a captain acknowledges the salute of a private of his company with studied politeness, and as though the latter were one of his own rank and class. And yet a man while talking to an officer, even for a lengthened period, must not for an instant lower his hand, this being probably a survival of the discipline which was once as severe here as it is to-day in Germany. There is even a legend that a former Tsar once sent off an entire regiment of dragoons to Siberia, without permitting them to return to barracks, simply because they failed to perform a certain manœuvre to his liking at a Petrograd review. And although at the present day officers and men off duty frequently address each other as " Brother " and " Little Father " respectively, discipline is never really relaxed; for even in time of peace, a soldier who, even when intoxicated, insults his superior officer, is at once tried by court-martial and very often shot. Such a breach of respect is, however, of very rare occurrence; for the mere fact that men are treated as their friends, even by field officers, precludes the former from taking a liberty, and one who did so would certainly be severely handled by his comrades.

Whenever I express my sincere admiration for the Russian Army to its English detractors they almost invariably reply : " Yes, but how easily it was beaten in the Japanese War ! " without apparently taking into consideration three important reasons for its defeat on that occasion, viz. : (1) the incapacity of its commanders ; (2) the enormous distance (6000 miles) from its base ; and (3) that the war was a very unpopular one, for half the army did not know what they were fighting for, or even against, some of the wilder Siberian troops picturing the foe as a fiery dragon of stupendous proportions and power ! Russia was also, at that time, seriously hampered by internal dissension which compelled the military authorities to retain a number of troops in Europe, whose services were urgently required in the Far East. She is now, however, fighting a traditional enemy whom even little children instinctively revile and detest, while every man in the country is well aware that not only his freedom, but his very existence, is at stake. Above all, the strategical conditions are now as much in Russia's favour as they were, in Manchuria, the reverse, while her troops acquired as much useful military knowledge and experience during the Japanese campaign as England after the South African War.

But anyway, Russia has now happily become our staunch friend and ally, wherefore it is satisfactory to reflect that, except on two occasions, she has never met with what can be called a really decisive defeat. On the other hand, she successfully resisted Napoleon for years, and eventually drove him out of the country with heavy loss; while in 1878 she completely routed the Turks, and would, if not restrained by the Powers, have occupied, if not annexed, Constantinople. Nor must one forget her brilliant military successes, against formidable odds, in Central Asia and the Caucasus, the once hostile races of which have now become peaceful and prosperous Russian subjects. To use a slang term, Russia, *in the end*, always " comes out on top," although at the outset of hostilities, and probably from characteristic indolence engendered by semi-Oriental methods, she generally gets the worst of it. The most crushing reverse, however, never seriously affects her, for the Russians are fatalists who, however gloomy the outlook, never give way to despair, being firmly convinced that, whatever happens in this world, in the shape of good or evil, is the will of God, and must therefore be submissively endured. And this, in warfare, is a wonderful consoler at times of depression and defeat.

Every one in England is naturally anxious to have done with the war, and I therefore constantly hear my compatriots express their impatience at the apparent slowness of our ally's operations on the Eastern front; yet this fact should never cause disappointment or anxiety, for (as I well know !) no Russian was ever yet in a hurry, and time, to him, is therefore of no importance so long as, in the end, he achieves his object.[1]   It must also be remembered that Russia cannot yet employ more than about a quarter of her forces simply because she cannot equip and arm the remainder.   No less than 18,000,000 men are available, and 12,000,000 of these are at present idle, and must remain so until the munition workers of other countries enable them to take their place in the ranks.   Russia's offensive is therefore at present only in its initial stage, for if the other Allies have now all they need in the shape of heavy armament, the former is still very inadequately supplied.   A Russian friend of the writer not inaptly described his country under present conditions, as an ocean, the incoming tide of which breaks upon an ironbound coast only to recede, and presently return with redoubled volume and strength.   So, he declared, will his countrymen come on, again and again, until the Hun defences are worn away, and that accursed race is submerged for ever.

For the Russian, like the British soldier, never knows when he is beaten.   "Ivan" will go on fighting as bravely as a lion and stubbornly as a mule indefinitely, if need be; and that is why, with such inexhaustible reserves, he must eventually wear down the enemy, who is nothing like his equal in point of numbers, and is, moreover, confronted by three grim forces which in the end repelled even Napoleon: distance, hunger, and cold.   We in England can only faintly realize Russia's latent but prodigious power, or conceive the overwhelming masses of troops which she can continue to throw into the field, if necessary, for the next twenty years.   And who can blame our lack of knowledge when the Russian Government itself occasionally underrates its military resources, as is shown by the fact that, a few months ago, the authorities decided to call up a territorial class which, it was calculated, would yield something like

---

[1] Their proverb, " What is slowly done, is well done," is exemplified by a peasant who, when making a horse-yoke out of a birch bough, was slowly bending the latter to its required shape by the aid of steam, when a bear standing by, thinking to accomplish the job more rapidly, snatched the wood away and crushed it with such force that it smashed into splinters.

400,000 men, and the call was promptly answered by nearly 1,000,000!

It may not be generally known that the present reforms in the Russian Army are chiefly due to the personal influence and efforts of the Ex-Tsar, who threw himself heart and soul into a work for which His Imperial Majesty's military knowledge and experience have rendered him eminently capable. The substitution, after the Japanese War, of young and energetic men for aged and incapable leaders, was almost entirely brought about by the Emperor, but only after powerful opposition on the part of those who naturally wished to retain their lucrative posts. The Kaiser was regarded as a man of unusual strength of character when he ruthlessly deposed Prince Bismarck, but the Tsar was recently confronted with a much more intricate problem before he was able to finally expel the band of sycophants (many of German origin) who had surrounded him ever since his accession to the throne, and who were chiefly to blame for the corrupt condition of the country and its army. Nicholas II. was also mainly responsible for an increase in the pay of officers, which now not only enables men of slender means, and perhaps superior military qualities, to obtain a commission, but also lessens the temptation to pilfer from regimental funds; a custom once so prevalent, that a colonel of a regiment frequently amassed huge sums of money by tampering with the forage for his horses or clothing for his men. It was also by the Tsar's personal intervention that the Russian flying corps, which has recently done such useful work, was entirely remodelled on French lines.

There can be little doubt that, with the exception of the more advanced Socialists, all classes of society in Russia are now solidly united against a universally dreaded and detested foe. Every Russian, of whatever creed or class, regards this war as a purely national struggle, and enough has perhaps been said to convince the most confirmed British croaker that " Russia's case is anything but hopeless," and that she has not yet been compelled to resort to agricultural implements as weapons of warfare! Moreover, a moment's calm reflection must surely show him that a nation which steadily continues to produce ever-increasing millions of men, and possesses such inexhaustible wealth and resources, can never be really or decisively conquered, either now or in the far-distant future.

A TOWN ON THE LENA IN SUMMER-TIME

CHAPTER XI

CIVILIZED SIBERIA

PART I

HISTORY—THE "TRANS-SIBERIAN RAILWAY"—ON THE
CHINESE FRONTIER

FEW people in England ever realize the stupendous size of the Russian Empire, proudly styled by its people "Polovina Mir," or "Half the World," which is, of course, an exaggeration, although Russian Asia alone covers an area of nearly 6,000,000 square miles. Mr. George Kennan, the American traveller, perhaps afforded the most graphic illustration of its enormous extent when he wrote as follows—

"If it were possible to move entire countries from one part of the globe to another, you could take the whole of the United States of America, from Maine to California, and from Lake Superior to the Gulf of Mexico, and set it down in the middle of Siberia without touching anywhere the boundaries of the latter territory. You could then take Alaska and all the states of Europe, and fit them into the remaining margin like pieces of a dissected map, and after having thus accommodated all of the United States, including Alaska, and all of Europe (except Russia), you would still have more than 300,000 square miles of Siberian territory to spare—in other words, you would still leave unoccupied in Siberia an area half as large again as the Empire of Germany!"

And all this is exclusive of European Russia, which has an additional area of over 200,000 square miles!

Thirty years ago, before the completion of the "Trans-Siberian Railway," Siberia was chiefly regarded in

103

England as a vast penal colony, to which political exiles were deported under atrociously cruel conditions. In those days, only a few capitalists and explorers ever gave a thought to the commercial or agricultural possibilities of a country which was practically as unknown to the majority of Englishmen as Central Tibet, and as many of the former may still remain in ignorance of the facts which led to the annexation of this vast and valuable territory, I will here briefly relate them.

Western Siberia was conquered in 1581, by a few hundred men under one Yérmak, a poor illiterate Cossack, who with a handful of desperadoes undertook the daring military operations destined to achieve such marvellous results. Previously to this Siberia had remained a *terra incognita* even in Russia until the middle of the sixteenth century, when the Tsar Ivan Vassilivitch sent an expedition across the Urals, defeating a few Tartars, who, however, quickly drove the invaders back into Europe. Disheartened by this reverse the Tsar next attempted to open up trade with Persia, but the imperial caravans were continually pillaged on the road by lawless Cossacks, led by Yérmak, who, however, was eventually defeated, and compelled to fly from his home on the Don, and take refuge with his followers on the banks of the Volga. Here Yérmak first learnt of the existence of Siberia—which was described to him as a country of fabulous wealth, under the rule of Koutchoum-Khan, whose dominions then only extended for a few hundred miles east of the Urals.

So it came to pass that Yérmak, allured by visions of fame and riches, set out in the summer of 1579 for the unknown El Dorado, with an armed but undisciplined rabble of 5000 men, whose progress was so slow, owing to lack of funds and transport, that over a year elapsed before they crossed the Asiatic frontier. Sickness, hunger and privation had by this time reduced them to under 1500 men, whom Koutchoum-Khan unexpectedly engaged with a formidable Tartar force just over the border. The battle which ensued was a desperate one, but although confronted by enormous odds, the gallant little band of Russians completely routed their foes. Yérmak then pushed on and occupied

Sibir, where he was installed as " Prince of Siberia " by his few remaining companions.

Here the invaders enjoyed for a time a well-earned rest, until Tartar intrigues caused further trouble, which urgently necessitated outside aid. A trusty emissary was therefore dispatched to Moscow to explain matters, and announce that Siberia had been conquered solely in the name of the Tsar. Nevertheless, the envoy approached the Holy City with serious misgivings, for there was not only a reward offered for the capture of his chief, dead or alive, but also for all his followers. Ivan the Terrible, however, on hearing the joyful and amazing news, granted every outlaw a free pardon, dispatched a large body of troops to their assistance, and simultaneously conferred wealth and the highest honours upon their adventurous chief, whose name is now almost as revered throughout the nation as that of Peter the Great. And amongst the princely gifts with which the messenger returned to his leader at Sibir was the suit of golden armour which, only a few months later, unhappily caused the death of its brave recipient.

The latter, now emboldened by the presence of imperial troops, recommenced operations by laying siege to a small fortress, which was expected to offer little resistance, on the Irtysh river. The Tartars, however, had in the meantime so successfully reformed their scattered forces, that Yérmak unexpectedly encountered a hornets' nest, which compelled him to fall back in disorder, closely pursued by the enemy, to his base at Sibir. And during the retreat thousands of Russians were slain, until one night Yérmak and a little band of men sought refuge on a small islet of the Irtysh, intending to resume their flight at dawn. But when the fugitives, exhausted by a long and harassing day, had fallen asleep, a force of Tartars silently landed and fell upon them so suddenly that only one man escaped, under cover of the darkness, to Sibir, with news of the disaster in which his chief had perished. The latter had fought fiercely to the last, cutting his way through serried masses of the enemy, before plunging into the river, where he endeavoured to board one of the boats which the latter had occupied. But the craft was moored some distance from the shore, and Yérmak was dragged under water to his death by the weight of the massive golden armour which had been presented to him by the Tsar.

The next expedition dispatched to Siberia was of such formidable proportions that it met with hardly any opposition, and speedily re-established Muscovite rule throughout the province of Sibir. The work of annexation was then extended, and fortresses erected at Tobolsk, Tará, and other strategic points from which the stream of conquest flowed eastward apace. Tomsk was founded in 1604 and became a base of further extension, while the now important town of Yeniseisk was founded in 1619, and that of Krasnoyarsk eight years later. Armed parties then marched on to Lake Baikal, and thence to the valley of the Lena, erecting stockades and subduing natives either by peaceful or forceful persuasion. Yakutsk was founded in 1632, and seven years later the Sea of Okhotsk was reached, although the Bouriattes and other indigenous tribes were not finally overcome until about the middle of the seventeenth century. Thus, in the short space of sixty years, and mainly through the courage and enterprise of one man, was added to the Russian Empire a territory of which centuries alone can truly reveal the prodigious wealth.

Siberia is, in England, generally associated with intense cold and eternal snow, and no one ever seems to picture it in summer garb, when it becomes one of the most temperate and fertile countries in the world. I have been there at every season of the year, and can therefore testify that if the cold has occasionally been beyond endurance, I have also on occasion suffered severely from the other extreme, a fact easily explained in this land of stupendous area, and therefore innumerable varieties of temperature. Thus, in the month of June, I have perspired in a thin flannel suit in the town of Tomsk, and, a few weeks later, have shivered in furs with 70° below zero on the River Lena! And I preferred the cold, for in Siberia (as in European Russia) few precautions are taken to guard against heat.

So much for the historical and physical characteristics of Siberia, following which a word as to the Trans-

Siberian Railway may not be out of place. A deal of nonsense has been written about the latter in order to attract English travellers bound to Japan, but these should beware of alluring and overdrawn advertisements. Personally I should always choose the sea-route in preference to that across Asia in cars not nearly so well-appointed as those of the "Wagons Lits" Company in Europe. I have travelled to the Far East both by land and by liner a dozen times, and give me the latter in preference to a train of exasperating slowness, where the outlook from your carriage window from Moscow to Manchuria is ever the same: in summer a dreary sunbaked waste, with intervals of pine forest; in winter a vista of perpetual snow—both being so monotonous that after a fortnight or so they have generally reduced me to a condition of apathetic despair. Climatically, the journey is agreeable enough, especially in winter, when Siberia is at its best, and when on most days there is a blue sky and dazzling sunshine which, at midday, often renders your heated compartment too warm to be pleasant, although outside the thermometer may register 20° below zero. But the air is dry and, even with a breeze (which will presently be torturing Londoners in the shape of a biting east wind), sometimes actually enjoyable. On the other hand, the food is (or was) atrocious, also the attendance; and although the beds are comfortable enough, the only bath in the train I last travelled in was generally used as a receptacle for storing ice, vegetables, and butcher's meat, and was therefore in a filthy condition when put to its proper use. Fortunately the station "restaurants" are as perfect as they are in Russia (and they are the best in the world); and the fares are extremely moderate, a first-class ticket from Moscow to Irkutsk (a ten days' journey) costing only £15.

It was in 1857 that an American first conceived this great railway, and although his project was abandoned, the Russian Government took careful note of the original surveys, and also of those which have since been made with a similar object by English and French engineers. The Trans-Siberian was undoubtedly a colossal achievement, and it is the longest railway in the world, but it cannot be compared, in ingenuity of construction, with the Canadian Pacific line, on which I have also frequently travelled. Yet I have occasionally read that the Russian line entailed greater difficulties, which is obviously absurd, for this track is mostly as level as a billiard-table, only the region around Lake Baikal and eastward of it being mountainous. Nevertheless no expense has been spared to make the Trans-Siberian (which is of uniform gauge with the European lines) as perfect as circumstances will permit. The bridges, formerly of wood, are now made of iron, the one over the Irtysh being nearly four miles long; a remarkable piece of engineering which, as it has to withstand enormous ice pressure, entailed an enormous expenditure.

The commercial possibilities of the Trans-Siberian cannot, as yet, be fully estimated, for its influence on commercial energy must, in years to come, affect the remotest part of Russian Asia. Even now, towns of considerable size have sprung up in all directions, although the country is, as yet, only sparsely peopled, its entire population being 1,000,000 less than that of London. It has now, however, largely increased, and will probably continue to do so so long as the goldfields attract prospectors, and foreign emigrants gradually realize that fortune awaits them, not only underground, but on the boundless and fertile prairie. I should explain that as regards agriculture Siberia is composed of three great zones—the upper or northern one, being the " Tundra," which extends across the country for about 5000 miles, and is useless for purposes of cultivation, for in summer it is like a soft wet sponge, into which you sink knee-deep, and which is only capable of producing mosquitoes. Immediately south of the " Tundra " comes the " Taiga," a forest belt of enormous extent, which contains valuable lumber of all kinds, the exploiting of which will be greatly increased by the facilities afforded by railway transport. The third and most important zone is the " Steppe " region, one of unfailing fertility which is yearly being more extensively brought under cultivation and where the soil is so rich that, as Siberians say, " When tickled with the hoe, it laughs with a harvest." This region must, in the near future, attract thousands of, not only Russian, but foreign capitalists, for the purpose of farming, horse and cattle breeding, and the export of grain.

Accidents are rare on the Trans-Siberian, but even the express trains travel at a snail's pace, and an enormous staff is employed to keep the track in order. The old post-road was (as I can testify) rather dangerous after dark, for it was infested with runaway convicts; but the railway is perfectly safe in this respect, and has never yet been the scene of a " hold-up." It is only beyond Irkutsk that the laying of the line presented anything like serious difficulties. Lake Baikal was the chief stumbling-block, and for a long time passengers had to cross it in a small steamer, preceded in winter by an ice-breaker, but the line now skirts the southern shores of the lake. From this point the track gradually ascends until it reaches the Yablonoi mountains, where it attains its highest altitude (3412 feet above sea-level), and passes through a region of impressive beauty and grandeur. There is from here a rapid descent to the plains, which continue until the Pacific Ocean is reached at Vladivostok, where the first stone of the eastern terminus was laid by the deposed Tsar (then Tsarévitch) on May 12, 1891.

Let me now describe my impressions of a country of which I had shared, up till my first visit, the vague and generally erroneous notions of my countrymen. My initial experience of a Siberian town was on a July day at Kiakhta, on the Chinese frontier, which I reached from the great wall of China, after a five weeks' journey across the Gobi Desert in a camel-cart.[1] This was before the existence of the railway, and the voyage which followed across Siberia to Europe was, therefore, accomplished with horses in a " tarantass," [2] a ramshackle vehicle on wheels which is used for posting in summer-time.

[1] See *Pekin to Calais by Land*, by the author.
[2] " A tarantass resembles a large cradle on four wheels. It is seatless, about seven feet long by five feet broad, and the luggage is packed in the well of the vehicle, a mattress being placed over the former on which the occupant reclines. There is a hood, from which an apron is fastened to the driver's seat to exclude wind and rain, but the carriage is springless, and suspended on two long slender poles " (*Pekin to Calais by Land*, by the author).

The little town of Kiakhta is worthy of description, not only on account of its proximity to the Mongolian frontier, but also because its manners and customs formed a striking contrast to other Siberian cities which I afterwards visited, and which have greatly improved, in every respect, since the construction of the great iron road. And even this remote place (through which all the overland tea from China passes) was a revelation to one who had anticipated finding, at most, a few squalid huts with possibly a military post, for even this would have been welcome after weeks in the wilds with only Tartars as companions. Judge, therefore, of my surprise when I rode into a town of attractive appearance, with public and private buildings, well-kept streets and squares, good shops, and a public garden with a bandstand! There were two or three churches; one a handsome building (erected by the local tea-merchants), the golden altar of which had cost £30,000, while its chime of bells had been dragged by thousands of horses for 2000 miles from Europe. Near this church was a new and imposing brick building which I eventually discovered was a college attended by over 100 students.

Having no letters of introduction, I went to the so-called inn to find that a foul, dark room, with a rickety table and two wooden chairs, was the sole accommodation provided, and that guests must find their own bed and refreshment. But there were then no inns worthy of the name in even the largest Siberian cities (except Irkutsk), and travellers had to put up at the post-houses, which generally contained a " samovar," eggs and black bread, although even these were unobtainable in the malodorous " Hotel Glembodski." Towards evening, therefore, of the day of my arrival I was literally starving in a land of plenty, for, being a Sunday, the shops were shut, and I could not purchase provisions.

So I strolled, friendless and well-nigh famished, to the public garden, where the band of a Cossack regiment was performing to a gaily-dressed assemblage, mainly composed of wealthy tea-merchants with their wives and daughters, the latter of whom sat listening to the music and flirting with officers, just as though this had been some French or German watering-place. One

A TOWN ON THE LENA IN WINTER

could scarcely realize that the loneliest desert in the world was only a couple of miles distant, or that this was the Chinese frontier, but for some pigtailed figures in delicate silken robes who mingled freely with that little concourse of Europeans.

The Siberian merchant is the soul of hospitality, as I happily discovered when, returning supperless to my unclean abode, I found its Polish landlord conversing with a frock-coated individual who addressed me in French, and who, on hearing of my troubles, invited me to accompany him to his home, an offer which, as it probably meant food, I gladly accepted. For I was now feeling actually faint from hunger, and was therefore much relieved to observe, on passing my host's dining-room, that supper was laid for a number of people.

My friend in need was a tea-merchant, who lived in a charming house, and whose wife's refinement and good taste were indicated by her drawing-room, which contained valuable pictures from Europe, and porcelain and other works of art from China and Japan. Here the guests assembled, and I watched their tardy arrival with pardonable anxiety, seeing that every minute was now increasing the discomfort caused by prolonged abstention from food. The supper-table which had presented such an inviting aspect was therefore uppermost in my thoughts, and my heart sank when, towards eleven o'clock, my host took me to inspect a consignment of tea-chests which were stacked in the yard, and which he proceeded, with maddening deliberation, to " taste," by driving a hollow piece of metal, like a cheese scoop, into each case, and withdrawing a small sample ! However, we found, on returning to the drawing-room, that all the guests had assembled, consisting of the local " ispravnik " and his wife—a stout and stern-visaged lady, a Cossack officer then quartered in Kiakhta, three young gentlemen and two young ladies of no special interest, a poor relation from nowhere in particular, and two professors, one of music and the other of chemistry, from the college. Only my host and his pretty wife spoke English, and the Cossack imperfect French, which, as I was then unacquainted with Russian, rather restricted my conversational efforts.

No one has a greater admiration for Russian life and character than myself, but while noting the many excellent qualities of our allies, it would only be misleading to ignore their few defects. And one of these is an utter disregard of punctuality with regard to meals— a failing which, I should add, is chiefly confined to Siberia. On the evening in question nine o'clock was the stipulated hour for supper, but it was nearly midnight before it was announced, and even then it was only with reluctance that the guests left a game of cards which, throughout the evening, had engrossed their attention. And even when at length the dining-room was reached we lingered for quite half an hour around a side-table set out with salted herrings, salmon, cheese and caviare, flanked by bottles of cognac, "vodka," and numerous liqueurs. Here every one gravely drank my health, turning his glass up, if I did not drain mine, to show that his was empty; with the result that, by the time supper was served, I had been compelled to absorb about a dozen glasses of "vodka," a fiery liquid which cannot be drunk with impunity.

Supper consisted of a dish of mutton cutlets and two diminutive chickens, a slender allowance for such a numerous company, but with the exception of bread and sweet biscuits, there was no other form of solid nourishment. There was no lack, on the other hand, of liquid refreshment in the shape of sweet "Sauterne" and sugary port wine (the latter bearing a well-known English label), but I searched in vain for claret, beer, or even water to slake the raging thirst induced by highly-spiced and salted "zakouski." Towards 3 a.m. the ladies retired, leaving the men to gather round the table and finish the evening (or rather morning) in the good old-fashioned way. In vain I protested that I never touched port, and that alcohol in any shape upset me; my companions ignored all excuses and insisted on my drinking with them in turn, much in the same way that the immortal Mr. Jorrocks and his huntsman, James Pigg, drank to the health of every separate hound in the pack when they had exhausted every other toast. For here, when the Tsar, Queen of England,

Emperor of China and other reigning potentates had been duly honoured, these Kiakhta revellers fell back, as a last resource, on their " noble selves."

It must have been about 5 a.m. (for it was broad daylight) when I was the innocent cause of a discussion which nearly resulted in a tragedy. The conversation having turned upon duelling, I related the story of the three-cornered duel in *Midshipman Easy*, which afforded the Cossack so much amusement that he retailed the anecdote, in Russian, for the benefit of the college professors; each of whom took opposite views of the question, one maintaining that this mode of conflict was permissible, while the other declared that it was cowardly and unfair. No three men, argued the musician, should be allowed to fire at each other, for one of them must be at a disadvantage; and the argument at length became so heated that my host was compelled to interfere. The Cossack then joined in, expressing his conviction that the matter could only be settled by personal combat, in order not only to satisfy the honour of the disputants, but also to test their respective theories. Nothing, he urged, would settle the matter but practical demonstration, and he would therefore be charmed to fetch his duelling-pistols and make a third! But fortunately this extreme course was not resorted to, for the captain's suggestion seemed to suddenly pacify the combatants, who thereupon shook hands, and ended by exchanging vows of eternal friendship.

It was past six o'clock when we separated, English bottled stout being previously handed round, a beverage which then cost about a guinea a bottle in Kiakhta, and was drunk out of wine-glasses! Then everybody kissed every one else (a trying ordeal to which, in Siberia, I have since frequently had to submit), and I retired to rest—on the drawing-room sofa, for, although the house was luxuriously furnished, apparently only the ladies were provided with beds. My host had disappeared when the Cossack, (who had consumed more liquor than any one else), buckled on his sword and strolled off to morning parade, still brooding over his rejected proposal, but now as sober as a judge. The professors also departed, arm in arm, in an opposite direction, down the

I

now sunlit street.   So ended my first " evening party "
in Siberia !

All this occurred some years ago, and I have merely
mentioned the incident in order to show that social life
has, in Siberia, greatly changed for the better, since
the railway has brought Europe into closer touch with
these outposts of civilization.   Such an evening as I
have described would, of course, be impossible under
the recent restrictions, nor would such a debauch now
be tolerated in any well-ordered Siberian household.

PART II

IRKUTSK—TOMS—KTOBOLSK

Irkutsk, which lies west of Kiakhta, is 4000 miles
from Petrograd—a journey which formerly took nearly
three months, although shortly before the war I did
it, by rail, in ten days !   It is called the " Paris of
Siberia," but I must confess I could never see any
resemblance between this unfinished, straggling city
and the gay French capital, although the former is
picturesquely situated in rugged Alpine scenery between
two rivers, the mighty Angará, and the placid little
Irkut.   The population numbers 60,000 and is naturally
rather mixed, for in the market-place you may see the
Celestial elbowing fur-clad Yakutes, and Central Asia
shaking hands with Japan.   The natives of the district
are Bourialtes, who are Buddhists and speak a mixture of
Mongolian and Chinese, although they are more intelligent than any other Siberian race, many holding
appointments as Government officials.

When I first visited Irkutsk there was one clean and
comfortable inn, which has now disappeared, to give place
to a number of so-called hotels, all equally bad and
expensive, which the railway has produced.   Of these
the " Métropole " is perhaps the best; but although the
name is suggestive of a gold-laced porter and marble
halls, it is a cheap, jerry-built building with an atrocious
cuisine and accommodation, although its charges are
equal to those of the Carlton.   On the last occasion

my room certainly contained an iron bedstead (an unknown luxury in the old days), but its sheets and pillows bore the imprint of many previous guests, and there was no bathroom in the house, the only washing appliance in my apartment being a brass tap fixed into the wall, which dribbled cold water into a dirty brass basin. The establishment, in short, was as dirty and comfortless as a fifth-rate London lodging-house, although other private residences around were almost palatial, being mostly owned by illiterate *nouveaux riches* who had amassed huge fortunes in the Amur goldfields. There is a wide social difference between the middle-class Siberian and his prototype in European Russia, which is explained by the fact that Siberian society largely consists of the descendants of convicts. Wealth apparently makes no difference to the garb of either men or women, most of whom, even though they be in affluent circumstances, present an untidy, even shabby appearance. It is only in winter that costly or cheap furs indicate a man's station in life, blue-fox or sable denoting the merchant, while astrakhan or sheepskin are worn by his clerk. Both, however, generally look as if they slept in their clothes; which, by the way, is not improbable. For I was once the guest of a Siberian Vanderbilt who lived like a prince, his house and its appointments having cost millions of roubles. The owner possessed priceless pictures and artistic treasures, horses and carriages, and conservatories of rare orchids and exotics, all brought from Europe. Even his bedroom was furnished *à la Louis XV.* by a famous Parisian upholsterer, and yet he slept every night, fully dressed, on three chairs !

Most of the buildings in the " Bolshaya," or main thoroughfare of Irkutsk, are of brick, and it is lit at night with electricity, although only flickering oil lamps illumine the back streets, through which, after dark, you must grope your way. The " Opera " (a new and handsome house) stands near this main street, which also contains two or three theatres, and some so-called music-halls, which blaze with light from dusk till dawn, and where suppers are served at little wooden tables, while painted harridans cackle, suggestive songs on a small stage, from which they occasionally descend to mingle with the crowd. Siberian millionaires spend their money freely, but most of those I met preferred the dubious amusements of their native city to the more refined attractions of a European capital. Many, therefore, took their pleasure sadly, but expensively, in these places, amid surroundings suggestive of a low-class American "dive"; and this was to some extent excusable, for the "Opera" was generally closed, and performances at the other theatres were of a very inferior description. But Irkutsk now has its skating-rink, and picture-theatres, and, for all I know, superior operatic and dramatic artists, and the evenings may be less dreary than those I passed there six or seven years ago, when, although I had hospitable friends, dinner was invariably followed by gambling for stakes far beyond my means. I generally returned to my hotel in a "droshki" at night, when it was well to be armed, for highway rob-beries and even murders were of frequent occurrence, and were generally traced to time-expired convicts in the lower quarters of the town. On the occasion of my last visit I was only here a week, during which period a woman was shot one evening outside the "Métropole" and a man stabbed to death, in broad daylight, on the busy "Bolshaya."

In summer-time Irkutsk society migrates for coolness and fresh air to Lake Baikal, about twenty miles away, and I retain pleasant recollections of a visit, in July, to the pine-clad shores of this the largest lake in Asia, which in places is said to be unfathomable. But its frozen waters present no attractions in winter, and this is moreover the pleasantest season of the year in Irkutsk, which in summer-time is unbearably hot and dusty. Yet the place is fairly healthy, except in the fall of the year, when lung disease and rheumatism are prevalent owing to cold and dense fogs. The spring is equally objectionable, for the melting and swollen Angará then causes inundations which are sometimes very destructive to life and property.

Tomsk is, next to Irkutsk, the largest city in Siberia; but although the former is 2000 miles nearer Europe, it is only reached by a branch line from the

Trans-Siberian, and is therefore, commercially speaking, a less important place. In former days, however, Tomsk was the only Siberian terminus in direct steam communication with Petrograd by river and rail; but this, although still maintained, has now been considerably reduced by the cheaper and quicker mode of transit direct by land to Moscow. Yet the river trip was, to my mind, preferable to the railway journey; and the ten days to Tiumen, and pleasant break across the Urals, succeeded by a four days' trip down the Volga to Nijni Novgorod, was as full of interest as the railway route is now dull and monotonous. The large paddle steamers which still ply in the summer to Tomsk from Tiumen and back are roomy and comfortable, and there is no pleasanter trip, especially for sportsmen, for the country teems with game of all kinds, and a shooting licence is easily procured. Navigation opens about the end of April and closes in October, and fares are even cheaper on board these boats than on the Trans-Siberian Railway.

Tomsk consists of an upper and lower town; the former, which is situated on a steep, granite cliff, comprising buildings which, at a distance, present a rather imposing appearance. In the lower, or business, quarter of the town, however, brick and wooden dwellings are confusedly jumbled together, and the broad, straggling streets are unpaved and, in summer, ankle deep in dust, or flooded by heavy rains which submerge the raised plank side-walks. When the roadway has thus been under water I have watched the arrival of tea-caravans, and seen carts which had come without a breakdown all the way from China overturned and wrecked, within sight of the steamer, in the treacherous pitfalls which here abound. In dry weather the dust here is so dense that on a still, summer's day it hangs over the town like a funeral pall; which is not inappropriate, for this is a most depressing place, less, perhaps, by reason of its lack of life and activity than the sombre aspect of the streets, where a few red-brick houses and green-domed churches form the only patches of colour. All around it is a vast prairie across which a rough track, formed by incessant traffic, leads to the steamer's landing-place some miles away; but it is only from the upper town that you can trace the course of the great River Obi, sluggishly rolling northwards, through interminable plains, with here and there a patch of dark pine forest to break their monotony.

The inn at Tomsk was worse than my Irkutsk " hotel," for I discovered, the day after my arrival, that the room assigned to me had lately been occupied by a smallpox patient. But when I indignantly complained of this outrage, the landlord merely shrugged his shoulders, and murmured that his guest had " only had a mild attack ! " thereby recalling the Irish peasant girl, who when reproved for deviation from the path of virtue pleaded that the result of her indiscretion was " only a little one ! "

I visited this town chiefly in order to inspect its prisons, and being furnished with Government credentials, enjoyed the hospitality not only of officials, but also of the mercantile community, which was certainly more amusing. For Tomsk, although a place of depressing exterior, can be socially very gay, especially in winter, when mining and agriculture being at a standstill, all classes in Siberia rest and take their pleasure, and there is plenty going on in the way of amusements. My evenings were usually passed at the theatre or club, where there was gambling every night, and for the highest stakes I ever saw, even in Russia. " Shtoss," a kind of simplified " baccará," seemed very popular, although it was a mere gamble, in which a card is named and an ordinary pack dealt, one to the right hand for the players, and left for the bank, which, of course, has the usual advantage. I have seen thousands of roubles staked nightly on this inane and senseless game, and during the winter race-meeting (for which horses are sometimes brought from Europe to run in deep snow !) even larger stakes are won and lost.

Although good looks are rare amongst Russian peasant women, this does not apply to those of the Siberian upper class, where pretty faces are more numerous in proportion to the population than in European Russia. Yet the life once led by the Siberian lady was anything but conducive to health or beauty, for she rarely took any form of exercise (in Siberia nobody ever walks or rides for pleasure), and in winter passed most of her time indoors, smoking cigarettes and reading French novels in a heated and unwholesome atmosphere. But these conditions have now entirely changed, and both sexes now employ their time more sensibly and profitably than even a decade ago. Frivolous feminine pleasures have been discarded in favour of intellectual pursuits, and greater interest is shown in the mental and physical welfare of the young. This is probably due to increased facilities of education, for while wealthy Siberians formerly sent their children to Europe to complete their studies, the latter may now graduate in almost any subject without leaving home. A voyage to Petrograd was, before the construction of a railway, such an undertaking, that parents often preferred to keep their daughters, or even sons, at home, under the care of incompetent instructors, rather than expose them unattended to the risk of an arduous and complicated journey. But Tomsk now boasts of a University for which a grant of 1,000,000 roubles was made by the State, and a similar sum by local subscriptions, where students may take up any branch of science or art. There are also high schools for girls, and as all this now applies more or less to every city in Siberia, the mental needs of the rising generation are well provided for. And it would be unjust, after enumerating his failings, to pass over the good qualities of the Siberian millionaire, who though often illiterate and ill-bred, is ever ready to put his hand in his pocket to further a good cause. At Tomsk, for instance, there are no less than a score of charitable institutions maintained solely by public subscriptions, and a beggar is therefore rarely seen in the streets. It should also not be forgotten that many of these men have received practically no education, and that the charity which they habitually practise covers a multitude of sins.

I have already referred to the innumerable feasts in the Russian calendar, and in addition to these every one celebrates a " name day " as well as the date of his birth. The former commences at the early hour of 11 a.m., when friends arrive with gifts and congratulations, returning to their respective homes at

2 p.m., but only to reassemble for dinner two hours later. The aforesaid meal, to which I was bidden, lasted about five hours, and consisted of nine courses, which commenced with pancakes fried in caviare, and ended with ices and pastry, the " name day " pie, consisting of various kinds of fish, eggs, rice and cabbage forming the *pièce de résistance*. Alcoholic beverages entered largely into the *menu*, and the prohibition of these must now greatly diminish the wild revelry which used to attend these entertainments. I have, for instance, vivid recollections of a certain bowl of " punch " which was composed of a bottle of champagne, half a bottle of brandy, four glasses of curaçoa and a similar amount of vodka, and which, before consumption, was set on fire ! Even General Hindenburg's favourite beverage, known as " East Prussian Cup," [1] can hardly be more potent than this Siberian compound, which I trust the reader may never be rash enough to try, even as an experiment !

In summer " aquatic picnics " are all the rage here. A river steamer is chartered by a number of towns-people, who, on this occasion only, ignore all social distinctions, the opulent merchant hobnobbing with any impecunious street loafer who may have contrived to save enough money to join the party. The former, however, engages a private cabin, where he entertains friends, while the latter can only enjoy himself on deck, not being admitted to the well-appointed saloon, where the upper ten lunch and dine. A string band accompanies the boat, which, after steaming up stream for several hours (with no special object) returns at sunset to her place of departure. At dusk a blaze of electric light is the signal for dancing which continues until midnight, when home is reached after (as the English reader may imagine) a somewhat dull and monotonous day. For during the excursion I attended there was little to do but eat, drink, smoke, or revert at intervals to what is known here as " conversation-siberienne," which is only another name for the cracking and con-

---

[1] According to the *Daily Mail*, " East Prussian Cup " contains a pint of stout, a bottle of champagne, a pint of brandy and a pint of burgundy.

sumption of hazel nuts, when there is nothing to talk about! During the afternoon there was a violent thunderstorm, and my host's daughter, with whom I was conversing at the time, seemed so preoccupied after a deafening crash of thunder, that I endeavoured to reassure her. "Oh! I am not in the least alarmed," she replied after a pause: "I was merely recalling the names of six bald-headed acquaintances," this being, the young lady declared, an infallible protection against lightning!

Tobolsk was probably selected as a fortress by its Cossack founder [1] by reason of its commanding site which, from a steep and rugged cliff, overlooks the grey waters of the Irtysh and a vast expanse of country. The town is picturesque and also interesting, for its citadel, comprising the Governor's palace and cathedral, was erected about the time of the annexation. There is a fine view from here of the crescent-shaped city, which mostly consists of low wooden buildings, some of great age, with here and there a glittering church dome. The streets are paved with planks, and driving at night is rather risky, for your "droshki" may be suddenly engulfed in some deep hole where the wood has rotted away, only to be repaired when it has widened into an impassable chasm. Tobolsk is, unlike other Siberian cities, very unhealthy, owing to the proximity of stagnant marshes which are productive of fever and malaria, and the winter here is even more severe than at Irkutsk. Summer is generally sunless and rainy, and exiles have told me that they would rather remain ten years at the mines than half the time here, even though they enjoy comparative liberty, and it is so much nearer Europe. The town was, before the war, infested with German manufacturers of leather, soap, and tallow, and the aggressive Hun was also worming his way into the boat-building industry (in which only Russians are here employed) when he was happily compelled to beat a hasty retreat or be interned.

If Lucerne and Berne are respectively famed for their "Lion" and "Bears," every stranger here is aggres-

---

[1] A stone obelisk has been erected to him at Tobolsk bearing the inscription: "To Yérmak—Conqueror of Siberia, 1581-1584."

sively reminded that Tobolsk also possesses an object of historical interest.   For on arrival at the landing-stage itinerant vendors will pursue him with walking-sticks, cigarette-cases, sleeve-links, and every imaginable and useless article fashioned in silver, ivory, or wood to represent the celebrated " Bell of Ouglitch," which, for tolling the signal for an insurrection in that town was banished to Tobolsk in the sixteenth century by the Tsar Boris Godouŕoff.   It was the custom, in those days, to flog Siberian exiles and remove their nostrils with red-hot pincers, but this was in the case of the bell obviously impracticable.   The Tsar was, however, facetiously inclined, and therefore decreed that the metal offender should first be publicly flogged and then (not being possessed of a nasal organ) have its ears filed off.   And this sentence was duly carried out, the " Ouglitch Bell," which for many years reposed in a church, having found a last resting-place in the local museum.

An interesting discovery was recently made here in the shape of vast subterranean passages which, running in all directions, were unearthed during some building excavations.   News of the occurrence was immediately wired to Petrograd, but, to every one's surprise, an order was returned to close the place up as quickly and secretly as possible.   The matter therefore remained a mystery, but as the galleries were driven only under the lower town, they were probably constructed by some ancient Tsar to be used in case of a revolt as mines.

Ekaterinburg [1] is more suggestive of some fashionable French watering-place, with its handsome stone buildings and *boulevards*, asphalte streets and excellent hotels, than a remote mining town.   The Urals, where it is situated, more resemble downs than mountains, and a few miles from the town, the stone pillar may still be seen which marks the border-line between Europe and Asia, and which in bygone days was the scene of many a sad parting, for all prisoners then passed it on their way to exile.   Ekaterinburg is rendered the more attractive by a clear and rapid river which, bisecting the town, forms in its centre a lake studded with fertile

[1] Founded in 1793 by Peter the Great, and named after Catherine of Russia.

islets where, on a summer's evening, pleasure boats afloat and crowded *cafés* ashore, impart an air of almost Parisian life and gaiety. And everything in the place conveys an impression of wealth and luxury, for this district is famed for its valuable deposits of gold, silver and platinum. Many English firms established here for their exploitation are also largely interested in iron, which is here so cheap and plentiful that it is made into walking-sticks, and precious stones are also found in the vicinity, amongst them the emerald, amethyst, topaz and pretty alexandrite, which, an emerald by day, becomes a ruby in the lamplight. The traveller is therefore constantly pestered by tiresome purveyors of gems, who are as wily and extortionate as their colleagues in Colombo, wherefore here, as in Ceylon, it is well to beware of worthless imitations.

So much for civilized Siberia. I shall endeavour in the next chapter to give the reader some idea of life in the remoter regions of a land of such enormous extent, that a political exile of my acquaintance once set out from Europe to travel incessantly for over a year, before finally reaching his destination in the Tsar's Asiatic Dominions.

CHAPTER XII

DARKER SIBERIA—YAKUTSK AND THE LENA RIVER

THE above heading is in no way connected with my experiences while inspecting the prisons of that great lone land which, in England, had ever been associated with the banishment of State offenders. As a matter of fact, the latter have always formed only a small percentage of the great army of criminal convicts of both sexes who are sent to Siberia, not only to expiate their sins, but to colonize. I shall now, however, ignore the penal question, and merely describe the strange towns and stranger people whom I met, not only on the uttermost confines of civilization, but also far beyond them, in the frozen North. Should the reader desire a detailed account of Russian prison life, it may be found in previous works dealing solely with my investigation of the Exile system which, at the termination of three years, convinced me that a long term of penal servitude in Siberia would be infinitely preferable to even a brief period of confinement in any English gaol.

Before we penetrate into the remoter parts of Siberia, let the reader take a map of the world on " Mercator's projection," and note how small and insignificant other countries (even our Indian Empire) appear beside this stupendous stretch of territory, more than six times the size of Australia ! Find the city of Irkutsk, and a long way north-east of it Yakutsk, which is not, as you might imagine in these lonely latitudes, a trappers' settlement, but a fair-sized town. Verkhoyansk, further north, is our next objective, whence we shall set out on a two months' journey nearly due east, to Nijni-Kolymsk, on the Arctic Ocean, which may indeed be described as " the end of the end " of the world, and where, so far as this book is concerned, our journey will end.

124

Let us say the reader wishes to proceed from Irkutsk to Yakutsk, beyond which no one who can possibly avoid it ever travels. A stranger will naturally have the vaguest notion of how to reach the place, and will only ascertain with difficulty, even at Irkutsk, that in summer he can travel there by small steamers plying on the Lena, or in winter-time by sleigh, on the frozen surface of the river, which then becomes a post-road, impenetrable forests and endless swamps rendering it impossible to travel on land. The summer journey takes about three weeks, but shifting sand-bars and other obstacles often cause delays, which must be patiently endured in conjunction with atrocious food and accommodation, and myriads of mosquitoes. Those compelled to go to Yakutsk, therefore generally choose the winter route which is perhaps the lesser of two evils; but in any case, the summer journey is one of incessant boredom and discomfort, while in winter there are daily privations and occasional hardships which can only be borne by a man accustomed to " rough it," in the severest sense of the word.

My " troika "[1] was changed at every post-house (of which there are one hundred and twenty-three between Irkutsk and Yakutsk), and my conveyance was a contrivance known as a Yakute sleigh and used nowhere else in the world. It consisted of a sack of coarse matting about four feet in depth suspended from a frame of rough-wooded poles, in front of which was a seat for the driver. Into this bag my luggage was first lowered, then a mattress, pillows and furs, and finally I lay down myself at full length on my belongings, with a thick felt apron as a protection in stormy weather or intense cold. I could have dispensed with the latter, for during sleep it rested on the face, causing frostbite, while in bad weather the thick heavy canopy cast me into outer darkness !

The whole journey may be described as one of maddening monotony with fairly frequent intervals of severe physical suffering. For, from first to last, the post-houses were squalid hovels where only black bread, salt fish, and occasionally a dubious egg were obtainable.

[1] A team of three horses harnessed abreast.

The provisions I carried had to be thawed out at every halt, and a case of Crimean claret which I had taken to enliven the first stages of the journey was found, when opened, to contain only red ice and broken glass! I carried, however, milk cut into frozen cubes in a net, and this, mingled with tea, was my only beverage.

Progress is so slow that after a few days the heart sinks at the appalling total of mileage to be covered, for advance is retarded by frequent accidents caused by logs frozen into the river ice, and other causes. A double row of pine branches indicates the track, but these at night are invisible, and there is then great danger from ice holes, caused by the hot springs which abound in the Lena. Blizzards were also frequent, when we would flounder about for hours lost in the deep drifts, and the wild, unbroken horses would sometimes bolt while one lay in a sleigh as helpless as a tinned sardine, and momentarily expecting a smash or plunge into the cold dark waters. Yet, on still clear nights, it was not unpleasant to lie back and watch an inky sky powdered with stars—the " Great Bear " now almost overhead, and the little " Pleiades " twinkling like diamonds against black velvet. And on sunlit days the heavens were equally beautiful, being unflecked by the tiniest cloud, and gradually fading from dark sapphire overhead to the tenderest turquoise on the horizon. But day after day and week after week the landscape was unutterably dreary and depressing, an endless vista of pine-clad cliffs between which the frozen Lena lay as broad as an arm of the sea,[1] and motionless as a corpse. The so-called villages were merely a few huts surrounding a post-house, and also a larger building surrounded by a palisade, where political prisoners are housed during this interminable journey, which, by the way, ordinary criminals never experience. After a week or so, I travelled like a man in a dream, wherein the jangle of yoke-bells and scroop of the runners seemed permanently hammered into the brain.

---

[1] The Lena has a length of 3000 miles, its tributaries being the Vitim, Aldan and Olekina rivers, 1400, 1300 and 800 miles long respectively. The Vitim runs through a rich gold-mining district, and the finest sables in the world are found in its vicinity.

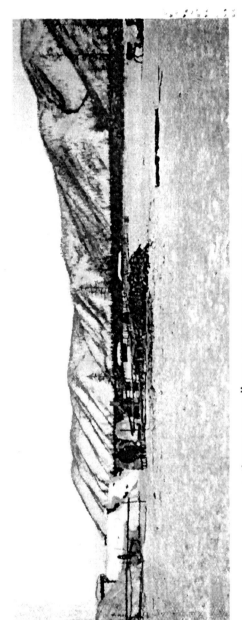

A "POST HOUSE" ON THE FROZEN SURFACE OF THE LENA

There are three small towns on the Lena between Irkutsk and Yakutsk (which I chiefly associate with the only three square meals I was able to obtain), and one of these, Kirensk, about half-way, was a pretty little place which afforded a brief but delicious interval of rest. And being a fine, bright day, it was really enjoyable to walk through a main street of neatly-built houses, two or three warehouses, and a store for the sale of provisions, clothing, and other necessaries of life. A couple of river steamers in course of construction, but now imbedded in the ice, accounted for the prosperous appearance of Kirensk, which actually boasted of an inn, where I fared sumptuously off decent food amid clean surroundings. Moreover, a fish I tasted here, called the " Nelma," which is found only in the Lena, and eaten in frozen slices, would certainly have found favour in a London restaurant.

The river here makes a detour of fifty or sixty miles, and in order to avoid this the post-road is laid for a short distance over the land, and through a forest so dense that my sleigh could scarcely get through it. Yet it was a relief to drive, if only for a few hours, through pine woods where the single telegraph wire which connects Yakutsk with civilization was our only guide. And here for the first time on this journey we encountered a wolf, which on first sight I took to be a mangy, half-starved dog, and which turned tail and fled at our approach. I mention this fact as, although I have travelled thousands of miles in the wildest parts of Siberia, I have never met these brutes in anything like dangerous numbers, and therefore imagine that reports of their boldness and ferocity may be somewhat exaggerated. I found in the inn at Kirensk (and nearly every post-house) cheap coloured prints which even here had been freely distributed by the German Government in order to excite animosity and ridicule against England. All were connected with the Boer War, in which (needless to say) the British troops were invariably depicted in the act of ignominious flight, one work of art representing three British generals upon their knees imploring mercy of Mr. Kruger!

One interesting event of that otherwise uneventful

journey was my meeting with the famous naturalist, Dr. Herz, who was returning to Petrograd with his newly-discovered mammoth, the discovery of which, at the time, aroused much interest in the scientific world. The prehistoric monster was being conveyed in sections, packed in twenty sleighs, to Europe, and had already thus been brought for over 2000 miles from the Arctic Ocean. The task of conveying it even as far as this had been almost a superhuman one, and Dr. Herz informed me that this was the most perfect specimen of the kind ever discovered. The animal had been found frozen into a massive block of ice, and had presumably fallen from a cliff near by, for its forelegs were broken, and there were other signs of injury. The beast measured more than twenty feet in height, and it was even possible to accurately calculate its period by undigested weeds found in the stomach. I am glad to be able to add that all difficulties of transit were finally overcome, and that this priceless treasure was successfully set up by scientists, and has now been relegated to the " Imperial Academy of Science " in Petrograd.

The town of Yakutsk (which I reached in twenty-seven days from Irkutsk) was founded by Cossacks early in the seventeenth century, and the old wooden stockade which they then erected was so strongly constructed, that it is still in a good state of preservation. It is said that the Yakutes granted these first Russian colonists as much land for the erection of a city as the latter could surround with 200 reindeer-skins, but the wily Cossacks cut the latter into such thin long strips, that they encircled many miles of ground. The town therefore covers a very large area, and looks at a distance rather imposing, although this impression is quickly dispelled on closer acquaintance, for the sombre wooden buildings, many rotting with age, and wide but lonely streets, present a lifeless and depressing aspect. Even the Governor's palace is a mean-looking, one-storied edifice, and there are no other public buildings with the exception of two or three handsome, golden-domed churches, which look rather out of place amid such squalid surroundings.

There was no inn here of any description, so I was

entertained by the Chief of Police, under whose guidance
I was enabled to study more closely the manners and
customs of the inhabitants. And I was surprised to
find that even isolated Yakutsk had its social side, and
that although in the streets only gold-laced officials,
burly Russian traders, and fur-clad natives were met
with, there was also an upper class which contrived
almost to enjoy life under especially adverse conditions.
The chief member of this " Society " was of course the
Governor and his staff, whose official exile was shared
by their wives and daughters. Then came the officials
according to rank, the mercantile community, and lastly
the political exiles, who to my surprise seemed to enjoy
as much freedom as any one else. A lunch therefore,
which was given in my honour by the Governor, assembled at least a score of guests, including several ladies,
some of whom were young, attractive and fashionably
dressed, although these were recent arrivals, and had
not acquired the " mildewed " appearance (I can think
of no other term) of the women who had resided here
for years. The *menu* was surprisingly elaborate,
and although I had suffered from starvation on the
road, the frequency of meals here was almost as distress-
ing as the pangs of hunger. My host, for instance, was
an orderly, business-like man, yet I never got to bed until
four o'clock in the morning, simply because supper,
the principal meal of the day, was only served at midnight. Breakfast, consisting of black bread, smoked
fish, and *cheese*, was served at 9 a.m., and followed at
midday by a heavier meal accompanied by beer and
liqueurs. At 3 p.m. there was a dinner of three courses,
and at 8 p.m. tea, accompanied by cakes and sweets,
while in addition to these repasts there was a sideboard
laid in the dining-room for a snack at any hour of the
day or night ! Every one rose very late and, as in the
Far East, retired for a " siesta " in the afternoon, an
arrangement rendered essential by the brief snatches
of repose obtained at normal hours.

Yakutsk, like all small towns, was a hotbed of scandal,
and the women especially seemed to pass most of their
time discussing other people's affairs, for none of them
appeared to have any rational or useful occupation to

K

mitigate an existence of hopeless monotony. I had heard in Irkutsk of the immorality prevalent here, and a stay of only ten days sufficed to convince me that the report was not entirely groundless. And this demoralization was scarcely surprising, seeing that although in summer-time women could obtain fresh air and exercise, in spring and winter they were kept indoors for days, and sometimes weeks, at a time by floods or intense cold. A prominent official told me that, but for the fear of publicity, things would have been far worse; and this condition of affairs is probably of long standing, for when my friend the late Admiral Melville came here thirty years ago (after searching the Lena Delta for his unfortunate shipmates of the *Jeannette*), the Governor informed him, on the occasion of a New Year's Eve reception, that, " on that night, as on no other, every man had his own wife instead of some one else's at his side ! " [1]

Nearly every night throughout the winter there is a social gathering of some sort, but there was a sameness about these entertainments which rendered them unutterably sad and depressing. There were only three pianos in the place, but the " gramophone " was ubiquitous and would grind away tune after tune, while the ladies sat around it in a silent circle, and the men played cards, or paced up and down the room, chatting and smoking cigarettes.[2] This is a singularly irritating habit peculiar to Siberia, where, when conversation flags, your host or companion will continue to walk to and fro for hours, murmuring the word " Da "[3] at intervals, while if you hazard a remark on any subject he will generally contradict you, more with the object of starting a discussion than because his opinion really differs from your own. The most important social

[1] *In the Lena Delta*, by G. W. Melville.

[2] The Russian Admiral, Von Wrangell, also thus described a visit to Yakutsk in 1820 : " The inhabitants are not in an advanced state of intellectual cultivation. They pass much of their leisure in noisy assemblages where eating and drinking play a principal part. After dinner (which is a very substantial meal) the gentlemen pass the afternoon with cards and punch, and the ladies gather round the tea-table."

[3] " Yes."

event was a monthly amateur dramatic performance at the club, which commenced at 6 p.m. and wound up with supper towards the small hours, although there had previously been plenty to eat and drink between the acts !

Life is more bearable here for men than women, for the former are occupied with official or commercial duties, and, if so inclined, can obtain excellent sport with rod or gun within a few miles of the town. The Verkhoyansk mountains can be reached in under a week in winter, and here there are elk, wild sheep and other big game; but, as I have already remarked, this mode of sport is not popular in Russia, and most of the men I met preferred to pass their leisure hours indoors with the fair sex, probably engaged in less healthful and innocent pursuits !

The feeling of gloom from which a stranger invariably suffers on arrival in Yakutsk is probably due to the fact that he has only reached the latter after struggling through a hell of monotony, hunger, and filth which will have to be undergone on the return journey—for there is no other way back to Europe, and the heart sinks at the thought. It was of course infinitely worse before the installation of the telegraph, which now at least keeps one in touch with the distant world of civilization. Yakutsk only possessed one so-called newspaper, a dry official monthly record, but telegrams received by the Governor were passed on to subscribers who paid for the privilege. The wire ends here and local news which filters slowly in from the Far North could generally be dispensed with, for it is generally associated with some death or disaster such as the tragic fate of the *Jeannette* expedition on the Lena Delta, or more recently the mysterious disappearance of Baron Toll, the Russian explorer, and his companions in the Liakov Islands.

Yakutsk has been described as the coldest place in winter and the hottest in summer in the world, but this is incorrect, for a daily record which I examined registered 78° Fahrenheit as the highest, and 69° below zero as the lowest for the past fifteen years, and I myself experienced a lower temperature further North. Nevertheless the soil is permanently frozen to a depth of 700 feet, and is only thawed, even during the hottest summer, for thirty or forty inches. Winter commences in September, and by the first week in October the country is icebound until May, when the Lena breaks up, flooding the country for hundreds of miles, and rendering Yakutsk an island, cut off by miles of water from any other land. The short summer is rendered very unpleasant by dust, dense fogs, and of course clouds of mosquitoes.

The Yakutsk province contains about 250,000 natives, and the town a considerable number, but they only associate on business with the Russians, so I saw little of them. Those who resided in the towns were not attractive, the men having sallow complexions, flattened nostrils, and straight coarse black hair, while the women were ungainly creatures, with faces thickly plastered with paint. But the Yakutes are proud of their lineage, and affect to despise the Russians, whom they say they only tolerate because of their money. There are many wealthy Yakutes, for they are such shrewd business men that Russians call them " the Jews of Siberia "; which is scarcely correct, for most of them are recklessly extravagant in the pursuit of pleasure, often gambling for large stakes, and squandering their money on women and riotous living. The men are also usually hard drinkers, although they rarely touch spirits, champagne being their favourite beverage.. Their costume is a blouse of cloth or fur, according to the season, baggy breeches, and high deerskin boots; that of the women, loose flowing draperies adorned in summer with bright silks and satins, and in winter costly sables and a head-dress of some valuable fur. Their language has one interesting peculiarity, for it so closely resembles Turkish, that a merchant from Constantinople could easily make himself understood in the market-place of this Siberian town. Numerous words expressing the same meaning are exactly similar, and the numerals up to ten identical.

There were only a couple of good stores here, where the most miscellaneous articles in the shape of furniture, wearing apparel, cheap jewellery, groceries and ironmongery were sold. I had hoped to procure valuable furs at a greatly reduced price, but found them almost as dear as in Petrograd, for the good old days are past when peltry was so cheap and European goods so expensive that an iron cauldron fetched as many sable skins as it would hold! In summer, however, a large " Aquatic Fair " is held on the Lena, on board numerous barges which drift down from its upper waters with the stream, and which as soon as navigation permits furnish not only the necessaries, but luxuries of life. These boats are towed back by steamers in the early fall, exporting furs, fish and ivory to the value of some millions of roubles. In the open season small steamers also run down the Lena to the Arctic Ocean, from which large quantities of salt fish, furs and walrus-tusks are yearly exported to Europe.

There is little doubt, in face of these natural resources, that in the course of a few years Irkutsk will be linked by rail from Yakutsk, for a line could be laid with comparatively little difficulty. Thirty years ago there was no steam communication of any kind, and it is now so inadequate to the commercial needs of this vast province, that it is practically certain that after the war special attention will be directed to the development of the Yakutsk district which will render imperative the construction of a railway to Irkutsk. For although so far north, even agriculture here is making great strides, as was proved by a visit which I made to a Skopt settlement near Yakutsk, where farming was successfully carried on, and which I shall describe in an ensuing chapter descriptive of " Curious Creeds." There is little doubt, therefore, that Yakutsk only needs capital, energy and enterprise to render it an important centre of commerce and civilization. Gold abounds in all the uplands of the Lena, many of them yielding (under present primitive modes of working) £500,000 sterling yearly. Platinum, lead, iron and coal are also known to exist in large quantities, and the trade of the place is now nothing to what it could be made in a short space of time, in capable hands. I passed through Yakutsk during a journey which I undertook by land to America, in order to ascertain the possibility of constructing a railway from

France to New York, in which the Béring Straits were to be negotiated by means of a tunnel. My expedition was the first to cover the entire distance, and while the conclusion which I formed at its termination inclined me to doubt whether the whole line would ever be laid, I was at the same time impressed with the enormous advantages that would be gained by the prolongation of the present Trans-Siberian Railway to the remoter regions of Siberia. For Yakutsk once reached, important branches could radiate in all directions from it as a mining and commercial centre; and I have heard Yakutsk merchants discuss the feasibility of a line to Gijiga (on the sea of Okhotzk), which would probably reap a rich harvest, for this system would open up Kamchatká with its valuable minerals, furs and lumber, and also Nelkan, near Ayan, where gold has been discovered in such large quantities that a well-known Siberian millionaire has commenced a narrow-gauge railway of 200 miles to connect the new goldfields with the sea. One may therefore safely predict that when wealth and enterprise have opened up the Yakutsk province, the banks of the Lena will swarm with large and prosperous towns, instead of being as they now are, a howling waste interspersed with a few small, poverty-stricken settlements.

CHAPTER XIII

FROZEN ASIA

LET us assume, before visiting Arctic Siberia, that London, and not Yakutsk, is the point of departure, as the reader will then more readily appreciate distances which, if merely given in round numbers, he would probably underestimate. " So many hundreds of miles " from one place to another in these frozen wastes convey very little to the dweller in civilization, even though the actual journey be one of interminable length, solitude and suffering. When, however, it is more graphically described as being " as far as that from London to Berlin," Constantinople, or some other well-known place, a clearer idea may be formed of the magnitude of mileage which, in the Far North, is often covered under almost impossible conditions. For instance, my journey from Yakutsk to the Béring Straits was about the same distance as from London to the Persian Gulf, a very ordinary journey in a genial climate by rail or steamer, but a very different proposition when the temperature averages 30° below zero, and the only mode of locomotion is an open sled drawn by dogs or reindeer !

It was with the latter that I journeyed from Yakutsk to Verkhoyansk (about as far as from London to Moscow), and I should explain that north of Yakutsk a few political exiles and the Cossacks who conduct them are the only travellers. Even natives are very seldom seen, and the Governor of Yakutsk, who had resided there for over twenty years, had never summoned the courage to embark even upon this comparatively short trip. A reindeer sled is the easiest primitive vehicle in the world over smooth snow, but is so light that, when the latter is rough, it rolls and pitches like a channel steamer. It is drawn by four deer, two abreast, without reins, the

135

team being driven by a thong attached to the off-leader, the traces being secured by a loop round the neck and inside the outer leg of each deer. The driver carries a long pole, not to urge on his team, but to sound deep snow, which, by the way, is essential for reindeer travel, for on ice they slip about like a cat on walnut-shells. On halting at night the deer are turned loose, and often wander away for miles in search of moss, although they never fail to return next morning. But at first it is rather disconcerting to see your only means of progress disappear, leaving you apparently stranded hundreds of miles from the nearest human "habitation"! Every fifty miles or so there is a "stancia" or deer-station, which is merely a log hut plastered with mud. The interior is a low dark den about six feet high, with a floor of beaten earth and window-panes of ice, surrounded by a rough wooden platform, a portion of which is strewn with fir branches for the use of guests. Here a pine-log fire blazed night and day, rendering the place intolerable when cooking operations were in progress; for the Yakutes prefer putrid to fresh food, and the stench of bad deer-meat or tainted fish often drove me out of doors into the ferocious cold. These natives are passionately fond of this revolting form of sustenance, and I once found an old man in a deserted hut lying beside a dead deer in an advanced state of decomposition. The poor wretch was apparently in great pain, and I inferred by signs that he had been poisoned by partaking of these disgusting remains!

If vermin could be numbered by their thousands on the Lena, there were certainly myriads here, for every deer-station was occupied by the Yakute owner, his numerous family, several deer-drivers, and occasionally cattle. When the inhabited "stancias" were more than two hundred miles apart there was also the "povarnia," a rough shanty generally half full of snow and partly open to the winds, with a bundle of firewood which the previous traveller had left for his successors, perhaps months before. Yet even these crazy shelters saved us more than once from death by exposure on this lonely and perilous track.

Half-way between Yakutsk and Verkhoyansk a range

NEARING THE " DIVIDE " BETWEEN YAKUTSK AND VERKHOYANSK

of mountains was crossed which from a distance looked like a perpendicular wall of ice. The sleds went by a circuitous and easier route, being unable to negotiate, near the summit, a precipice of 1000 feet spanned by an ice-ledge about three feet wide. On the downward side, in order to descend a snow slope about a mile in length, the deer were fastened *behind* the sled to restrain them; but the pace gradually increased until all control was lost and we dashed into a deep snowdrift at the bottom, where men, deer and sleds were mixed up in inextricable confusion, and whence the sled which followed us looked like a fly crawling down a white wall. The temperature that day was 45° below zero, but I hardly felt the cold, although the next morning, as I had not removed my stockings on the previous evening, one of my feet was badly frozen. A change of footgear at night is essential when sleeping here in the open, or perspiration formed during the day congeals during sleep into solid ice.

The scenery here in winter-time is of wondrous beauty, and notwithstanding all the suffering and privation, it was almost enjoyable in fine weather to glide swiftly under pine branches glistening with hoar-frost, while occasional rifts in the forest disclosed a glimpse of snowy peaks glittering against a sky of cloudless blue, just such views as you get in Switzerland, although palatial hotels, snug chalets, and tinkling cow-bells were unfortunately wanting! Smoking would at such moments have been an additional consolation, but in these abnormally low temperatures a cigar becomes glued to the lips, and the stem of a pipe blocked with frozen nicotine.

Verkhoyansk, which is generally reached in about a fortnight from Yakutsk, is called by Russians the " Heart of Siberia," but political exiles know it by another name which is also preceded by the letter " H," but has a different meaning! It consisted of forty or fifty mud-plastered log huts in various stages of decay and half buried in snow-drifts over which ice windows peered mournfully. Glazing is cheap in these parts, for you simply cut a block of ice six or eight inches thick from the nearest stream, lay it on the roof of a hut until required, and then fix it with snow; which soon freezes, the cold being so intense that notwithstanding internal warmth one ice window generally lasts throughout the winter. I thought that a more gloomy God-forsaken spot than Verkhoyansk could scarcely exist on the face of this earth. But I had yet to see Sredni-Kolymsk. Only the Chief of Police, and half a dozen political exiles, and a few Yakutes formed this little colony. Yet the Russian official received me in the familiar grey and scarlet uniform, reminding me that even this remote corner of the empire was under the eagle eye of the secret police !

An empty hut was assigned to me which, although devoid of furniture, was weatherproof and snug enough with a roaring fire, which was badly needed, for Verkhoyansk is the coldest place in the world. During my stay only 50° below zero was experienced, but I encountered, about 200 miles north, 78°, which froze the breath into powder as it left the lips. Yet I can safely say that I have felt chillier in London on a damp December day than in this phenomenal but dry and still atmosphere ! For, by a merciful dispensation of Providence, there is never, in anything more than 40° below zero, any wind, or no human being could survive it.[1]

The political exiles here declared that they had little to complain of except of course utter stagnation, severe climatic conditions, and a chronic insufficiency of food. Winter, they said, was preferable to summer, which, however, had one compensation in the shape of constant daylight; for candles could only be purchased at a ruinous cost, and they practically lived in darkness. Deer meat was the chief article of food, but tea and sugar were so dear that the former was boiled over and over again until it was tasteless, and sugar held in the mouth and removed to serve another time. Vegetables, although cultivated at Yakutsk, were here unobtainable, and although wild flowers grew freely in July and August, they were as scentless as *immortelles*.

There is only one (so-called) mail a year from Verkhoyansk to Sredni-Kolymsk, which is carried in sleds by the Cossacks, who convoy a consignment there every twelve months of from three to half a dozen political

---

[1] Eighty-one degrees below zero was once registered at Verkhoyansk: a record throughout the world.

exiles.[1] This journey,(about as far as from London to Constantinople) can only be accomplished in winter, for it lies across a region which unless it is in a frozen condition no man can traverse. Moreover, numerous lakes and rivers have to be crossed, which in their natural state would present insuperable obstacles, for boats are, of course, unobtainable, and a considerable portion of the distance lies beyond the limit of trees.

It took me over three weeks to accomplish this voyage with reindeer, and now the " stancias " were so far apart that we generally had to rely for shelter on the " povarnias," which I have already described.

> " League on league of Desolation,
> Mile on mile on mile without a change,"

aptly describes the huge desert of snow which, in winter, separates Verkhoyansk from the Polar Sea. And so sparsely is this region peopled that even a whole town can vanish from off the face of the earth, and no one be any the wiser. As a proof of this, Mr. George Kennan relates the following anecdote, which is endorsed by official statistics.

" In 1879 there lived in the city of Pultava a poor apothecary named Schiller, who was banished as a political offender to a village in the Province of Kostroma. Schiller finding life tedious, ran away, and about this time the Tsar issued a command directing that all exiles found absent from places of banishment without leave should be sent to the Province of Yakutsk. When, therefore, Schiller was re-arrested, he was banished to Irkutsk, and the Governor-General of Eastern Siberia was requested to place him under police surveillance in some part of the territory named in the Imperial command. The Governor-General (who had only recently come to Irkutsk) was not familiar with the vast region entrusted to his care, and therefore directed that Schiller be sent to the town of Zashiversk, which was (supposed to be) situated on the River Indigirka, a few miles south of the Arctic Circle. A century ago Zashiversk was a town of considerable importance, but it lost its pre-eminence as a fur-trading centre, fell gradually into decay, and finally

---

[1] Before the recent revolution.

ceased to exist. Its location, however, was still marked on all the maps, and ' tchinovniks ' in Irkutsk were still pocketing the money appropriated for repairs to its public buildings; when, as a matter of fact, it had not contained a building or inhabitant for more than half a century, and forest trees covered the ground it had once occupied. Poor Schiller, after being carried three or four times up and down the Rivers Lena and Indigirka in a vain search for a non-existent Arctic town, was finally brought back to Yakutsk and a report was made to the Governor-General that Zashiversk had ceased to exist ! The Governor-General therefore ordered that the prisoner be taken to Sredni-Kolymsk, which place, after more than a year of constant travel, the unfortunate druggist eventually reached."

I employed on this journey over 1000 deer (many of which perished); and as we gradually crept onward into the unknown, a sense of unspeakable loneliness seemed to increase with every mile we covered. Now that shelter was so rarely available, an additional cause of suffering was want of sleep; for in the open, on closing the eyes the breath in a short time formed a layer of ice over the face which, melting in the warmer region of the neck, gradually trickled down next the skin until by the morning every stitch of underclothing was saturated. If slumber was prolonged for any time the mouth and eyelids would be closed by thin ice, and one would be awakened by choking and gasping for breath.

I reached Sredni-Kolymsk in brilliant sunshine, but the aspect of that dismal settlement seemed to darken the landscape, and fill the mind with a vague sense of gloomy unrest. A double row of tumbledown log huts, clustered around the ruins of a wooden church, formed the main street, which was surrounded by perhaps a score of other equally squalid hovels. All around a desolate plain of snow with patches of Arctic vegetation fringing the frozen River Kolyma—over all the silence of death. The place looked less like an abode of humanity than one deserted by trappers or decimated by deadly sickness; yet presently one or two skin-clad haggard-looking wretches emerged from the huts, and nodded a cheerless welcome. The very air seemed tainted with death and disease, and the place to scrawl the word "Despair" across the desolate world.

There were about 200 people here, including one official, and fourteen exiles who needed no guards, bolts or bars, for nature supplied all three. Death would surely have followed any attempt to escape, for hundreds of miles must be traversed in any direction before reaching any sign of help or humanity. Natives of the Yakute tribe formed the remainder of the population, and this was fortunate, for Sredni-Kolymsk was the starting-point of my further journey of 2000 miles along an uninhabited coast to the Béring Straits. And these people possessed a few dogs, which eventually enabled me to reach them.

I found here fourteen political exiles, two of whom were women, and one of the latter being Theisa Akimoff who attempted to assassinate the deposed Tsar at his coronation.[1] The others had been convicted of such serious political offences that they had been condemned to death, the capital sentence having been commuted to perpetual banishment in this Arctic "Inferno." It is now, however, my object merely to describe how ordinary mortals live in these remote regions, and not to discuss the justice or otherwise of Russian penal methods, although I may add that I have recently been informed that Sredni-Kolymsk has now been abolished as a place of exile. That it was only known during its existence to the dreaded "Third Section," or secret police, is indicated by the following remark which was made to me by one of the exiles here: "If the Emperor," he said, "could only be informed of the life we lead in this ghastly place, he would do away with it to-morrow."

Sredni-Kolymsk is, in summer, as isolated from the rest of the world as a desert island, by flooded marshes, swamps and lakes which extend inland in every direction for over 1000 miles. A sled skims easily over their frozen surface, but from June till September the soil is so wet and spongy that you can only walk a few yards with the utmost difficulty. Summer here consists of a few weeks of damp and cloudy weather, when, even on a fine day, the sun looms through a curtain of mist, while swarms of mosquitoes add to other miseries, the sole

[1] See chap. iii. p. 20.

protection against these pests being a heap of damp moss which is kept perpetually smouldering on the threshold of every dwelling, suffocating the inmates with clouds of acrid smoke. The huts were about six feet high, and each contained only one room with a floor of beaten earth, on which a few planks were laid for a sleeping-place. An old kerosene tin formed the only seat in a hovel I entered, of which the occupant (an exile) kindled a few sticks on the open hearth which burnt brightly for a moment and then flickered out, whereupon he clambered on to the roof and closed the chimney with a bundle of rags. This is the Yakute mode of warming an apartment, for firewood is so scarce that even in the depth of winter the warmth from an ordinary fire can never be enjoyed. At this season salt fish and rye bread are alone obtainable, but in the spring-time better food is provided in the form of geese, duck, and, until the autumn, fresh fish. Cold and hunger were, however, less dreaded than the uncanny and unbroken silence of winter, and this fact I learnt from the Chief of Police as we stood one evening watching the frozen river darkening in the dusk. "The stillness here is worse than anything," he declared. "Day after day, year after year, not a sound except the dull roar of ice when the Kolyma breaks up in the spring. I have stood here at midday and heard a watch tick in my pocket, and although only a few months have elapsed since my arrival, I shall apply for leave next year, or——" and he tapped his forehead significantly.

If summer here possesses one advantage arising from more abundant food, it also produces more sickness, especially malaria and smallpox, while some of the Yakutes suffered from leprosy. There is also a mental disease peculiar to these regions which is more dreaded than any bodily ailment, and is common to both sexes, who reside here for any length of time.[1] The attack is

---

[1] The Russian explorer, Von Wrangell, mentions an apparently similar mental disease as existing in these regions in 1820. He writes: "There is here (Sredni-Kolymsk) that singular malady called *mirak*, which, according to the universal superstition of the people, proceeds from the ghost of a much-dreaded sorceress, which is supposed to enter into and torment the patient. The *mirak* appears to me to be only an extreme degree of hysteria; the persons attacked are chiefly women" (*Siberia and the Polar Sea*, by Von Wrangell, 1829).

A POLITICAL EXILE AT SREDNI-KOLYMSK HOLDING A FROZEN FISH

usually sudden; a previously sane and intelligent person proceeding to shout, sing and dance for no apparent reason, and also to imitate the voice and actions of others who may be present at the time. The sufferer becomes in most cases permanently deranged.

Although I only remained here ten days, it seemed on the day of my departure as though weeks had elapsed, so intolerable were the monotony and depression. I may mention that we were the first strangers from the outer world to visit this place (with the exception of officials, exiles, and Cossacks) for over forty years, the last being two shipwrecked sailors from the ill-fated Arctic steamer *Jeannette*. And I embarked from here on a hazardous journey to the Béring Straits almost with a sense of relief, notwithstanding serious misgivings that these unhappy beings might be the last fellow-creatures I should ever behold on this earth.

CHAPTER XIV

SOME CURIOUS CREEDS

RELIGIOUS dissension in Russia has existed for centuries, according to Stepniak (the famous Socialist), who writes that, as early as 1370, a sect was founded in the town of Pskov, by one Strigolnik, whose doctrine rejected the sacraments and priesthood, and only tolerated confession if a penitent prostrated himself and confessed his sins to mother earth. The Strigolniks led a severe monastic life, devoted to fasting and prayer, and so despised their less ascetic fellow-townsmen that the latter resented the insult, and the dissenters were therefore quickly suppressed in the forcibly unpleasant manner which, in mediæval days, was usually employed.

The Greek Church in Russia is generally associated with almost tyrannical intolerance, and yet there is no country in the world where so many forms of faith are practised, of course in secrecy, for severe penalties are visited on dissenters from the orthodox faith. The latter somewhat resembles the Catholic religion, for the Holy Virgin and the saints are worshipped, High Mass is said, and confession is compulsory, although a priest is not only permitted, but encouraged to marry, and instrumental music in churches is prohibited. The Greek Church imposes innumerable fasts, and its saints-days number nearly half those in the year, while services are conducted in the ancient Sclavonic dialect, only sermons being delivered in the modern Russian tongue. Lent being very strictly observed, no meat is eaten for the six weeks which precede Easter Day, when the universal gaiety which prevails is often due to physical, as well as spiritual, reasons. An orthodox Russian's religion enters into the most trivial details of his daily life, and even before starting on a short journey his entire household

144

prays that safety may attend a traveller, even though he be an unorthodox guest; indeed, I could occasionally have dispensed with these ceremonies when hurrying to catch a train, or starting off in the wilds with an unruly dog-team! In the same way, soldiers on active service seldom venture to attack without being previously blessed by a "pope," thousands of whom accompany the army on campaign. Even houses and rivers are blessed by the clergy in order to ward off destruction by fire, or to ensure a plentiful supply of fish!

The Russian "pope" is generally well paid for his services, and in former days was therefore often tempted to over-indulge in the "vodka," which flowed freely on feast-days. It was my privilege to enjoy the friendship of the late Procurator of the Holy Synod, M. Pobedonostzeff, who devoted the last years of his life to remedying this evil, and generally raising the tone of the rural clergy; while, a few weeks before his death, he abolished hereditary priesthood, which was obviously open to many objections. The Jews [1] were also granted greater privileges under this humane and distinguished official, and it is only fair to add that the Russian Government was less responsible for the "Pogroms," or street massacres, which, at the time, aroused such indignation throughout Europe, than infuriated Christian citizens whom even strong military forces were unable to restrain.

The Russian Lutherans number several millions, and Catholics are almost as numerous, but both these, although practically nonconformists, are only interfered with by the State if they attempt to make converts from the Greek Church. All other dissenters are known as "Raskolniks,"[2] although this term really only applies to the "Staro-Viéri," or "Old-Believers," whose tenets are closely allied to the Greek Church, and whose creed, although illegal, is therefore regarded with greater leniency by the Holy Synod than any of the proscribed sects which I shall presently enumerate. This tolerance is probably due to the fact that many members of this

[1] The Russian Empire is said to contain more than half the Jews in the world.

[2] The word "Raskolniks" signifies "to split asunder," and is thus descriptive of seceders from the Orthodox Church.

L

sect are influential members of society,[1] devoting a considerable portion of their wealth to the maintenance and education of the poor. The " Raskolniks " chiefly inhabit the northern parts of Russia, to which they were exiled in olden days, and where they made many converts amongst the Lapps and Samoyédes.

The " Staro-Viéri " cannot, perhaps, be called dissenters in the true sense of the word, for in remote places they often employ an orthodox " pope " to conduct their services, while the most trivial causes seem to have led to the separation of the churches, such as making the sign of the Cross with two fingers instead of three, and other equally minor methods of worship. Scrupulous cleanliness is maintained by every " Old-Believer," who will not eat out of a plate or drink from a cup which has been used by any one but himself, these articles being at once destroyed if " polluted " by any one but their owner.

There are no less than a hundred proscribed sects in the Russian Empire, which, as they are scattered, not only throughout European Russia, but also Siberia, gather many adherents amongst the simple-minded, superstitious peasantry. Space will only allow of a description of the most important, amongst these being the " Dukhobortsi," who number about 50,000, and chiefly reside in Southern Russia. The late Count Tolstoi was a great admirer of these people, whose faith specially appealed to him, chiefly because, being mostly of humble origin, their religion is based on the equality of man. This socialistic doctrine in an autocratic country at one time subjected this sect to much persecution, and Catherine II., although friendly with the " Old-Believers," was one of its bitterest opponents. Yet, notwithstanding their progressive proclivities, the " Dukhobortsi " are now peaceable citizens, and therefore enjoy freedom and privileges which were denied them in olden days. They do not worship the Supreme Being, believing that the Deity dwells in the soul of every man, revealing its spiritual influence through his mind and actions. The ordinary conception of Immortality is not admitted, nor the existence of Heaven or Hell, for the " Dukhobor " regards the promises of a future life as set forth by the Scriptures

[1] They number about thirty millions.

to apply only to human existence. The world will never, he avers, be destroyed, or depopulated, but eventually good will overcome evil, and all will be harmony and peace on earth, where conditions of human life will continue to exist, in their present state, for all eternity.

The "Dukhobortsi" possess no sacred buildings, having a strong aversion to any kind of religious ceremony. Baptism, marriage and burial are therefore solemnized by a simple declaration, usually made by the head of a family, who officiates as priest. Some years ago a party of these people settled in Canada, where they were at once arrested by the police for appearing in public in a state of nudity, this practice originating from the fact that, so long as Adam and Eve remained in a state of nature, they retained their chastity! The "Dukhobortsi" are, to a man, "conscientious objectors" to military service, thereby occasionally exposing themselves to as much contempt and ridicule as those misguided beings who, in England, now seek to cloak their cowardice under this feeble and palpable pretext.

The "Molokani," or "milk-drinkers,"[1] seceded from the "Dukhobortsi" about the end of the eighteenth century, then forming an entirely independent community, which has so rapidly increased that they are now more numerous than the original sect of which they formerly formed part. The "Molokani," unlike the "Dukhobortsi," believe in a future existence but not in Hell, maintaining that sinners are punished in this world, not in the next; however much a man has transgressed, all will be forgiven him. Their meetings are held in an ordinary dwelling-house, and they are of the simplest description, one person reading passages from the Bible and then expatiating upon the text. I have heard some of their sacred music, which is very beautiful and less mournful than that of the Greek Church, being generally in the major key. A "Molokani" marriage is solemnized by the reading of suitable passages from the Bible, followed by a brief exhortation from an elder; and divorce, although sanctioned, is very rare.

The "Molokani" are strict vegetarians, who consider

[1] So called because they keep no fasts and drink milk freely during Lent.

it sinful to sacrifice animals for food, total abstainers, and, like the " Dukhobortsi," are so averse to conscription that they are always assigned to non-combatant sections of the army.

Although of comparatively modern origin, the " Stundists " have now become a very influential sect, which originated at Odessa, on the Black Sea, but now has followers in many other parts of Russia. The founders are said to have been German Lutherans who migrated to the fertile black-lands about sixty years ago, and the faith somewhat resembles that of " Christian Science," for although the Scriptures are read, the clergy is replaced by elders, who conduct services at which any member of the congregation may address the remainder. Many of the Stundists are wealthy, and as the poorer members are generally thrifty, law-abiding people, they are rarely interfered with by the authorities.

The " Old-Believers," " Dukhobortsi," " Molokani," and " Stundists " are, perhaps, the most important religious sects in Russia; but there are, of course, innumerable others, a few of which lean towards mysticism and even pagan worship. These include the " Stranik," a kind of hermit, who forsakes civilization to lead a lonely and primitive life in the forests; the " Philippovtsi," who regard suicide and the killing of their friends as virtues; the " Moltchatni," who, like the Trappist monks, take vows of eternal silence; and the " Skaurny," a dancing sect resembling our English Shakers. I have personally only come in contact with the members of three of these minor communities, viz : the " Napoleonists," " Skoptsi," and " Shamans," who, however, are perhaps the most curious and interesting of them all.

I met the " Napoleonist " some years ago, on the shores of Lake Baikál, and although the former thereby ran the risk of a long term of imprisonment, he was not afraid to impart, under vows of strict secrecy, the principles of his mystic faith to an Englishman. I, therefore, learnt that the " Napoleonists " (who reside only in Eastern Siberia) exclusively worship the Great Emperor, regarding his departed Majesty not only as the coming Messiah, but as their actual ruler, thereby disavowing all allegiance to the Tsar. My informant produced a small plaster bust of Bonaparte, which he worshipped every night, and assured me that Napoleon's spirit had flown from St. Helena to the shores of the great Siberian lake, where it was only awaiting a favourable opportunity to resume a mortal shape. An enormous army would then be raised to overthrow the Románoff dynasty, and the world would gradually be subjected to the Muscovite yoke, under Bonaparte, when those who had remained faithful to him would enjoy eternal peace and prosperity.

On another occasion I visited a small colony of the "Skoptsi," near Yakutsk, to which place they had been banished for religious offences, but where they had contrived, even in these Arctic wilds, to raise a flourishing agricultural settlement on the outskirts of the city. Cultivation of any kind had, before their arrival, been deemed impossible in this inclement region, but now the Skopt exile amasses wealth, while the poor "moujik" gazes enviously at his fertile fields and sleek cattle, and wonders how it is all done. And his surprise is only natural, for the yearly sale by these people of corn and barley (formerly unknown) now realizes over a million roubles! Moreover, only thirty years ago the entire Yakutsk district contained but a few head of miserable half-starved cattle, whereas the Skoptsi now export, every year, two million roubles' worth of frozen meat to various settlements on the Lena, and provide the market at Yakutsk with several kinds of vegetables, where formerly only potatoes were obtainable.

I found the little community which had accomplished this agricultural miracle at Markha, near Yakutsk, where every soul in the place was a Skopt, and where the scrupulous cleanliness of the village was in agreeable contrast to the dirt and squalor of others in the vicinity. The Chief-Elder's well-built wooden house was comfortably furnished, and contained an extensive library, while his sitting-room was adorned with palms and flowers, obviously artificial, but which were none the less cheerful and comforting on that grey and wintry day. And, to my surprise, my host gave me an excellent lunch and plied me with champagne, for these people, although misers at heart, are fond of displaying their wealth, which is generally considerable. Yet they are generous and kind to their poor, as was shown by an institute maintained here for the aged and needy of both sexes.

My Skopt entertainer was a bright, intelligent person, well posted in current subjects of interest even in distant Europe, but he and the rest were, notwithstanding their friendliness and hospitality, the most repulsive collection of beings I have ever beheld. The men, both young and old, were stout and ungainly, with smooth, pasty faces, and a shrill treble voice, while the women looked emaciated and prematurely aged. Not being then acquainted with the revolting practices of this sect, I ingenuously remarked on the apparent scarcity of very young people in Markha, and was informed that the " White Doves "[1] are bound by vows of absolute chastity, both sexes so mutilating themselves that they can neither beget nor bear children. They therefore seemed to regard the acquisition of riches as their sole pleasure in life. When a Skopt dies his property should legally revert to the State, but he generally conceals it in some remote place where, if not discovered, it indefinitely remains. The Skopt religion seems to be founded on the text : " If thine eye offend thee pluck it out," for it argues that a man should be as sexless as an Angel, in order to gain the approval of his Maker, quite ignoring the deadly sin which is committed to attain this end.

The " Khlysti " derive their title from the word " Khlyst," a whip, and date back to the sixteenth century, calling themselves the " People of God," although they are known to the orthodox church simply as " The Flagellants." The exact principles of this faith are rather hard to define, although it is probably remotely allied to Christianity, for the " Khlysti " declare that Our Saviour occasionally re-visits this earth in human shape, a suitable member of the sect being generally deputed to impersonate Him. I could never glean, even from Russians well read on the subject, what transpires during the services held by these people, which take place at dead of night and with the utmost secrecy, every member being admitted by a different pass-word. Some say that the proceedings are harmless, although it is known that both sexes dance together in a state of

[1] The " Skoptsi " are known by this name in Russia.

nudity and whip each other with birches until a state of religious frenzy is attained, often ending in a fit, or loss of consciousness. Others aver that these ceremonies lead to acts of the grossest immorality, although the Khlysti are, in everyday life, generally staid and respectable people. Marriage amongst them is, however, unknown, a man living for a time with the partner of his choice, and, when tired of her, selecting another, which the woman is also free to do.

"Shamanism" (one of the oldest religions in the world) is chiefly practised by the Yakutes, Tchuktchis and other fur-clad races, for amongst civilized Russians it is practically unknown, and only a few Europeans have therefore beheld the weird doings of this community in the depths of the forest or out on the lonely "Tundras." My friend, Mr. J. Stadling, the Swedish explorer (who some years ago led an expedition through Northern Siberia in search of André), has made a special study of the Shaman faith, of which the following may be taken as a lucid description :[1] "The Shaman universe," he writes, "consists of a number of planes, or worlds, separated from each other by intermediate space. The seven upper planes constitute the kingdom of light, and seven, or more, lower ones the kingdom of darkness. Between these upper and lower layers the surface of the earth, or habitation of mankind, is situated, whence the latter is exposed to the influence of both the upper and lower world—i.e. the powers of light and of darkness. All the divinities which create and preserve the children of men have their abode in the upper planes, or world of light, while the planes of the lower world harbour evil spirits ever seeking to destroy humanity. In the highest plane of all (the 'Seventh Heaven'), the Great Tangára (as he is called in Northern Siberia) is enthroned and exalted far above all good or evil, for this pagan deity meddles but little with the Universe, caring neither for sacrifices nor prayers. In the fifth or ninth plane of the lower world the Prince of Darkness sits on a black throne, surrounded by his Satanic court. The intermediate planes are the abode of spirits of various degrees of light and darkness, some being the ghosts of human

[1] *Through Siberia*, by J. Stadling, London, 1901.

beings.   These, however, are able to influence the destiny of man for good or evil; whence the necessity of the 'Shaman,' or Priest, who alone is privileged to communicate with the spiritual world."   There would thus seem to be some sort of affinity between this ancient faith of savage races and the modern and civilized Theosophy of which my friend, the late Madame Blavatsky, was such an able exponent.

I once met at Tomsk, in Western Siberia, a fur-trader who had actually witnessed a Shaman ceremony, which he thus described : " I came on them by accident in a lonely part of the forest, but concealed myself behind some undergrowth.   In a circle of flaming logs I beheld perhaps a dozen natives seated around a priest, or Shaman, who was clad in a long white robe.   Round his neck was a circular brass plate signifying the sun, and all over his body were suspended bits of metal, small bells and copper coins.   The ceremony performed by this strange being seemed to consist of circling round, without cessation, for nearly an hour, at the end of which he commenced to howl and foam at the mouth, to the violent excitement of his audience.   The gyrations gradually increased in rapidity, until at last the dancer fell heavily to the ground, face downwards, apparently in an epileptic fit.   The meeting then commenced to disperse, and I fled as quickly and silently as possible, for had I been discovered my life would certainly have paid for my intrusion."

The museum at Yakutsk contains some interesting relics pertaining to Shamanism, amongst others articles found in the tomb, presumably, of an important personage, for it contained valuable jewellery, arms, and personal effects.   I noticed that everything, from the corpse's shroud to a brass tobacco-box, had been punctured with some sharp instrument, and a Russian friend explained that all personal property buried with a Shaman is thus pierced with a dagger, in order to " kill " it before interment !

I only once saw a Shaman priest in the flesh, and this occurred in a post-house in Arctic Siberia, where I was awakened at dead of night by an object in shapeless grey rags, with a pale, evil countenance which, dimly revealed by flickering firelight, leered at me from a tangled mass of coarse grey hair. Every movement of the creature was accompanied by a tinkling sound caused by scraps of iron, rusty nails, copper coins and other metal rubbish which dangled around its body from head to foot. And its presence was so unspeakably foul and repulsive that it tainted the already fetid air with a faint, sickly odour of corruption. How, or why, this apparition entered the place I never knew, and it was stealthily departing when my Cossack attendant, aroused by the creaking of the door, promptly fired his revolver at the retreating figure, with as little compunction as though it had been a weasel or rat. "One of those cursed Shamans," muttered my "orthodox" companion, lying down again with a grunt of disappointment; "pity I missed him!"

CHAPTER XV

SOME STRANGE RACES

THE native races who, from time to time, have come under British rule may be numbered by their millions, yet Russia's alien subjects, although less numerous, are almost as varied as those who swear allegiance to King George. I have drunk "koumiss" with the Kirghiz, shared a "narghileh" with a Bokháran, and eaten whale-blubber with Tchuktchis in the frozen north, and as all were more or less interesting from various points of view, a brief description of some of the tribes with which I have come in contact may here not be out of place.

The most numerous non-Slavonic subjects of the Tsar are the Tartars, who now number over 3,000,000, and who, since their first invasion of Russia early in the thirteenth century, have so largely influenced the course of Muscovite history. Many of them are now as well educated and prosperous as Europeans, for they are a clean and temperate people, which cannot always be said of the "moujik," although, unlike the latter, they have a characteristic Asiatic distaste for hard work of any kind. The men are generally middle-sized and muscular, with a sallow complexion, broad nostrils and beady black eyes, while the women disfigure themselves by plastering their faces with paint, and generally lose their good looks by becoming stout and ungraceful at an early age. The Tartars are, of course, strict Mahometans, many becoming "mullahs," or priests, who, after completing their education at a large Mahometan College at Ufa, occasionally make the Mecca pilgrimage, in order to attain more religious influence amongst the faithful on their return.

Many Tartars in the Volga districts have adopted

154

European dress, but their heads are always shaven in the Mahometan fashion, and covered, even when indoors, by a linen skull-cap. The women are never permitted to perform manual work of any kind, for the men are generally well-to-do, and able to employ as many labourers as are necessary to cultivate their gardens and fields. A wealthy Tartar's wife is therefore generally a spoilt, indolent creature, whom her husband loves to bedeck with costly silks and jewels, and these are worn even when living in the Steppes, where these people lead a nomadic life in tents, being chiefly engaged in roaming over limitless plains, herding and grazing horses, although even here their canvas dwellings are always luxuriously furnished. It was in one of these " yurtas " [1] that I first tasted " koumiss," or fermented mares' milk, and have no desire to repeat the experiment, although I know of several cases of advanced consumption which have been completely cured by a lengthened treatment of this nauscous beverage.

The " Tchuvash " are another branch of Tartar origin, who inhabit the Orenburg district, and who bear rather an evil reputation, as, unlike most Tartars, they are confirmed thieves and drunkards, who, having become Christians, are rather despised by their compatriots. The Christianity they practise is, however, anything but orthodox, and includes strange rites (probably of Shaman origin), while their mode of divorce is especially curious. When the decree is pronounced, husband and wife lie on the ground, secured together, back to back, by a cord, which is severed by a mutual friend of the couple, both of whom are then free to marry again.

The Tartar race consists of so many branches and dialects that it would be impossible, in a work of this nature, to describe them in detail. Those who impressed me the most (and with whom I am best acquainted) were the Kirghiz, for they, more than any, have retained their Oriental surroundings and habits, and greet you with a " salaam " instead of " zdrazdvouite," [2] while their villages have an essen-

[1] Tent.   [2] Russian " Good-day."

tially Eastern appearance, the wooden huts being interspersed with brick mosques and minarets, from the summit of which you may hear, every evening, the "muezzin" calling the people to prayer. The Kirghiz generally live in the vicinity of grazing lands, for they live by their horses, which are famed for their speed and endurance, although thousands of them perish in winter, when no fodder is provided. For in the Steppes a sudden rise of the thermometer frequently melts the snow, which on re-freezing is converted into solid ice, through which the poor beasts cannot get at the grass beneath. In the spring-time they are, therefore, reduced to bags of bones, but soon recover under the influence of summer sunshine and rich vegetation. It is a case, however, of the survival of the fittest, wherefore the Kirghiz horse is even, if possible, hardier than the Siberian pony. The late Captain Burnaby mentions a chief of this tribe who once galloped two hundred miles in twenty-four hours over steep and difficult country, and his mount was none the worse at the finish.

I have always found the Kirghiz cheery and good-tempered, hospitable and fond of a joke, but such terrible gluttons that I have seen three of them dispose of a fair-sized sheep at a single meal! But they are tough, wiry fellows, who generally die of old age or accident; and a Russian doctor told me that their longevity was chiefly due to "koumiss," which men, women and children imbibe in enormous quantities.

The Bashkir Tartars, who inhabit the Ural region, are nomads like the Kirghiz, and only reside in villages during the winter, living in tents at other seasons of the year and tending droves of horses, of which some of their chiefs own two and three thousand. But the Bashkirs are also good agriculturists, and are renowned as expert bee-keepers, their hives furnishing some of the best honey in Russia. They are also fonder of field sports than other Tartar tribes, especially hawking, and breed an unusually large kind of falcon, with which they are able to hunt foxes and even wolves.

Space compels me to pass over the interesting people whom I have met, from time to time, in Russian Central Asia (which people rarely realize is nearly as extensive as our Indian Empire),[1] while the Georgians, Circassians, and others who inhabit the Caucasus will be described in a following chapter. Travelling due north, therefore, from the Kirghiz country, we shall bid farewell to the Tartars at Kazan, on the Volga, and, after an arduous journey, reach the Arctic Ocean, the coast of which, from North Cape to the Béring Straits, is sparsely peopled by some of the strangest people in existence. These will become gradually wilder as we progress eastward, easy reach of civilization rendering the Laplander, at the western extremity of these Arctic wastes, a decent member of society as compared to the depraved and filthy " Tchuktchi," who inhabits the north-eastern coast of Siberia, at the other end of the line.

The Samoyèdes, who inhabit the shores of the Arctic Ocean from the Yenesei River to the White Sea, number about 25,000, and are almost as civilized as the Lapps, for many of them are Christians, and frequent association with Europeans has rendered them morally and mentally superior to their eastern neighbours, the Ostiaks, who may be described as the first step in the descending scale of civilization. The Ostiaks (about as numerous as the Samoyèdes)[2] are found in the vast tract of country lying between the Obi and Yenesei rivers and the Polar Sea. In summer they wander up and down the banks of these rivers, living in birch-bark tents, and earning a livelihood by fishing, the produce of their nets being salted and exported (via Tobolsk) to European Russia, but in early autumn the rivers are gripped by ice, and the Ostiak then returns to his winter quarters and reindeer on the coast. During summer he lives entirely upon fish, often eaten raw, his winter diet consisting of bear-flesh, game, and reindeer milk. Compared with tribes further east the Ostiaks are friendly and hospitable, possessing but few firearms, and generally using the old-fashioned bow and arrow to bring down the blue fox and other valuable fur-bearing animals. These people had the quaintest

---

[1] It has an area of 1,325,530 square miles, that of India being 1,802,000.

[2] Scurvy and a yet more loathsome disease introduced by Russian fur-traders is slowly decimating this tribe.

method of measuring time I have ever observed, even amongst savage races, for, when I set out on a short journey, they said it would take me twenty " kettles " to accomplish.   And I only afterwards discovered their meaning, which was to the effect that I should arrive at my destination in the same space of time as would be needed to consecutively set cold water in the said kettles on the boil !

I have never visited the Ostiak in winter quarters, but arrived one evening at one of their summer en- campments, and was nearly torn to pieces by half a dozen large, savage dogs, which they never move with- out.   The latter were, unlike their owners, the most sagacious beasts I ever saw, and also the cleanliest, for every morning I saw them go of their own accord to the river, and bathe like human beings !   An Ostiak encampment has, even in summer, a depressing aspect, and it looked on this occasion, when viewed by the light of a crimson sunset, the picture of desolation. In the foreground columns of grey smoke rose sluggishly from two or three grimy tents, while skin-clad forms flitted silently to and fro getting in the nets and canoes for the night.   And it took me some time to become inured to a faint, sickly odour which is peculiar to this tribe, and is caused by their repugnance to salt, although it is provided for them, at considerable expense, by the Government.   Some of the Ostiak women would have been almost attractive if their teeth had not loosened and dropped out, owing to a lack of this essential article of diet.   Most Siberian tribes regard their women as beasts of burthen, but the Ostiaks appeared to treat their wives with kindness and respect.   The Samoyède woman, on the other hand, is invariably persecuted, and, as the men consider child-birth degrading, the unfortunate mother is constantly maltreated until it is born.   A woman during pregnancy is tortured until she confesses with whom she has been unfaithful, often naming an imaginary lover in order to escape further ill-treatment, although even if she be proved unchaste a small sum of money, or its equivalent in drink or tobacco, compensates her husband.

I once lived for some months amongst the Dyaks of

Borneo, and was, on this occasion, much struck with the many points of similarity between them and the Ostiaks, although the former are a far finer race. The dug-out canoes used here were identically the same in shape and construction as those I had seen in Central Borneo, and the Ostiak paddles were carved with much the same patterns, a curious coincidence which may interest students of ethnology.

You must go far afield even from the remote town of Yakutsk (already described) to find the indigenous native of that enormous territory, which, although very sparsely peopled, is nearly the size of Europe; and this, I may add, is only one of many such districts in Siberia! The Yakute is shorter and slighter than the Ostiak, and is also less hospitable and more mercenary, although, unlike most of these tribes, he is cleanly and well dressed, his fur garments being ornamented with intricate patterns, while the women wear white deer-skins and a rather becoming head-dress of the same material. The wealthier Yakutes wear sables, of which the finest in the world are found in this district, and sold, even here, for large sums to Russian traders for sale in the capitals of Europe. The Yakutes are per-haps the most intelligent of these Arctic tribes, and many are clever craftsmen, who, like the Chinese, will copy almost anything given them for that purpose. An exile at Yakutsk told me that, being in want of a fork, he commissioned a Yakute to make him one of wood, a silver one being used as a model, and was much sur-prised to receive the next day a perfect imitation of the original article skilfully made of iron.

The Yakute winter dwellings are made of logs, which, being protected by banks of earth, afford more warmth than those of other natives. Human beings, cows and calves share these " yurtas," and even occasionally reindeer, for the latter provide these people with cloth-ing, food and drink, and are therefore carefully tended, the more so that a species of intoxicant, nearly as potent as " arak," is derived from their milk. The latter is generally accompanied, at festivals, by a kind of cake made of fir-tree bark, powdered very fine, which reeks of turpentine, but which is here regarded as a luxury. Epidemics of smallpox are common in this district, and Russian traders frequently come upon a village deserted by all but dogs and reindeer, while the corpses of those who have succumbed lie rotting above ground. And most of them die, for when a Yakute is attacked by this dreaded disease a cup of water and bundle of fire-wood are placed within reach, and he is left to his fate.

The Tunguse country extends from the Yenesei province to the Pacific Ocean, and also along the whole length of the river Amur. This is the most numerous tribe in Siberia (numbering about 50,000), whose customs show traces of Japanese influence, for steam communication has for years existed between the Amur and Japan. The Tunguses are, however, dying out, owing to the yearly increasing influx of Russian and Chinese emigrants, whose more modern methods of trade are gradually depriving the Tunguses of their former means of existence by the sale of fish, furs and fossil ivory.

It may interest the reader to know how these tribes dress in winter, in order to withstand the ferocious cold, and my own costume may serve as an example, for (except the underwear and " duffle " suit) it was supplied to me by a Yakute. My apparel consisted of two pairs of flannel singlets and drawers, thin deerskin breeches, and three pairs of thick woollen socks reaching over the knee, over which I wore a jacket and trousers of " duffle " (a kind of thin felt), and deerskin mocassins (leather would instantly freeze the feet), secured around the leg by thongs. Over this was a second pair of thicker deerskin breeches, and a loose, heavy coat of the same fur reaching to the knees, with a wolverine hood almost entirely concealing the face, which, in order to avoid frost-bite, must always be kept smeared with vaseline or some other oily substance. Under this hood I wore two close-fitting worsted caps, and over them a deerskin cap with ear-flaps. Two pairs of thick worsted gloves and finger-less bearskin mits reaching to the elbow completed the outfit, and I may add that I have often shivered, even under this mountain of material, on (for these regions) a comparatively warm day !

TCHUKTCHI WOMAN AND CHILD, MIDWAY BETWEEN KOLYMA RIVER
AND BÉRING STRAITS

(Author's tent and Tchuktchi walrus-hide hut in background)

Of the natives inhabiting Kamchatka and the shores of the Okhotzk Sea I have no personal knowledge, although I have, on two occasions, had to live for weeks at a time with their northern neighbours, the " Tchuktchis," and to share a walrus-hide hut with over a score of these unsavoury people, under conditions which, on the first occasion, nearly cost me my life. Indeed, had I not been rescued by a belated whaler in the late autumn, when ice was closing round the coast, severing all communication until the following summer, nothing could have saved me.

There are in all about 12,000 Tchuktchis, some of whom inhabit the Arctic coast from Tchaun Bay to the Béring Straits, and rely on the sea for a living, while others wander about the mountains of the interior with herds of reindeer. These natives are nominally Russian subjects, yet for two centuries they have resisted conquest, and to this day pay no taxes, nor, indeed, have they ever set eyes on a Russian official.[1] For, strange as it may seem, the Great White Tsar himself has less influence here than the skipper of the grimiest American whaler, so long as the latter appears every summer with a plentiful supply of the vile concoction known as whisky, which these natives receive in exchange for whalebone, walrus tusks and furs. Indeed, were it not for the San Francisco whalers the Tchuktchis would probably disappear, in a very short time, from the face of the earth.

I have, as I have said, twice lived with the Tchuktchis : once in '98, when I endeavoured to reach Paris by land from New York, and failed to get further than Oumwaidjik, one of their settlements on Béring Straits. Here, when the American revenue cutter which landed me had sailed away, I was regarded as a prisoner by the chief of the place, who appropriated my belongings and subjected me to such brutal treatment that, had

---

[1] "These people for many years resisted every attempt made by the Russians either to subdue them or to pass through their country. Of a force numbering two hundred armed men, who were sent into their territory, rather for the purpose of scientific exploration than with any views of conquest, not a soul returned, nor has their fate been ascertained."—Professor Eden.

M

it not been for my timely rescue, just before the closing
of navigation, I must have perished. I therefore
avoided Oumwaidjik on my second, (and successful),
journey from Paris to New York, and lived at Whalen,
a village consisting of about 300 less objectionable
natives and thirty walrus-hide huts (eighty miles north
of Oumwaidjik), until a crossing of the Straits was
rendered practicable. But even at Whalen my position
was rather precarious, owing to the fact that, however
well disposed the Tchuktchi may be when sober, he
invariably becomes, when drunk, a homicidal maniac.[1]
And my arrival on this occasion was celebrated by a
feast, at which so much " tanglefoot "[2] was consumed
that by sunset every man in the place was intoxicated,
with the exception of the chief, in whose hut I concealed myself until the trouble was over. Nevertheless,
all his companions were armed with Winchester rifles,
and reeled throughout the night about the settlement,
firing ball-cartridge in every direction, and vowing
vengeance on the white man whom a few hours before
they had greeted with effusive hospitality! And the
next morning, when sober, every native was again quite
friendly; but as these entertainments took place about
twice a week during my two months' stay, I gradually
realized that Whalen, although perhaps less dangerous
than Oumwaidjik, was anything but a desirable residence!

The village is situated on a sandy beach at the foot
of precipitous cliffs, and, as I reached it late in the
spring, I could not stir many yards from the place
owing to deep slush and melting snow. I therefore
never saw an inland Tchuktchi, but those on the coast
seemed fairly intelligent (when sober), and possessed of
great physical strength, owing to a life of incessant peril
and activity, in summer fighting furious gales in flimsy
skin boats, in winter hunting walrus and seal in the
cold, dark silence of the ice. The men wore a deerskin
garment reaching a little below the waist, and secured

---

[1] European whalemen are occasionally killed during these orgies,
and during the few weeks I was here two natives were shot.—Author's
note.

[2] A slang term used by whaling men for the cheap intoxicant which
they sell to the Tchuktchis.

by a walrus thong, and hair-seal breeches and moccasins, topped by a close-fitting fur cap like a baby's bonnet, while all carried an ugly-looking knife in a leather sheath. The women were small in stature, and some would have been pretty but for hard, weather-beaten features, caused by exposure to all kinds of weather. Nearly all had teeth of snowy whiteness, much disfigured by the constant chewing of sealskin to render it pliable for making moccasins and other articles. Only the women tattooed their faces and wore deerskin " combinations," trimmed at the neck and wrists with wolverine, their hair being dressed in two long plaits intertwined with beads, copper coins, and other cheap trinkets procured from whalemen. The garments of both sexes were occasionally trimmed with coloured fur, of bright red or green, worked into intricate patterns, and I wondered how they obtained the dye, until I discovered that the green tint was extracted from the urine of dogs, and the red from a rock some distance away in the interior.

I can safely say that the Tchuktchis are. without exception, the filthiest race, both in their mode of life and bodily habits, in creation. Were I to describe one-tenth of the revolting incidents which I witnessed during my stay even at Whalen, (at Oumwaidjik it was worse), the reader. would lay down this book in disgust. I will therefore only briefly explain that these people wash, not in water, but a certain emanation of the human body, and that their upper garments are so made that the hand and arm can be thrust right into them to relieve the annoyance caused by vermin. And these are the least repellent of the sickening practices in which I saw the Tchuktchis habitually indulge.

There is a theory that the latter originally migrated here from the American continent, but this, I think, is doubtful, as, although they are barely thirty miles apart, there is no resemblance whatever between the Alaskan Eskimo and his Siberian neighbours. For even natives of the Siberian settlements varied with regard to language and personal characteristics, and although at Whalen I was well treated, I was warned not to go near East Cape, only four miles away, where the natives were said to be "dangerous." Moreover, the dialect spoken at East Cape differed from that at Whalen, which latter was again different from that which was spoken at Oumwaidjik.

The hut in which I lived at Whalen was of walrus hide, and measured about forty feet round and fifteen feet high in the centre, the only aperture being a very low doorway. Dogs roamed freely about a large outer chamber stored with hunting and fishing tackle, and which led into a similar inner space screened with deer-skins, where the inmates ate and slept. The darkness here was dimly illumined by seal-oil lamps, which were never extinguished, maintaining night and day a temperature of over 85° Fahr. And the heat and stench were beyond description, for although, at night, men, women and children stripped naked, the perspiration poured off them, while the days were even worse, for then the unspeakable filth of the place was more clearly revealed. The daily meal—which, having no provisions, I had to share—consisted of seal-meat, occasionally varied by stale goose eggs and fish-roe, flavoured with seal-oil; also a kind of seaweed found in the stomach of a dead walrus. When smoking the Tchuk-tchis used a tiny brass Chinese pipe, and did not emit, but swallowed the smoke, while the cheapest American tobacco was so precious that it was only chewed and passed from mouth to mouth until the flavour had been completely extracted. When smoked—on rare occasions—it was eked out with seal hairs!

As the weather got warmer, life would have been more bearable had it not been for the drink-feasts, which constantly recalled the unpleasant affinity between a barrel of whisky and bloodshed. When I arrived here most of the fiery spirit left during the previous summer by the whalers had been consumed, but the chief (although himself an abstainer) had contrived to brew a special brand of his own, which he would first retail to his less temperate companions, and then barricade himself and prepare for squalls. This beverage was even stronger than the American "tangle-foot," and was made by mixing together one part each of flour and molasses with four parts of water and then

A TCHUKTCHI "WITCH" NEAR TCHAUN BAY (N.E. COAST OF SIBERIA)

letting the mixture ferment. My host's distillery consisted of a coal-oil tin, an old gun-barrel, and a wooden tub, the mash being placed in the tin, from which the gun-barrel, which served as the coil, led into the tub, which was filled with cracked ice. A fire was then built under the tin, and as steam rose from the heated mess it was condensed in the gun-barrel by the ice in the tub, to drop, in the shape of liquor, through the gun-barrel into a drinking-cup. It therefore took a long time to obtain even half a pint of the poisonous stuff, which, however, made up in strength what it lacked in quantity.

The Tchuktchis must have some sort of religion, for they occasionally performed strange rites, one of which was to throw pieces of walrus or seal meat into the sea to abate its fury, and there were other signs of their belief in a Supreme Being. I also ascertained that when a Tchuktchi's end is easy and painless he is condemned to eternal torment, while a violent death ensures eternal peace. This belief probably accounts for the "Kamitok," a ceremony practised only by these people, and which I witnessed at Oumwaidjik, where an old man was strangled with a walrus thong because he had become too old to work. The victim, oddly enough, seemed to evince less interest in his impending execution than the distribution of "tanglefoot" by which it was preceded, when every one drank to excess, only the executioner remaining sufficiently sober to give the *coup de grâce*. Women, I was told, are never put to death in this manner.[1]

I sometimes went seal-hunting at Whalen, but this is poor fun in very cold weather, when you have to watch a hole in the ice, sometimes for hours together, before the animal's head appears; which, moreover, it often fails to do! But walrus-hunting is glorious sport,

[1] "One of the attendants I had with me in the Kolyma country was a man of fifty, and the father and elder brothers had already followed in the way of their ancestors (by the 'Kamitok'). Once, while stricken with a violent fever, instead of taking the medicine that I gave him, he inquired anxiously if I were sure he would recover at all, otherwise he felt bound to send for his son and ask for the last stroke."—*A Strange People of the North*, by Waldemar Bogoras, *Harper's Magazine*, April 1903.

involving a certain amount of risk, for when one of these beasts is sighted, and even if it is blowing a hurricane, the "baidarás" (large walrus-hide canoes) put to sea, and it is a race who shall first reach the monster, which is now no longer dispatched with harpoons, but firearms. The walrus I saw killed measured ten feet long, and had quite that girth, and must have weighed over a ton, yet he was reckoned rather a small one !

The Whalen natives were fine athletes, and I frequently saw them racing, wrestling, and even boxing with an old set of gloves which they had obtained from a whaler. The women also had a game which resembled "tossing in a blanket" (a walrus hide being substituted for the latter), and the one who attained the greatest height was proclaimed the winner, and kissed by the chief—a ceremony which here consists of rubbing noses while murmuring "Oo." Once there was a "walrus dance" in one of the huts, when both sexes appeared in a state of nudity, wearing only sealskin moccasins. This weird entertainment was preceded by the beating of sealskin drums, after which two naked women, sitting astride, were carried in on a long plank, upon which they performed a series of contortions somewhat resembling the *Dance du Ventre*. Relays of girls continued this exercise until exhausted by their efforts, when flesh cut from the newly captured walrus was handed round, to be washed down with copious draughts of "tanglefoot." It was then time to beat a hasty retreat and conceal myself until the next day, by which time most of the revellers had regained their sobriety and composure.

It was, of course, an interesting experience, but, as the reader may imagine, I was not sorry when, one bright summer morning, the American revenue cutter *Thetis* anchored off Whalen, and my second enforced residence of over a month amongst the Siberian Tchuktchis was safely brought to an end !

CHAPTER XVI

KIÉFF AND LITTLE RUSSIA—AN EVENING WITH A NIHILIST

EUROPEAN RUSSIA possesses almost as many varieties of climate as her gigantic neighbour, Siberia, and every mile you go south, from Petrograd or Moscow, the more attractive the country becomes, especially to those easily elated or depressed by immediate surroundings. For Northern Russia is, even in summer, a land of grey days and gloomy landscapes, whereas down south blue skies and brilliant sunshine, verdure and flowers, impart a welcome warmth and gaiety to both nature and humanity. A native of the Crimea is, therefore, usually more genial and attractive than an inhabitant of, say, Archangel, just as a Neapolitan's mental outlook is, generally, more cheerful than that of a Swede.

The belt of rich black soil known as the " Ukraine " [1] (which extends across Russia from the Austrian frontier to the Asian Steppes), divides these two zones, and Little Russia's chief town is Kiéff, which flourished before even Moscow sprang into existence as a settlement of log huts. The former was, therefore, the first Muscovite capital, and it now enjoys the anomalous distinction of being not only the most ancient, but also most modern city in the empire, with imposing stone buildings and broad, crowded thoroughfares, which present a business-like, up-to-date aspect, more suggestive of some prosperous town in the Western States of America than a holy place of pilgrimage, to which thousands of the orthodox faith annually resort for healing, fasting and prayer. There are, therefore, hundreds of churches here, besides monasteries, convents and other sacred

---

[1] The wonderfully fertile nature of this soil is ascribed to the slow decay of the grass, many centuries old, of the steppes.

167

buildings, which, however, are all so scattered as to attract little attention, and the visitor's first impression of Kiéff is that of a commercial, yet fashionable, centre, well provided, for those who can afford them, with every comfort and pleasure in life. Petrograd, notwithstanding its hidden life of extravagance and dissipation, is dull and commonplace; Moscow is saddened by association with mediæval crime and calamities; but Kiéff possesses all the charm and few of the disadvantages of other Russian towns, which, in the provinces, are so exactly alike, that one is outwardly typical of them all. There is always a Governor's Palace—in various stages of splendour or decay—any number of churches, a dilapidated and generally empty theatre, military barracks, a " Gostimoi-Dvor " and a prison, with a space of ground called (by courtesy) a public garden. Kiéff, however, is not only essentially original, but is also the healthiest place in Russia, owing to the bracing air of the steppes, and scrupulous cleanliness of the city, which extends for nearly ten miles along the right bank of the broad, swiftly-flowing Dnieper.

The place contains about 500,000 inhabitants, and comprises four distinct districts, which may almost be called separate towns. Podol, the commercial quarter, skirts the river, and above it, on a steep declivity, is Lipti, the residential quarter, and an enchanting spot in summer, with its handsome villas, embowered in dark, luxuriant foliage. North of this is Kiéff proper, which contains the University and Cathedral of Saint-Sophia, a building erected in the eleventh century, but so constantly repaired and added to, that it is now a huge and towering structure with over a dozen large golden domes. Here also are the theatres, best hotels, and shops, which latter are quite as modern and well-found as those of Petrograd or Moscow. Petchersk, the fourth district, is well worth seeing, for it is honeycombed with caves and catacombs which, in olden days, were used as places of refuge and monastic cells, and where, during holy festivals, one can scarcely move through the dense crowds of pilgrims, of whom 300,000 annually visit this ancient and revered monastery. The " Lavra," as it is called, contains the embalmed remains of over a hundred saints, one being that of a holy personage who lived for fifteen years buried up to his neck in the ground, from which his head may still be seen protruding.   The latter is said to sink a little lower into the soil every century, and a monk gravely informed me that the day of judgment would simultaneously occur with its entire disappearance !   The " Lavra " covers an enormous extent of ground, and you may wander for days through its interminable streets, alleys and courtyards—in one of which latter, beggars are always clustered around the ever-open door of a church, in the dim recesses of which wax tapers shed their mellow light, through a haze of incense, on faded tapestries and jewelled images of saints.   The citadel once stood near here, but its site is now occupied by a modern arsenal, whence there is a fine view of the surrounding country, while, at night, a great cross on the statue of Saint Vladimir, is lit by electricity, and shines, at night, over many miles of surrounding country.

Although the cathedral and churches of Kiéff are endowed with less wealth than those of Moscow, the former contain many valuable pictures and works of art, notably the sanctuary doors of the Ouspensky Church, which are of solid silver and exquisite workmanship.   Kiéff is rightly described as " Holy," for early in the tenth century Prince Vladimir forcibly converted its people to Christianity by baptism in the Dnieper, and built many of the churches which the place contained a hundred years later.   These were, however, pillaged and destroyed when the town was seized by the Tartars in the thirteenth century, being eventually retaken from them by a Grand Duke of Lithuania, who, in 1386, added Kiéff to the kingdom of Poland.   It was not, however, until 1686 that, after a protracted and desperate struggle, the city was finally ceded to Muscovy, together with the rich provinces of Little Russia, Podolia and Volhynia.

Pilgrims of all classes flock here at certain seasons of the year from all parts of Russia and even Siberia, many suffering from incurable diseases, for Kiéff is as renowned for its marvellous cures as Lourdes in France. Some people come merely to pray, often for the furtherance of some special object, and these when wealthy, generally leave thousands of roubles in aid of charities when they depart;[1] while the poor peasant, who cannot afford a ticket to the Holy Land, visits Kiéff instead, in the firm belief that his soul will derive as much spiritual benefit as from the longer and more expensive journey.

The exhilarating, open-air life here reminded me of Paris, especially in the spring-time when parks and gardens were a mass of flowers, bunches of which were sold in the streets for as many kopecks as they would have cost roubles in Petrograd. There were also leafy *boulevards*, where one could sit in a *café* and drink *bock* amongst men who appeared less preoccupied and women who looked gayer and prettier than those of other Russian towns, perhaps because of pure air and clear sunshine. And the evenings were equally enjoyable, when a theatre or music-hall generally preceded a stroll through the starlit streets, or supper *al fresco* in some public garden, under electric light, with a "tzigane" band as an accompaniment. These places were always amusing, for Kiéff is a favourite meeting-place of every variety of the Russian race—Poles, Ruthenians, Caucasians and Jews; while, before the war, even wealthy Rumanians were lured here, certainly less by religious motives than business, or some other less serious and profitable object.

Yet this is by no means solely a city of pleasure, although its industries are mostly agricultural, and the atmosphere is therefore unpolluted by factory smoke. Kiéff's commercial prosperity is chiefly due to the cultivation of beetroot (for it is the centre of the sugar industry in Russia), and is therefore the resort, in springtime, of a host of refiners, who come here to sign contracts with the growers, and also enjoy themselves *en garçon*, or with their wives and families. The town then becomes so crowded that hotels raise their prices, and for about a month there is a ceaseless round of amusements and gaiety.

It has been suggested, since the outbreak of the war,

[1] One monastery alone is said to have an annual revenue of many million roubles.

that Kiéff would make an admirable capital from every point of view, and it is within the bounds of possibility that, when Russia annexes Constantinople (which in the ordinary course of events, she must surely do), the greater part of her trade and industries will be transferred to the southern provinces, thus relegating Petrograd and Moscow, commercially speaking, to a secondary position in the Empire. This, at any rate, was the opinion of an influential merchant whom I met here, and I quote it for what it is worth. He added that such a change would be popular, if only because this is a purely Slav city, which, unlike Petrograd, has never been tainted by Teutonic influence and customs.

Being desirous of seeing Little Russia at its best, I drove, in summer, from here to Kharkoff in a " tarantass," a vehicle drawn by three horses yoked abreast. The middle one bears a high-arched wooden yoke, or " duga," with jangling bells, and advances at a rapid trot, while the horses on either side gallop, with heads turned outwards, at such a sharp angle that they frequently blunder into the ditch, whence, however, they generally quickly extricate themselves without stopping the team. But I have noticed that Russian horses seem endowed with super-equine intelligence, and when in a difficulty never plunge and struggle, but lie absolutely motionless until help arrives. And they scarcely ever shy, this being perhaps due to the fact that they wear no blinkers and can therefore see all that is going on around them.

I have seldom enjoyed a journey more than this one through the Ukraine,[1] which is, in every respect, a pleasant contrast to the bleak and cheerless northern provinces. Little Russia is, of course, the most fertile region on earth, but so are parts of Siberia, and I was here less impressed by the richness of the soil and prosperity of the peasantry, than the attractive appearance not only of the people but also of their villages—now no longer surrounded by dreary plain and pine forest,

---

[1] The name " Little Russia " originated in the fourteenth century to distinguish this region from " Greater Russia," which lies to the north. Russians generally call the former the " Ukraine."

but by fields of golden corn and rich pastures, where sleek cattle browsed in the shade of oak and chestnut trees. The houses were built, not of wood, but plaited wicker-work plastered with clay and surmounted by a neatly-thatched roof, and their walls, which were either whitewashed or of a light rose or green colour, were in cheerful contrast to the sombre, weather-bleached buildings of Greater Russia. And yet the former are more cheaply and rapidly erected, many portions, such as the roof, window-frames, door-posts, etc., being kept ready for sale at the nearest " Gostinnoi-Dvor," or bazaar. And even the humblest dwelling has its carefully tended garden, where the sunflower always predominates, for it is cultivated here on account of its seeds, which are consumed in huge quantities by people of all classes from Kiéff to the Black Sea. And I passed my first night in no grimy post-house, but a clean, sweet-smelling cottage, with lattice windows overlooking an orchard gay with pear and apple-blossom; while my evening meal was served, not on greasy oil-skin, but a spotless linen tablecloth, with (wonderful to relate) no crawling " Tarakans " to mar its snowy surface. Moreover, I slept in soft sheets, a luxury which I had never previously enjoyed throughout many thousand miles of travel in Russian rural districts.

The Malo-Russians [1] are largely interbred with the Polish race, and it is probably from the latter that they derive their love of art and pleasure and a partiality for cheerful surroundings. The " Great " Russian is generally careless and slovenly as to his dress, but his southern neighbour loves bright colours and fantastic costumes, and devotes as much attention to his personal appearance as to his garden, which says a great deal. Thus, on this occasion, my host's pretty wife (who looked sixteen, but had six children) wore the picturesque national dress—a white, delicately-embroidered bodice, short grey shirt and turquoise-velvet " kakoshnik," which set off her soft brown hair, while the owner's diminutive feet would certainly have aroused admiration in Bond Street or on the *boulevards*.

The moujik of the north is bearded like the pard,

[1] Malo-Russia, " Little Russia."

but men here, as a rule, wear only a moustache, and a century ago shaved even their heads like the Tartars, leaving only a long lock over the forehead. Natives of the " Ukraine " were, therefore, formerly called " Tufts " by the " Greater Russians," the latter being termed " Goats " (on account of their hirsute appearance), in retaliation! I also noticed that the "Malo-Russians" are less subservient than those of other districts, rarely addressing one as " Beloved one," " Little Father," " Sweet Pigeon," and other extravagant terms which are lavished on even a humble stranger in other parts of Russia. For the Malo-Russian formerly acknowledged but one master—the Tsar, and therefore greeted every one else, except officials of the highest rank, simply as " Barin " or " Sir."

I lingered on the road for nearly a week between Kiéff and Kharkoff, for this is truly a land not only of music and song, but "with milk and honey blest." Everything grows in abundance, grain of all kinds, tobacco, and especially fruit; for the tiniest cottage has its orchard, the produce of which is generally sent to Kiéff, which is justly famed for its jams and preserves. And, from first to last, I drove over excellent roads through a panorama of verdant hills and dales, park-like grazing-lands and clear, rapid streams, alternating so frequently with stretches of dark forest, or belts of lighter woodland, as to dispel any semblance of monotony. And every day we passed bands of gypsies, camping by the wayside, and causing as much anxiety, with regard to the security of village poultry-yards, as they do in the English shires. Most of these " tsiganes " were Rumanians, working as tinkers, basket-makers, or musicians. And many of the latter, who have achieved fame in Parisian restaurants and *cafés*, have drifted there from Wallachia, notably one wandering and swarthy artist who eventually married a well-known Belgian princess. It is only fair to add that here, as elsewhere in Europe, the gypsies are mostly honest, law-abiding people, who are eyed with distrust chiefly by reason of their wild, barbaric appearance.

The heat in the day-time was rather oppressive, but sunset usually brought a cool, refreshing breeze from the

Dnieper. And it was pleasant, on a still evening, to sit out in the gloaming and listen to the distant voices of women returning from the fields, as they joined in some sweet, plaintive air of Little Russia; while, in the village street, men danced to the twanging lilt of a " balalaika," or played " landrail," a game in which two long lines are attached to a post driven into the ground. To the former are attached two blindfolded players, one of whom has a short club and the other hand-bell, which he occasionally rings to indicate his position, the discovery of which ensures him a sound drubbing from his antagonist.

Dwellers in Petrograd or Moscow will tell you that the Malo-Russian is lazy and deceitful, and this may be partly true, but any minor defects these people may possess are certainly atoned for by their attractive social qualities. On the other hand, the toiler of the Ukraine is (unlike the northern moujik) no passionate lover of the soil, which he regards merely as a means of maintenance for his family, with the addition of a certain amount of amusement for himself, and his indolence is perhaps partly due to the fact that the land here is so fertile that these are easily obtained. The women, unlike the men, are thrifty and industrious, and, when not working on the land, are generally employed in making embroideries (which have only of late years reached London and Paris) or weaving carpets, which, being not only artistic but cheap, find their way to all parts of Russia. Good looks prevail to an unusual extent amongst the fair sex, who are not renowned for their virtue, marital infidelity being of common occurrence. Some writers ascribe this laxity of morals to lack of religion; for both sexes, although nominally of the orthodox faith, evince so little interest in spiritual matters that this is about the only district in the Empire where there are few, if any, sectarians.

The Malo-Russian's chief defect is lack of humour, for his dreamy, sensuous nature seeks refined and artistic pleasures rather than the insidious but sordid joys of " vodka " and the " traktir." He is, however, no fool, and as shrewd as any one else at driving a bargain, although sadly improvident, having for centuries past

A TCHUKTCHI GIRL FEEDING THE DOGS

made no attempt to guard against the droughts which occasionally devastate this district, fortunately without any permanent ill-effects. During their continuance, however, Little Russia is anything but " the blest," for the earth is then parched and rent with enormous fissures, and not a drop of water is procurable for man or beast. Even the Dnieper is then reduced to the dimensions of a narrow, sluggish stream, and although artesian wells and other modern appliances would modify this evil, their adoption never seems to have occurred to the careless, self-indulgent Malo-Russian, who, being a spoilt child of nature, never realizes that the latter can occasionally become a harsh and even cruel mother. The swarms of locusts which, at certain seasons, ravage the crops are almost as destructive, but these are of course unavoidable, and the same may be said for the spring floods, which occasionally lay waste large tracts of cultivated land.

I have sometimes travelled for weeks through the wilds of Siberia without setting eyes on fur or feather; but the Ukraine and steppes team with animal life, wolves being so numerous that nearly every dwelling is surrounded by a thick thorn-hedge, ten or twelve feet in height, as a protection at night-time. Every household is also guarded by a number of dogs, which, as they occasionally interbreed with the wolves, are unusually wild and savage. The former are never kept in-doors, or even fed by their owners, and therefore have to find their own victuals, often being reduced to fruit and grapes, which I have seen them devour with apparently as much relish as a piece of butcher's meat. The fields of Little Russia swarm with mice, which sometimes play havoc with the crops; but the most curious animal I saw was the " Suslik," which is less common here than in the Asian Steppes, or Mongolian Desert of Gobi, where I encountered thousands. The " Suslik," which is something between a squirrel and a marmot, is very hard to catch, but its burrow has always two entrances, and Malo-Russians secure the little beasts by pouring water in at one end, and seizing them as they emerge from the other; for the fur is soft and delicate, and fetches a good price in Kiéff, where it is used as a lining for ladies' evening cloaks. There is also any amount of game here in the shape of sand-grouse, duck, teal, widgeon and snipe, hares and rabbits, which (as elsewhere in Russia) are rarely shot at by local sportsmen, and therefore easily obtainable.

Summer here is very enjoyable, but the " Ukraine " is at its best in May; when nature is awakening from her long winter sleep, the woods and meadows are ablaze with lilac and laburnum, and violets, daffodils and daisies peep out of the long grass, which for months has lain under a heavy blanket of snow. The first two or three days of warmth and sunshine produce a rapid and luxuriant growth of trees, grass and flowers which is elsewhere unknown, and it is only here that you can truly appreciate the delights of spring-time, which in other countries are generally so overrated. And, later on in the season, the evenings, when the long grey twilight is succeeded by only a few starlight hours, have a charm all their own, although the " white nights " of August, when sunset and sunrise are so imperceptibly merged that there is no real darkness, can only be enjoyed much farther north.

Kharkoff is a university town which entirely lacks natural beauties or archæological interest, for it is a comparatively modern place which only dates from the seventeenth century. It is also much behind the times, especially with regard to hotels, and although I expected to find in a place of this size a bed and washing appliances, the former had no sheets or pillows, and the latter consisted of the little brass tap let into the wall, which I had hitherto imagined was peculiar to Siberia. Kharkoff was, in short, so dull and unattractive that my stay there would have been very brief, had I not promised a political exile to deliver a letter to his brother who resided in the town. The writer of the missive had just served a sentence of ten years in the Nertchinsk silver-mines when I met him, living under police supervision, at a village in Eastern Siberia. His offence had therefore been a serious one, and his younger brother (whom I will call Serge Androvitch) had heard nothing of the exile since his banishment. Knowing, however, by experience that association with even the relatives of a political prisoner in Russia is apt to be dangerous, I waited until after dark before calling upon Androvitch, who was employed as a minor Government official, and occupied, in a squalid suburb, a small, poorly-furnished flat. And its owner seemed fully prepared for my arrival, which, having some knowledge of the secret and rapid mode of communication between revolutionaries of all countries, scarcely surprised me. I once heard of the suicide of an exile whom I had met years before in Sredni-Kolymsk[1] from a friend of the latter living in Soho, although how the latter received the news has ever since remained a mystery.

Androvitch, who greeted me cordially, at once gave me to understand that he was working for " the cause " in conjunction with a young lady who shared his apartment, and who I therefore assumed was either his wife or sister. But I was then unacquainted with the domestic methods of the Russian Nihilist, or rather " Socialist," for the former term is never used in revolutionary circles, the members of which prefer to style themselves the " Intelligentia." And I learnt, during the course of the evening, that there were numberless secret societies in Russia varying from those composed solely of Terrorists to others as harmless as the " Primrose League," although even the latter were eyed askance by the Secret Police. Serge, therefore, spoke with reverential awe of his brother, who had belonged to the former category, while my host modestly owned that he was only a humble disciple in the great scheme of social regeneration.

Both Androvitch and his mysterious friend proved interesting companions, with whom I freely discussed topics the mere mention of which would, in any public place, have entailed our immediate arrest and probably severe punishment. Kharkoff, they told me, was an important base of operations, and two or three important leaders generally resided there, while many of Serge's friends had been exiled for political offences which this beardless youth proceeded to defend and justify with all the assurance of an experienced man of the world, although the united ages of the girl and himself

---

[1] See chap. xiii.

cannot have exceeded forty years ! But I had when in Siberia frequently noticed the juvenile appearance of most of the exiles. Men and women, banished for political crimes, were generally middle-aged and even elderly; but the majority looked like mere boys and girls, more fitted for the playground than a political conspiracy. For in Russia mere children occasionally get bitten with a mania to " go out among the people," or, in other words, to disseminate revolutionary views amongst the lower orders. And thousands of young people of the better class are lured into the Socialistic net by old and experienced agitators, who are actuated solely by mercenary motives, and who themselves keep safely in the background.

There is little doubt, however, that Russian youth is more precocious than that of any other country. Mr. R. Reynolds,[1] for instance, mentions the case of a boy of fourteen from Petrograd, whom he met at a French watering-place, and who was about to write a play dealing with the Paris of Louis XIV., the characters of which were all either reprobates or courtesans. " The three of us supped " (writes Mr. Reynolds) " in a restaurant, and ' Shura ' (the lad in question) laid down the law on politics, religion and the problems of life with amazing assurance. He told us he was not called upon to take an active part in politics, but that he should, when invited to do so, ' support the Socialists.' . . . ' But, you see,' he explained, ' life holds only three, things worth troubling about : Eating, drinking and making love to pretty women ! '

" This engaging youth then departed, remarking that his father would be annoyed if he stayed out later than 2 a.m. He also informed us that, at the age of twenty-five, he intended to shoot himself, as life after that would not be worth living ! "

The same author relates that a deputation of school-children once visited the Petrograd *Rus*, a liberal paper, and requested the editor to publish their views on social reform—one of their suggestions being the substitution of " free love " for the marriage ceremony !

Serge Androvitch belonged to a type of youth of whom

[1] *My Russian Year*, by R. Reynolds.

I had met many in Siberia, and whose conversation was freely interlarded with revolutionary jargon, yet who, when invited to explain the practical aim and working of their secret mission in life, seemed to have the vaguest ideas as to how mankind was to be socially improved and regenerated.   Thus Serge's views on the freedom of the people, liberty of the press, restriction of education and so forth, were expressed in a parrot-like manner which seemed to indicate that he was merely echoing phrases expressed by fluent orators at some revolutionary meeting;   for when my young friend became natural his remarks were devoid of all originality, clearness, or depth of thought.   But a fairly long and varied experience has shown me that Socialism, in Russia, is in many cases taken up by young and impulsive people as a fad, rendered irresistibly attractive by reason of its atmosphere of romance, personal risk, and especially the chance of notoriety, which always appeals to the vain and immature mind, and which is probably responsible for the crimes of violence which here invariably follow the assassination (or execution as it is called) of some distinguished personage.

The revolutionary youth of both sexes in Russia are easily recognized, for the men affect an eccentric style of dress, wear their hair very long, and are rather chary of soap and water; while even young and attractive women cut off their luxuriant tresses and display an utter indifference as to their personal appearance.   Serge had, on this occasion, discarded his official uniform for a shabby velveteen jacket and flowing red tie; while the girl's ill-fitting, rusty black gown and closely-cropped head detracted from what would otherwise have been a comely face and slim, graceful figure.   Liouba had, it appeared, only met Serge a few weeks previously, and I was assured by the latter, without a trace of embarrassment, that their relations were purely platonic.   And this was probably true, for in the revolutionary world a couple often elect to live together under conditions entirely dissociated with anything approaching love or sensuality.   Young people of this category regard themselves and are regarded merely as sexless fellow-workers, in whose relations the heart and emotions play no part, and as most of the women of this class, with whom I have come in contact, have been what Americans call " homely," this fact is perhaps less strange than it might otherwise appear. Moreover, in Russia, a man's constant association with a woman of his acquaintance in any class of life, even if she be married and beautiful, creates no scandal, as it would in other countries, for the bond between them may, and frequently does, arise from a purely intellectual affinity. And so it is when students of opposite sex, living in a university town, agree to live together, for the simple reason that mutual interests and objects in life have brought them together as intimate friends, and nothing more. And this was the case with my host and his companion, who was a medical student at Kharkoff University. And the latter herself informed me that it was customary for girls who " go out among the people," to choose a male partner towards whom they were absolutely cold and indifferent from a sexual point of view, but whom they thought might prove useful as a collaborator in the difficult and dangerous task which they had sworn to perform. Occasionally, she added, but very rarely, they married in the end, but that otherwise, if the man attempted to overstep the platonic barrier, separation was almost invariably the immediate result.

My experience of these loveless and sterile unions was limited to Kharkoff; but, on the other hand, I could quote many instances of almost sublime self-sacrifice on the part of revolutionary women whose male " comrades " have fallen into the hands of the police. Official statistics show that hundreds of them annually, and of their own free will, accompany not only their husbands, but lovers, to Siberia; a notable instance, in the latter case, being that of Baroness Rehbinder, who followed Dr. Weimar (the Empress-Dowager's physician) to the life-long banishment which he had to endure for the attempted assassination of a court official.

Androvitch seemed less interested in his brother's health and welfare than the condition of the Siberian peasantry, amongst whom, as he was compelled to admit, the " propaganda " had fallen on very barren ground. The moujik, he declared, was an ungrateful mortal, who, notwithstanding all that had been done to ensure his freedom, had never evinced the slightest gratitude towards his would-be benefactors. My host related an incident in proof of this fact, and described how two peasants attended the execution of a famous Socialist leader, from whom the former had received many kindnesses and favours. "He is to be hanged to-morrow morning," said one; "let us go to the execution." "Why," said the other, "you don't want to see the poor devil suffer?" "Oh! no," was the rejoinder; "but we might get a bit of the rope, and it brings good luck!" "Is it worth our while," added Serge, "to endure imprisonment and exile, and even risk death, for such thankless dogs as these?" And my obvious but unspoken, reply was, "Then, why do it?"

I may here mention that I have never, even in Siberia, heard political exiles of either sex display personal animosity towards the Emperor or any member of the Imperial Family, their enmity being chiefly directed against the system of government of which their Majesties form the figurehead. The "Tchin" or "Bureaucracy" seemed to be the object of their special detestation, and next to it the priesthood, many members of both these professions having during the past few years been "removed" to the next world by violent means. Serge, however, informed me that the Terrorists in favour of assassination were now few in number and gradually dying out. It had, he said, been realized that political crime and bloodshed only impeded the cause of reform, and he added that the murders of the Grand Duke Serge, Trépoff, Stolýpin and others had been strongly condemned by the more influential leaders of his party.

Neither Androvitch nor his pretty little friend professed the "orthodox" or any other faith, for in nine cases out of ten the Russian Socialist is also an atheist. Liouba was a delicate, frail-looking creature, with pale pathetic features and wonderful dark eyes, which flashed with indignation when she informed me that, only the week before, a young student and his girl-friend had been sold by a "comrade" and lodged in the city gaol. The girl declared, however, that the possibility

of such a fate did not worry her in the least, or
even the fear of death itself, provided she were not
incarcerated in the fortress of Schlüsselburg, the most
dreaded place of confinement in Russia; for those con-
signed there are lost for ever to the outer world.[1] But
Liouba's equanimity with regard to an enforced residence
in the generally dreaded land of exile was, perhaps,
inspired by a letter which she had just received from a
friend who had been deported to a town in the province
of Yakutsk, and which I was permitted to read.

"Doushka,"[2] it ran, "do not fret about me, for I was
never happier in my life. It is rather dull here, of
course, after Kiéff; but exile has at any rate released me
from a husband who has, for some time past, bored me
to extinction with his intolerable jealousy and stinginess.
Here, however, I have found some old friends, and
received nothing but kindness from even new acquaintances, and, although the days are rather dreary, our
evenings are enlivened by music, dancing and theatricals.
I never knew what domestic freedom really meant until
I came here ! "

Toward midnight I rose to depart, but my companions
insisted on my first sharing their frugal supper, for
Russian revolutionaries have apparently the same partiality for late hours as their more lawful compatriots.
And as Androvitch prepared the meal, Liouba produced a "balalaika" and in a clear, sympathetic voice
sang a melody well known on the Volga river, near which
she had passed her childhood. But the singer was continually interrupted by Serge, who, even while laying the
table, continued to execrate the evils of autocracy and
tyranny of kings. "We want a wider horizon," he kept
repeating. "We are now deaf and dumb ! We must
have education for the people, and absolute freedom for
all ! " And I could almost hear the wild-eyed, dishevelled
orator who had not only instilled my hospitable
friend with his seditious principles, but taught him the

---

[1] This, by the way, is the only Russian prison which I was not
authorized to visit, although it was described to me at Sredni-Kolymsk
by Madame Akimova, who had awaited trial for four months within
its gloomy walls.
[2] Darling.

appropriate gestures wherewith to express them. For Serge, as an original exponent of Socialistic doctrines, was a dismal failure.

The life of a Russian Revolutionary, of whatever class, must be one of perpetual anxiety, and his incessant dread of the police was indicated, on this occasion, by a trivial incident which occurred soon after we sat down to supper. While Serge was relating, in a loud and excited tone, certain facts concerning the assassination of M. Stolýpin, there came a resounding knock at the door, which startled me almost as much as my host, for I knew the unpleasant consequences which might follow my rather imprudent visit. Nor was I reassured by the nervous agitation displayed by my companions, who sat staring blankly at each other, evidently in expectation of the dreaded command to " open in the name of the Tsar." It was, therefore, with much relief that I saw my host's pale and anxious face relapse into a sickly smile at the sound of a familiar voice, and the next moment the door was unbarred to admit an intimate friend and student at the University. The newcomer was, it appeared, also a " comrade," who, while Liouba brewed fresh tea, entertained us with the account of an apparently fruitless mission from which he had just returned in the service of " the cause." Needless to say my farewell was indefinitely postponed by the new arrival, and it was only by the grey light of dawn that, just before parting, we solemnly arose, and stood round the table to sing, almost in a whisper, a pathetic melody in minor, which, although strictly prohibited in European Russia, is sung without hindrance by the political exiles in Siberia.[1]

But everything in this chapter pertaining to the revolutionary movement should be written in the past tense, for anarchy, in Russia, is now as dead as the proverbial doornail, and Serge Androvitch is fighting bravely for the National Cause, instead of the Empire, which he once so ardently desired to overthrow.

[1] This prison-song has been translated and published by the author, and may be obtained at Messrs. Weekes & Co., Music Publishers, Hanover Square, W.

CHAPTER XVII

THE CRIMEA—THE INTERIOR

" IF that place belonged to us," observed an American tourist, as one bright summer's day we neared, from seaward, the harbour of Sevastópol; " I guess we would make it the beauty-spot of Europe ! " " But," I replied, " the Crimea is that already," while sorely inclined to add that its natural beauties would scarcely be enhanced by transatlantic turmoil, mammoth hotels, and surging crowds. For there scarcely exists, throughout the world, a more enchanting spot than this, which in England is generally less associated with a perfect climate and exquisite scenery than with the protracted but futile campaign which, half a century ago, laid waste its fertile provinces and fair white towns. " An emerald in a sea of sapphire ! " exclaimed my companion; and the simile was really not exaggerated when, on that occasion, I first beheld the lovely shores of Taurida, glittering in the sunshine under a sky of cloudless blue.

No Russian need seek the French Riviéra in winter, for he can always here find a nest of warmth and flowers, protected from the bleak north wind by the precipitous chain of mountains which screen the southern coast of the peninsula, which, by the way, is about the size of Sicily.

The Crimea is always delightful, but I prefer it in winter, for in summer the heat is often oppressive, and I have known it 94°, (and even more), in the shade in August, although the nights were generally cool. Only October and November are damp and unhealthy, especially on the north-eastern coast, where chilly mists roll in from the " Putrid Sea," a shallow lagoon formed by a long sand spit in the Sea of Azov. Fever and ague

184

are then prevalent, also rheumatic complaints, for which latter nature has provided a cheap remedy in the shape of the black mud which bubbles from a number of miniature volcanoes near the town of Kertch—and which apparently possesses wonderful curative powers. A Scotch merchant at Rostov-on-the-Don told me that he had vainly tried every imaginable remedy in England for neuritis, but had been instantly cured by the mud-baths of Kertch, the marvellous properties of which were known even to the Scythians who inhabited the Tauric peninsula [1] many years before Christ.

Kertch is a dull and dismal town, although its situation at the narrow inlet to the Sea of Azov invests it with considerable commercial importance. Nothing now remains of the old Tartar stronghold which has been converted into a modern and malodorous seaport, where, since the Crimean War, vast sums of money have been expended on the erection of fortifications which would stand no earthly chance against modern engines of destruction. On the day of my arrival a driving mist obscured the town, the narrow streets of which resembled rivers after a week of incessant rain, so having landed from the grimy little British collier which had brought me from Taganrog, I straight-way hired a carriage to convey me to Sevastópol, (with the accent on the penultimate), by way of Yalta, and the loveliest stretch of coast-line in the world. Kertch certainly contained an " hotel," but one of such appalling aspect that I preferred to return to the *Tynemouth*, and share a greasy steak and onions with her burly skipper, before setting out, later in the day, for Theodosia.

There is a railway to the latter place from Kertch, but the line was now blocked, by an accident to a bridge, for a couple of days. Nevertheless, had I for a moment anticipated the discomfort of that two days' drive to Theodosia, I should certainly have awaited a resumption of traffic, or proceeded there on board the little *Tynemouth*, although the sea journey

---

[1] The Russian name " Taurida " is derived from this, the Crimea having only been ceded to Russia by the Porte in 1784. " Crim " or Crimea is a Tartar name.

was, the skipper averred, as unpleasant owing to fog and heavy weather as the one by post-road. Indeed, his summary of the situation coincided with that of the nigger when consulted on a choice of routes: "Whichever road you travels, I guess you'll be d——d sorry you did not take the other!"

Yet even the *Tynemouth's* stuffy saloon combined with dryness, warmth and food, would have been infinitely preferable to those interminable hours of wet, cold and hunger, through a country so shrouded in mist that we had to grope our way for quite a third of the journey. I could only procure a " telega," or country cart, where I reposed upon dirty straw, while although the vehicle was provided with a hood, the latter was so dilapidated that the rain poured through it like a sieve, until night fell, and the " troika " was as often in the ditch as out of it. Once we were hopelessly lost for over an hour in the darkness, owing to the stupidity of my squat Tartar driver, whom I could not even curse with any sense of satisfaction, for he only spoke his own language. Fortunately I possessed a large scale-map, and eventually by the aid of this and a horn lantern we managed to stumble, like drowned rats, into a squalid hovel, where I gathered, by signs, that I must pass the night. It was now midnight, and we had been on the road ten hours, having covered in that time under twenty-five miles !

The " post-house " at Argin contained two rooms, or rather dens, the filth of which I have seldom seen equalled in a human habitation. One was occupied by an aged and unsavoury Tartar and his equally repulsive wife, the other was for the use of guests; and here I waited in the cold and darkness until a tallow dip was brought in to reveal the hideous squalor of the place, which contained only a narrow divan, evidently intended as a sleeping-place, although legions of vermin scurried gaily over its now threadbare and discoloured surface. A broken window was stuffed with bits of rag, and the open hearth contained only a little heap of cold, grey ashes. My heart sank as, soaked and shivering, I surveyed those once whitewashed walls, now glistening with filth and damp, while the rustle,

TCHUKTCHI BOYS AT EAST CAPE (BÉRING STRAITS)

outside, of ever-falling rain was accompanied, indoors, by the monotonous drip, drip of water as it soaked here and there through the rickety roof. But, anyway, here I had to remain until daylight, inhaling an overpowering stench of sewage from an open cesspool just beneath the window, which suggested the possibility of typhoid as a climax to this charming journey. How I survived it without at least contracting pneumonia remains a mystery, for the rain having soaked through my portmanteau, I was practically wet through for forty-eight hours. There was no food of any kind at Argin, but fortunately plenty of fuel; and I sat before blazing pine-logs until dawn, sharing my only tin of sardines and some biscuits with my Tartar driver, whom I had not the heart to send in such weather to the stables. And, late the next night, I reached my destination, after just such a day as the previous one, although on this occasion monotony was dispelled by an upset caused by the breaking of an axle, luckily within reach of a village and forge. So much for the journey by post-road from Kertch to Theodosia, which I have described at some length in order that others may profit by my inexperience, and, if placed in similar circumstances, travel by rail or sea!

I contrived at Theodosia to procure a more comfortable carriage and better team, also a Russian "yemstchik." And now I could afford to linger amidst such pleasant surroundings—for from here on to Sevastópol the journey was so enjoyable that I was able to recall its initial stages with much the same feelings as a man who awakens from nightmare in a comfortable bedroom.

The scenery on leaving Theodosia was rather monotonous, for most of the Crimea north of the littoral range of mountains is composed of steppes resembling those of the mainland. In these northern districts Tartars are chiefly met with who differ essentially from those inhabiting the southern coast, the former being rough, but kindly, people, of the Mongolian type, mainly employed in the breeding of horses, sheep and cattle, while those on the littoral, having in other days freely interbred with the Greeks and Genoese, are more

refined in appearance and manner, and also more indolent—probably by reason of a more sunny and
enervating climate. Personally I preferred the Tartar
of the plains, who, though rude and uncouth, was
much franker in his dealings and more generous than
those I afterwards met on the coast, where even any
small attention had generally to be paid for. In the
north, on the other hand, I was more than once the
guest of Tartars who refused payment of any kind,
but this never once occurred on the shores of the Black
Sea.

So leisurely was Ivan's rate of progression that we
took three days to reach Karasou-Bazar, sleeping *en
route* in tiny Tartar villages, which were few and far
between, for the country here is very sparsely cultivated. Yet we constantly passed ruins, tombs, tumuli
and other indications that, thousands of years ago,
this must have been a thickly populated region, with
thriving cities and towns. It was now late in the
summer, and the beneficial effect of the rains, which
every spring render the land green and fertile, had
worn away, and one gazed on every side on a parched
and arid waste, the Northern Crimea being cursed with
a lack of water, which, however, abounds on the coast.
For although the peninsula has numerous rivers, these
become in dry weather insignificant streams, or even
rivulets, and there is no attempt at irrigation save by
means of shallow pits dug by the Tartars and called
" auts," which are practically useless. And yet,
centuries ago, the Tauric peninsula exported huge
quantities of corn to Greece and other countries, while
now the Crimea has to depend chiefly upon Russia and
Siberia for her supply of grain.

On nearing Karasou-Bazar I passed what appeared
to be a mass of modern fortifications, erected on the
summit of a hill of considerable height, but on closer
approach found, to my surprise, that the place merely
consisted of chalk cliffs which had been fashioned by
nature into the almost perfect semblance of a fortress.
Karasou-Bazar was, after the Muscovite annexation,
assigned by Catherine II. to the exclusive occupation
of the Tartars, so that even to-day everything about

the place, from mosques and minarets to pariah dogs, savours of the Orient, and there is a general impression of hoarded wealth and open squalor about its dark, narrow streets, permeated with a typical Eastern odour of coarse perfume, roasting meat, wood-smoke and sewage. I had to leave the carriage outside the town and proceed on foot through narrow, tortuous streets, with raised and narrow footpaths, and huge stepping-stones placed at intervals, to afford a crossing when, during the heavy spring-rains, these malodorous alleys become foaming torrents. And I wandered for perhaps an hour through endless avenues of low, flat-roofed mud houses with windowless walls, with here and there an open gateway disclosing a small courtyard with its patch of verdure, shrubs and flowers, and generally a marble fountain plashing in their midst. But it was impossible to linger anywhere for long, for beggars, of both sexes, and loathsome exterior, swarmed around me in such crowds, that more than once I had to threaten them with a stick to escape from their clutches.

There was, of course, no inn of any kind, and a glimpse of the native " caravanserai " was so uninviting that I decided to lodge with a Tartar friend of Ivan's—a tobacco merchant, who, with no thought of remuneration, entertained me in a clean and comfortable dwelling, which after my previous experience of native households came as an agreeable surprise. For it contained several rooms almost luxuriously furnished in Tartar fashion with soft and capacious red-velvet divans, walls hung with costly embroideries and Caucasian armour, and cool red tiles strewn with bearskins and small but exquisite rugs from Bokhara. There were, of course, neither tables nor chairs, so I had to sit on the floor while discussing my first decent meal *à la Tartare*, which commenced with onion soup, followed by trout, in rich yellow sauce, roast lamb, skewered " kababs," fried in grease, vegetable marrow stuffed with savoury herbs, and a variety of highly coloured, unwholesome cakes and sweetmeats. Crimean wine accompanied the repast, which concluded with " Beckmess," a syrup of sweet and sickly flavour made of fermented apples. Coffee, " narghilehs " and cigarettes were then handed round, before I sought my couch, where, it is perhaps needless to add, my slumbers were somewhat disturbed !

Crim-Tartars appear to regard appropriate hours for meals and repose with the same indifference as most other Eastern races, who generally sleep when they feel tired, and eat when they are hungry. I was already aware of this Oriental idiosyncrasy, but was certainly somewhat startled when, the morning after the aforesaid banquet, my host suddenly appeared in a weird white garment, to awaken me at 5 a.m., although I knew he was well aware that my departure was only fixed for midday. Yet this matutinal intruder placidly seated himself on my bed, (or rather divan), and, as he was unable to converse, continued to smilingly contemplate my recumbent form for nearly an hour, before this trying ordeal was fortunately terminated by the entrance of Ivan. The latter then informed me that it is an old Tartar custom to visit guests at dawn in order to inquire whether they have slept well—a kindly attention which, if practised, say, in England, might conceivably result, under certain conditions, in grave bodily injury—to the host !

Notwithstanding the kindly aid and protection of the Empress Catherine, Karasou-Bazar is now commercially on the down grade, for there is no bazaar to speak of, and the various trades and industries are here scattered all over the town, whereas in more prosperous Eastern cities each has its own street or quarter. The place was once famed for its arms and cutlery, but the staple article of commerce now consists of lambskins, which are chiefly used to make the typical Astrakhan bonnet worn by the Cossacks, and numbers of them are therefore exported to Kertch and the districts of the Don. Perhaps the most novel and interesting sight here was the gipsies' quarter, which I stumbled upon by accident, and found these strange people living in little reed shanties, plastered with mud, or dark, narrow caverns roughly scooped out of the side of an adjoining hill. Their occupants were scantily clad, repulsive-looking creatures, more suggestive of animals than human beings, while children of both

sexes almost in their teens were running about the place
in a shameless state of nudity. I should add that these
gipsies were descendants of some who had settled in
Karasou-Bazar perhaps a century before, and had none
of the wild and attractive characteristics peculiar to the
Romany race—of which these appeared to be very
degraded specimens. There were perhaps a hundred in
all, who, so far as I could learn, were utterly destitute,
subsisting on charity, theft, or the occasional sale of
their female children, if young and pretty, to some
opulent Tartar or dealer in human flesh. Although the
Crim-Tartars are strict Mahometans their women appear to enjoy much more freedom than in other Moslem
countries. The " yashmak," for instance, is now seldom
seen in the interior, and never on the coast—an innovation perhaps welcomed by the young, but certainly not
by their elders, for, aided by this veil, a plain and middle-
aged female, if only possessed of dark expressive eyes,
could formerly attract as much masculine attention as
the loveliest of her sex. And an Eastern woman's eyes
are in public her sole attraction, for she is generally
short in stature, always clothed in balloon-like garments
that compel her to walk with a waddle. My host's
twin daughters, slim, graceful girls, wore, when indoors,
a rather becoming costume, consisting of a closely
fitting heliotrope silk tunic, with wide skirts falling to
the knees, loose thin muslin trousers secured round the
ankles, and a little white-cloth fez, adorned with old
golden coins; but when dressed for the street, they
resembled animated bolsters, and presented an almost
grotesque appearance. Both were good-natured, cheery
little souls, devoid of shyness, who played the guitar,
sang me Tartar love-songs, and, when we parted, presented me with some dainty silk handkerchiefs of their
own embroidering. Tára, the youngest, was like her
father, intensely superstitious, wore all kinds of amulets
and charms to avert the evil eye and other calamities,
and when I expressed my admiration for a costly ring
she wore, frowned mysteriously and laid a finger on her
lip, for I had yet to learn that among these people any
female article of jewellery has only to be praised by a
male stranger to be immediately stolen or lost! Nor

must you openly approve of your host's horses and cattle, or they will inevitably die !

It is thirty miles from Karasou-Bazar to Simpheropol, and at Souy, about midway, the country began to assume a less desolate appearance, while "Tchatir-Dagh," the highest peak in the maritime range, was here dimly discernible on the southern horizon. Nearing Simpheropol mud dwellings gave place to much more pretentious buildings, of European architecture, each with its smooth lawn and rose garden, embowered in oak and chestnut trees. And, from here onward, the scenery became, every day, more varied and picturesque, until I reached Yalta, that priceless gem of nature, which cannot be adequately described, and which must be seen to be fully appreciated.

Simpheropol (pronounced like Sevastopol) [1] is essentially Russian, and therefore presents a striking contrast to dirty, sleepy Karasou-Bazar, being now the capital of the Crimea, which was built, after the Russian accession, over the ruins of "Ak-Metchet," formerly an important city, under the Khans. There is still, of course, a Tartar quarter, but most of the town now consists of fine Government buildings, modern streets and boulevards, several churches and good shops; also a railway station, on the main line from Petrograd to Sevastopol. "Simpheropol" is derived from two Greek words signifying a "meeting-place," and was aptly named, judging from the cosmopolitan element it contained in the shape of Russians, Greeks, Rumanians, Turks, and especially Jews, who seemed to outnumber all the rest. There were several hotels, one with an excellent restaurant, where French cooking was very acceptable after my previous gastronomic experiences; and the strains of a military band in some public gardens, the tooting of motor-horns, clattering of droshkies and other signs of European civilization set me wondering whether mouldy old Karasou-Bazar, with its mediæval methods, filth and flies, could really only be a score of

---

[1] The pronunciation of many Russian towns entirely differs from their appearance in writing. Thus the city of "Orel," pronounced as it is written, would convey nothing to a Russian, who only knows it as "Areeol." And there are many similar instances.

miles away! But the market was the sight of the place, with its flower-bedecked stalls and great piles of superb grapes and peaches, plums and nectarines, any of which you could buy more than you could carry for half a rouble; while the delicious " karpouz," or water-melon, for which the Crimea is famous, was equally cheap. Here the vendors were chiefly Tartars; and this and strings of camels, which continually delayed the traffic even in those spacious streets, were about the only Eastern touches about Simpheropol, which is, perhaps, more picturesque but otherwise quite as un-interesting as any third-class modern European town. A genial colonel of Cossacks, whom I met at the hotel, entreated me to ascend the " Tchatir-Dagh," which, the colonel explained, lay on my way to Yalta, and whence, he assured me, I should obtain the finest view in the world. This was clearly an opportunity not to be missed, and, although strongly averse to mountaineering in any shape, I promised my friend I would take his advice.

My way to the coast now lay due south through a well-cultivated country, with villages as neat and prosperous-looking as those west of Simpheropol had been foul and poverty-stricken. Rows of fertile green pasture now separated yellow fields of corn and maize, nearly ready for the sickle, while the roadside was bordered by leafy orchards with trees weighed down by ripe, luscious fruit. Kilbouroun, approached by a stately avenue of poplars, was my first halt—a pretty little place composed of a double row of low, vine-trellised houses, surrounded by a cluster of low, green hills, one surmounted by a frowning Tartar fortress, which, in conjunction with a turquoise sky, clear sunshine and barbaric costumes, was irresistibly suggestive of a rustic scene from some comic opera! It would have been quite in keeping if some peasants, drinking outside the village " traktir," had suddenly broken into a stage chorus.

It was but an hour's drive from here to Buyuk Ankoi, where I slept in the hut of a Tartar who provides saddle-horses for the ascent of the mountain, the summit of which is about 5000 feet above sea-level. But the place was so cold and draughty, and fleas so numerous,

o

that I was glad to make a start at 3 a.m., in bright moonlight which, clearly revealing an apparently perpendicular peak, rendered me doubtful as to whether its ascent would prove as easy as the colonel had predicted. I have always had a dread of height and anything approaching hazardous climbing, and can no more explain this failing than account for the fact that the presence of a rat in a room fills me with abject terror, although, when in the wilds, innumerable rodents must, from time to time, have crept over my unconscious body when asleep. And in the same way I have occasionally, when in remote places, been compelled to negotiate some giddy height simply because my objective lay beyond it and there was no other way round. This occurred during my land journey from Paris to New York, when in the Verkoyansk mountains, (of Arctic Siberia), I had to clamber up an ice slope overhanging a dizzy precipice of several thousand feet. In Switzerland it would have been a case of ropes and iceaxes; but in those benighted regions I wore heavy iron horseshoes clamped to my feet! and somehow got over, although to this day I do not know how I ever negotiated that ghastly passage, where a slip must have meant certain death.

However, the ascent of Tchatir-Dagh proved easy enough, which is more than I can say for the gait of my diminutive steed, which came down with me twice while on smooth, level ground, although in steep, stony places he was as nimble as a goat. The ascent was at first very gradual, up an almost drivable road through a forest so dense and dark that my guide had to precede me with a lantern. But we presently left the woods for an open space of wild, heather-grown moorland, thickly strewn with huge granite boulders which rendered progress very difficult. Half-way up the mountain the sun rose, only to disclose a dense sea of mist on which we looked down as from an island; but this was quickly dispelled, and on reaching the narrow pathway, hewn through solid rock, which leads to the summit, the day had become bright and cloudless and almost too warm to be pleasant. Here I dismounted, left my pony with the guide, and climbed alone up the side of a cliff with a drop of a couple of thousand feet, which, however, was only seldom visible through the chinks in a wall of loose rocks and boulders. It was very tough work for about half an hour, owing to the loose stones which kept slipping away from under my feet, and also to steep limestone ledges, six to eight feet high, which, as I had no companion, were only scaled with some difficulty. But at last, at eight o'clock, I stood upon the summit to find that my military friend had not exaggerated, for seldom have I ever overlooked such a glorious expanse of land and sea as that which now lay stretched at my feet. Away to the north the barren steppes rolled away like an ocean to the sky-line, with only two little islets to break their dreary expanse; the yellow mosque, drab roofs and green courtyards of Karasou-Bazar, and the golden domes and green-roofed buildings of Simpherópol, the modernity of which was indicated, even at this distance, by a tiny cloud of steam rising from the railway station. One could distinguish, as though a line had been drawn, the arid northern plains from the fertile fields and valleys of the south; while, nearing the Black Sea, the rugged range, of which Tchatir-Dagh is the eastern extremity, formed a second and more substantial barrier, which seems to have been specially designed by nature to protect and shelter the narrow but exquisite strip of coast between Aloushta and Sevastópol. It is only a hundred miles in length, although you might travel ten thousand without finding its equal!

It was no easy job to descend alone, and some time elapsed before I could find my guide, who had strayed some distance away to feed the ponies on a steep and scanty patch of herbage further down the mountain. We then made a hasty meal off eggs and black bread, which I washed down with wine of the country, though my guide preferred "Bouza," a mawkish Tartar beverage made of millet, which he produced from a battered tin flask in his saddle-bags.

On the downward journey I examined a curious cave, which, although I could scarcely crawl through the low, narrow entrance, is said to contain an endless succession of chambers which apparently penetrate into the very

bowels of the earth.   There were two of these huge
caverns, the one I visited being appropriately named
Foul-Kuba,[1] for the 'atmosphere resembled that of a
charnel-house.   This, however, was not surprising when
I discovered, by the light of a candle, that the floor
of the place was composed of a soft mass of human
skulls and bones, the remains, as I afterwards discovered, of a force of Genoese invaders who were smoked
to death here by the Tartars in the thirteenth century.
This gruesome chamber led into a more spacious one
quite eighty feet in circumference, and supported by
stalactites which glittered brightly even in the rays of
my feeble tallow dip.   I then entered yet another and
even larger hall, where, however, the air was so oppressive that I retraced my steps, although some years ago
a French scientist advanced steadily for several hours
without reaching the heart of this subterranean mystery.

Buyuk-Ankoi was reached by midday, and here I
found the man who had provided my horses greatly
perturbed, one of his four-legged cripples having suddenly been seized with staggers in the yard.   I was
about to suggest a very simple remedy when a lad ran
out, of the post-house with a couple of eggs, which his
master eagerly snatched from his hand and proceeded
to smash on the patient's forehead, violently rubbing
the raw yolk into the poor brute's eyes and nostrils.
This, some Tartars declare, is an infallible remedy for
any equine complaint, which, however, on this occasion
completely failed.

An hour later we were on the road, and I sat down
to supper the same night, after a pleasant but uneventful drive, in a modern and garden-girt hotel, overlooking the sea, in the pretty coast town of Aloushta.

[1] Also known as " Byng-Bash," or the " Cave of a Thousand Heads."[1]

CHAPTER XVIII

THE CRIMEA—THE COAST

Two days are seldom alike while driving along the Crimean coast. For instance, you may sup one night off sour milk in some grimy Tartar hovel, stifled by wood smoke and devoured by fleas, and the next morning lunch off an *omelette soufflée* and " Aspic " of quails in the Hôtel Splendide at Yalta, which is quite as luxurious, and rather more expensive, than the Hôtel de Paris at Monte Carlo. This, indeed, was my own experience.

But Yalta, that glittering Mecca of the Russian aristocracy, is some distance from Aloushta—a modern, but sleepy, little place, bearing about the same relation to its fashionable neighbour as Saint-Raphael to Cannes or Nice. It is chiefly frequented in summer by tradesmen and minor Government officials who come here with their families to bathe, fish, and otherwise amuse themselves without troubling their heads about the " upper-ten " at Yalta, where prices are, of course, beyond their means. And here I may remark, *en passant*, that snobbery is quite unknown in Russia, where people are generally content with their social surroundings, however commonplace and humble the latter may be.

And those of limited income may well be satisfied with Aloushta, which is situated at the mouth of a picturesque gorge which here cleaves the mountain range from north to south, and which in hot weather affords a pleasant retreat under the shake of oak and chestnut trees, amidst wild flowers, fernery, and rippling brooks and waterfalls. The town has some historical interest, being surrounded by ruins where old Greek weapons, coins and other objects may still be found, while a dilapidated tower still remains of the formidable fortress' which was erected here by the Emperor Justinian, as a defence against the Goths and Huns, 500 years B.C.

Many centuries later, Aloushta became, under the Genoese, a place of mercantile importance, although it now contains only a few small shops where household and tourist necessaries are sold. There is a fine view from here of the "Tchatir-Dagh," which acts as a barometer, for when the peak is concealed by mist, rain is sure to follow, though this is a rare occurrence.

But Aloushta is not a mere pleasure resort, its sheltered position and many mountain streams rendering it an idyllic spot for the cultivation of the grape, wherefore its vineyards are justly noted for their pure and delicate vintages. When in Russia I always drink Crimean wine, but had no idea, until I visited an estate near here, that the country produced so many varieties : still and sparkling, red and white. I should be afraid to say how many kinds I was pressed to sample by the hospitable proprietor, who, had I not finally and firmly declined to partake of more, would certainly have sent me back to my hotel in a most regrettable condition ! For he plied me with locally grown Burgundy, Bordeaux, Sauterne, hock, and even Tokay, all excellent of their kind, and of which the more matured fetched high prices in Petrograd. The Aloushta vineyards covered over 3000 acres, but were only a few of many scattered along the coast, where many little towns have their grape-cure, with a resident physician during the months of August and September.

The culture of the Crimean vine was originally introduced by Prince Woronzoff, who, in the early part of the last century, was the first to appreciate and take advantage of the favourable climate and rich soil of the littoral, for the wine industry had previously only been attempted north of the Tauric Chain, in a bleak and un-protected position where it was doomed to be a failure. And this first speculation met with such success that the Prince then formed a company to cleanse and drain the coast towns, erect " casinos " and hotels, and con-vert the Crimean seaboard into a fashionable winter resort, a scheme which, as it was honoured with imperial patronage, speedily bore fruit. A century ago the south coast was a desert, whereas now it attracts people even from the remotest parts of Siberia.

On leaving Aloushta, the broad and excellent road reaches a height of several hundred feet before descending again to Buyuk-Lambat, one of the loveliest spots on the coast, where we drove through avenues of leafy chestnut trees with, on the one hand, the blue, sunlit sea, and on the other, a smiling panorama of pine forest, golden cornfields, and green vineyards, with here and there the red-roofed villa of some prosperous grape-grower peeping out of the vines. And behind the ever-enchanting landscape were always the mountains softened by haze and distance, with their wooded slopes and snowy limestone summits, which, however, attain no great height, save where the Ayug-Dagh, or " Peak of the Bear," towers 1000 feet above the rest. One might have been somewhere between Beaulieu and Menton but for the Eastern aspect of the villages with their flat-roofed mud huts, skin-clad Tartars, strings of camels, and little brown children who pursued us with bunches of wild roses and mimosa. The natives here are more demonstrative than those of the north, and generally gave us a smiling " Salaam—Aleikum," while all seemed happy and contented, as well they might in this land of eternal sunshine.

At midday we reached Partenite, a pretty little village with a " Restaurant " by the sea, which was already occupied by a merry party from Yalta, for this is a favourite place for picnics. Several motor-cars had brought these guests, to be presently joined by friends who rowed ashore from a large steam-yacht in the harbour. And I sat down to breakfast in dusty tweeds amidst daintily-gowned women and well-groomed men, with some reluctance, until invited by one of the party to join them at coffee, for an Englishman, in Russia, is ever welcome. And a pretty girl among them informed me that Partenite was once the residence of the Prince de Ligne, one of Catherine of Russia's numerous lovers, and herself showed me the walnut tree under which the Prince was wont to compose impassioned poems to his imperial mistress.

From Partenite to Yalta the scenery, although ever beautiful, assumes a more artificial aspect, created by numberless private residences which have sprung up, within the past few years, around the famous watering-place. These are of all sorts and sizes, from the stately marble mansion of the millionaire, approached by gilded iron gates and a private road, to the wooden creeper-clad villa which, although less pretentious, suggests a proportionate outlay of wealth and atmosphere of luxury. Beyond Partenite there were some public gardens, a miniature edition of Kew, where I loitered so long that our destination was reached only after sunset.

Yalta by night was not unlike Monte Carlo, although by daylight it is even more picturesque. There is the same impression of wealth, extravagance, and social unrest; of palatial "restaurants" and red-coated " tziganes "; of shops bedecked with costly gems, expensive flowers, and the latest Paris fashions; of clean white streets and gaily bordered lawns; but—there is no gambling—at any rate of the kind which attracts an ever-hopeful army of victims to the Devil's Garden, although the place is patronized, both in winter and summer, by very wealthy people, willing to pay the same enormous prices all the year round. I went to the best hotel, where an immaculately attired German manager eyed my travel-stained clothes askance, but apportioned me a luxurious apartment, furnished with a bath and every modern convenience. Fortunately I never travel without a dress suit, for nothing else was worn in the " Restaurant," where the women, although exquisitely gowned. had not changed their day costume —for in Yalta no lady wears evening dress except at a private house. There was, as usual in Russia, a preponderance of military uniforms, and some gold-laced naval officers from Sevastópol, but surprisingly few of the *demi-monde*, which is generally so numerous in health and pleasure resorts. This element may be undesirable, but it certainly infuses an air of gaiety, which on this occasion, was rather lacking; and therefore, having smoked a cigar, I was thinking of retiring, when approached by a grey-haired and affable stranger in evening dress, who spoke excellent English, and handed me a visiting card bearing his name, address, and the significant words : " Roulette-Baccará " in one corner. The thing looked suspicious, but, impelled by curiosity, I strolled out shortly afterwards to a house with three sumptuously furnished rooms, two of which contained a gambling table and the third an inviting cold supper. Many players had already arrived, and I recognized at least one distinguished personage connected with the Court, who, although the " Villa Kasbek " was obviously a *tripot*, was plunging heavily. The " Baccará " table was unapproachable, but I took a vacant place at " Roulette," which was not so popular, and, strange to relate, left the place a winner. My modest stakes, however, were invariably placed on the even chances opposed to the heavy wagers of a gilded and slightly inebriated youth who sat opposite, a simple little system which I have worked with success even in that international stronghold of knaves and crooks, Port Said !

There are so many places of interest within easy reach of Yalta that one need never be dull for an hour in the day-time. I did not visit Livadia, (which was occupied by the Imperial Family), but there are now private residences almost as beautiful and extensive as that of the late Emperor. Unfortunately the harbour here is very exposed, but several vessels, including the Imperial yacht *Standart*, were moored inside the breakwater constructed of recent years to afford an anchorage during the tempestuous weather which, at certain seasons, rages in the Black Sea. And talking of the *Standart*, I have only once had an opportunity of seeing the ex-Tsarina, and this was at Yalta, where I had never previously set eyes upon the woman whose secret and baneful influence might, but for recent events in Russia, have caused irreparable injury to the cause of the Allies. Her late Majesty was on this occasion driving into the town from Livadia, in a pony-cart, accompanied only by the Grand Duchess Olga, and no one would have dreamt that the owner of that pale, girlish face, with its sad, delicately-chiselled features, would in a few short years be implicated in a tragic plot which has staggered the world and for ever deprived the Romanoffs of all their former might and power. It had, however, for long been an open secret in Russia that the Empress suffered from a form of nervous disease which rendered her morbidly susceptible to the influence of people around her, especially if they happened to be clever and unscrupulous members of the opposite sex, and of this failing the German Government was not slow to take advantage. Yet although many secret agents and spies in the Kaiser's pay have, since the outbreak of war, enjoyed the ex-Empress's special favour, I am credibly informed that no one ever attained a greater hold over her than the unspeakable scoundrel, Rasputin, whom, by the way, I met some years ago at Tomsk in Siberia, where his predilection for women and alcohol was already' notorious. How this uncouth boor ever became an illustrious and gifted lady's constant companion and adviser remains a mystery, (for there can be no foundation for the infamous slanders which have been freely circulated), although Rasputin's treachery probably proved a blessing in disguise. For had it not been for his assassination and the public inquiry which followed, the conspiracy would have continued to ripen until it would probably have been too late to avert or repair its disastrous effects. Fortunately the Russians are a forgiving race, and make allowances for the fact that the woman who once ruled them was a German, not only by nationality, but by instinct and preference; who, although she adored her husband, never really loved her adopted country, and only reluctantly embraced the Greek faith under the very strongest pressure from the Court of Berlin !

I travelled from here to Sevastópol in a motor-car by invitation of its owner, a wealthy Californian whose acquaintance I made, 'appropriately enough, in an American bar, and who was touring Europe in company with an English valet and a French poodle. Our casual friendship was cemented by the fact that we possessed mutual friends in the Klondike, where, during the first days of the gold rush, Elisha B. Kellogg had rapidly amassed a large fortune. So I accepted this friendly offer only to regret, within a few hours, that I had deserted Ivan and his old shandrydan, which, although the American's " Mercédès " was the latest thing in speed and luxury, would have been far preferable. Had we travelled at anything like a moderate pace all would have been well; but my companion was obsessed with a desire to tear madly along, devouring space without even a glance at the scenery, and with a mind solely centred on the fact that some place or other must be reached at a certain hour for the purpose of refreshment. So this exquisite drive, to which I had planned to devote at least three days of lazy enjoyment, was accomplished in under twelve hours, during which I bitterly realized how sadly an American millionaire can take his pleasure. Fortunately my friend's guide at Yalta had informed him that distinguished travellers invariably halted at certain points of interest on the road, and these Mr. Kellogg elected to visit, as he expressed it, " according to schedule." But for this we should certainly have reached Sevastópol " in record time ! "—or in under an hour, as the distance is only fifty-five English miles !

One of these places, (at which I was permitted to regain my breath), was a village called Mishov, which is rendered interesting by the fact that here once lived a certain Princess Galitzin, a famous beauty and universal favourite at the Court of Alexander I. Suddenly wearying, however, of worldly pomps and vanities, the Princess retired into private life and devoted herself with such zeal to religion and the welfare of the poor, that the Tsar, rendered uneasy by her advanced views and increasing influence over the people, was compelled to exile the woman, who had once been the object of his warm admiration, to the Crimea. Here the Princess, undeterred by a sentence of banishment, resumed her spiritual crusade amongst the Tartars, assisted by one who had in brighter days been her constant companion, and who now further proved her loyalty and affection by sharing her misfortunes. This lady was known in Russia as the Comtesse Guacher, although most people at Court were aware that the name had been adopted by the notorious Comtesse de Lamotte-Valois, who in Paris was publicly branded on the Place de La Grève, for complicity in the scandal connected with Queen Marie Antoinette, Cardinal de Rohan and a diamond necklace. As years went on Princess Galitzin recovered a portion of her confiscated fortune, and with this she purchased the estate of " Gaspra " (which adjoins Mishov), where she built a charming residence, in which she continued to reside, until her death, with the devoted friend who had voluntarily shared her exile.

Although the most alluring aspects of nature entirely failed to arouse Kellogg's enthusiasm, he seemed deeply interested in Madame de Lamotte-Valois, probably because the latter was associated with some shady transaction concerning a valuable piece of jewellery! Yet Kellogg, though a rough diamond, was an entertaining companion, with startling views on life expressed in a dry, quaint manner which would have made his fortune on the music-hall stage; while, although practically uneducated, this *nouveau riche* displayed a shrewd perception of men and human nature. His views, however, on mythology, which were propounded while examining an ancient group of statuary at Gaspra, were sadly elementary, and recalled those of that famous stage-manager, the late Charles Harris, who, while rehearsing a ballét at the Empire Theatre, was advised by a friend to include the Three Graces in a final scenic display. "*Three Graces on a stage of that size!*" yelled Harris; "why, they will never be seen! We must have a dozen at least!"

Shortly after leaving Mishov we passed Aloupka and its castle, a quaint combination of Moorish and Gothic architecture, built some years ago by Count Vorontzoff at a cost of many millions of roubles, for its construction entailed a huge excavation from the sheer side of a cliff, and its interior is said to equal even that of Livadia in luxury and splendour. But even the Livadia gardens cannot be compared to those of Aloupka, where nature and art have been cunningly blended with marvellous effect. The charm of the place defies description, and I could have wandered for hours amidst those shady avenues, carpeted with smooth green sward, " pergolas " of roses, jasmine, and clematis; groves of orange and magnolia trees, traversed by paths, with herbaceous borders of every imaginable flower; and forests of fern with their miniature grottoes, fountains and lakes. Even down the face of the cliff, which, in front of the mansion, slopes sharply down to the sea, azaleas and rhododendrons grew freely amongst pine and walnut trees, from the branches of which hung festoons of twining creepers; while nearing the beach, narrow walks wound in and out among the rocks, every cleft of which had been carefully filled with earth for the cultivation of some rare exotic. But we had barely entered this modern Garden of Eden when the sky was suddenly obscured by a dense white mist which completely blotted out the lovely surroundings. These fogs are prevalent in early autumn, but seldom last long, and when we reached Simeis all traces of this one had disappeared.

We lunched here in a garden off roast larks wrapped in vine leaves, wild asparagus, and delicious honey, for which latter the place is famed. And the sunshine and warmth, scent of cherry-pie and mignonette, and drowsy hum of bees seemed for a time to soothe my restless friend, whom I therefore persuaded to remain for longer than usual, in this seductive spot of which Castelnau, the French traveller, wrote : " La suisse est fertile en charmants paysages, mais on l'oublie en voyant le vallon de Simeis ! " The lower slopes of the hills around it are densely wooded; but at one place, towards their bare and rocky summits, a tiny village was perilously perched on a fragment of cliff which had slipped from the mountain side to pause midway, and which looked as though a touch would complete its downfall.

These landslides are more frequent a few miles further, near the Phoros Pass, where there is a rather dangerous bit of road under beetling crags and tapering *aiguilles*. Portions of these occasionally become detached to fall on the road below; and on one occasion, about a century ago, a gigantic mass of rock came crashing into the valley to destroy a whole village. From here it is but a short distance to the Tartar village of Baidar, approached by a pass 3000 feet in height, where is a great granite gateway, which might have been designed as a picture frame to the glorious panorama beyond it. The Baidar Pass is now drivable, but could formerly only be negotiated on horseback over the " Devil's Staircase," by a narrow pathway hewn out of the rock, where dizzy chasms were crossed on trunks of trees. And here we said farewell to glorious scenery and soft balmy air—for The Baidar-Gate is the dividing line between the sunlit coast, " where there is little rain and no snow," and a cloudy and sterile region where we sadly bade adieu to glorious scenery and soft balmy air. The reader may already have wondered how the Crimea can be so warm in winter, when hundreds of our soldiers perished there, during the war, of arctic cold; well, for the simple reason that only desolate downs and sand dunes, which for most of the year are covered with snow and swept with icy gales, lie west of the Baidar Pass. It is almost as though you opened the door of a well-warmed house, to walk into a cold and wintry street. To-day, for instance, we noticed, for the first time, a sharp nip in the air, while the temperature at Sevastópol was 15° Fahr. lower than it had been on the preceding day at Yalta. Moreover, the sun seemed less brilliant, and the sky less blue, as if in harmony with the now grey and sullen landscape.

There is little of interest about Balaclava, save its association with the famous Charge of the Light Brigade, of which a memorial, erected near the Valley of Death, remains as a record.. So we drove straight on to Sevastópol, to reach it as the town and its frowning forts were bathed in the glow of a crimson sunset. This is undoubtedly one of the finest military harbours in the world, and enormous sums have of recent years been spent upon its fortifications, which, before the introduction of modern siege guns, were supposed to be impregnable. Only a few tramps and sailing vessels lay at anchor in the long, land-locked arm of the sea, which was, however, crowded with Russian warships, destroyers and submarines; and the incessant clatter of hammers, creak of machinery, and screech of steam sirens, were somewhat trying after the peaceful seaside towns and villages. Sevastópol would be attractive but for the incessant glare, for there is little shade, and nearly every building is composed of limestone of a dazzling white which, in bright weather, is very trying to the eyesight. The place is essentially Russian, and Tartars are seldom met with in its busy streets, or indeed strangers of any nationality, for I was apparently regarded as a spy by all around me, and therefore carefully avoided military ground. Little now remains of the ruins caused by the siege, though one may still faintly distinguish the " no man's land " which lay between the Russian earthworks and batteries of the Allies. A memento of the war also exists in the shape of some guns on the Esplanade facing the harbour, which are generally pointed out to tourists as having been captured from the British. But this is quite erroneous, for they were borrowed from us by our Turkish allies, who lost them at Balaclava, and are therefore, perhaps, the identical field-pieces which Lord Cardigan was ordered to re-capture, and which led to his disastrous, but ever-glorious, charge.

Other objects of interest pertaining to the siege may be seen in the house of the late General Todleben, who presented it to the town to be used as a museum. This I did not visit, but walked out to the Malakoff, which is worth seeing if only to realize the magnitude of the feat accomplished by the French, when on the 8th of September, 1855, this hitherto invulnerable fortress was captured, with characteristic dash, by Chasseurs and Zouaves, a brilliant victory which conclusively sealed the fate of Sevastópol. Over 30,000 Russians perished in the Malakoff's defence; a number which may now seem insignificant, but which was, in those days, of considerable importance.[1]

My American friend displayed as little interest in military relics and reminiscences as in the beauties of nature, and on the morning following our arrival, the automobile, English valet and canine appendage, were transferred to a steamer leaving direct for Odessa, their owner having expressed his intention of proceeding to Vienna as rapidly as gold and petrol would carry him. I have generally observed that, when visiting Europe, Americans are irresistibly attracted by any city or place but the one in which they happen to be located. So I here bade the Klondiker farewell, and all success on his erratic flight through Europe, in which I had certainly no desire to participate !

Nevertheless I missed, at first, the companionship

---

[1] "The Tricolor flag was hoisted and the Imperial eagles planted on the Malakoff within ten minutes of the French quitting their trenches." (Letter from Captain the Hon. Harry Keppel, R.N., to Sir Edmund Lyons, Naval Commander-in-Chief.)

of this record-breaking fiend, although it was as well that the latter did not accompany me to Kherson, where he would surely have been detained for two or three days by heavy rains and impassable roads, and probably developed symptoms of homicidal mania. And it was only in order to visit a sick friend that I went there myself, for Kherson is a busy but dull place, the journey by rail to which was tedious and wearisome. It was, however, interesting to find that Howard the philanthropist died here in January 1789 of pneumonia, and not, as many people imagine, of gaol fever in England. And, by the way, I noted that a monument erected to the memory of this famous Englishman, near the Church of the Assumption, sadly needs repair.

Russians call Odessa a little Paris, and though the simile is exaggerated, it is perhaps the most agreeable city, next to Kiéff, in Russia. The place is, however, little more than a century old, which may partly [1] account for its cosmopolitan character, and the fact that it is really less suggestive of Paris than of a mixture of San Francisco and Marseilles. For there is little to connect the town with Russia but its typical Greek churches and Slavonic shop-signs, while even the names of the streets are also written up in Italian. But whoever selected the site must have had an artistic eye, for nothing could be finer than the approach from the sea, where the golden domes and white buildings of Odessa are visible for a great distance, the town being situated on a lofty eminence overlooking the spacious harbour, the improvement of which must have entailed an enormous amount of expenditure and labour.

The population of Odessa must now be close upon 500,000, composed of so many nationalities that trade here is largely in the hands of foreigners — French, Italians, Greeks, and a few English. But the Jews are the most numerous; and nowhere else in Russia are they so cordially detested, chiefly because by dint of tenacity, thrift, and cunning they have gradually contrived to attain not only commercial, but political influence.

---

[1] Odessa, then known as " Hadji-Bey," was captured in 1788 during the Russo-Turkish War, and the treaty of Jassy (in 1791) secured to Russia the territory from the Bug to the Dniester.

SPRING-TIME AT WHALEN (ARCTIC OCEAN)
(X The Author)

Many a ragged, ringleted Hebrew has drifted here from Poland or Rumania, to blossom, within a few years, into a sleek, frock-coated financier, who has generally practised usury in addition to some other line of business. But the abolition of alcohol must have been a serious blow to Israelites of the lower class, who owned most of the bars and grog-shops.

A steep road leads from the landing-quay to the town, which owes its beauty and prosperity to the Duc de Richelieu, who was its Governor in 1803, and who was responsible for the French aspect of the principal streets, with their beds of flowers and rows of acacia trees, conveying an impression of gaiety and tidiness which partly justifies the alleged resemblance of this city to the capital of France. Odessa even now is ever growing, and new suburbs are rising up in all directions, with buildings built of bright-coloured stone obtained from adjacent quarries, which is, however, so friable that blocks of granite had to be imported from Italy for the principal thoroughfares, which are beautifully paved. And variety lends a certain charm to both the public and private dwellings, which bear traces, not only of Russian, but also French and Italian architecture.

This is in every way an expensive place, and the shops in the Rue de Richelieu (some of which are owned by Frenchmen) afford every opportunity for extravagance, while there is here no " Gostimoi Dvor " to lure purchasers away with its cheaper prices. But the " pearl of the Black Sea " has one great disadvantage in the shape of a variable climate, and it is never safe to go out at any season of the year without an overcoat, owing to sudden changes of temperature. I have landed here, in early autumn, when a bitter east wind compelled people in the streets to wear furs and sheepskins, only to discard them on the following day, which was sultry and oppressive. And this sort of thing goes on throughout the year, while as a rule, the weather in summer is only too often dull and overcast.

Odessa has flat and uninteresting surroundings, and its " datcha " life in summer is a poor imitation of those around Kiéff and Moscow. Shrubs and flowers are only raised with difficulty in the adjacent country,

P

although the town has plenty of water, and public and private gardens abound and flourish. Some of the former had open-air theatres and restaurants, but it is generally too cold, even in September, to sit out of doors late at night. · But climate excepted, there are worse places than this to spend a week in, provided a stranger is provided with letters of introduction. For hospitality is always freely extended here, especially to the English traveller, who will therefore do well to avoid the hotels, nearly all of which are inordinately expensive.

CHAPTER XIX

THE CAUCASUS (1)

SOME years ago I travelled by land to India from Russia,[1] and should probably never have visited the Caucasus had it not been situated on my line of route from Petrograd to Bombay. Time was, then, of importance, and it was therefore only on a later occasion that I was able to wander, at my ease, through that region of snowy peaks, dense forests and blue lakes, which little more than half a century ago was infested by brigands and cut-throats, but which is now regarded as a Russian Switzerland, and visited, in summer, by a yearly increasing number of tourists.

Caucasia, which is bisected by the Caucasus, a continuous chain of mountains extending from the Black Sea to the Caspian, has now a population of about six millions, but Russia was compelled to fight incessantly for nearly two hundred years before its numerous and warlike tribes were finally brought into subjection. The indigenous races are Caucasian and Mongolian, but there are now many Russians, exclusive of Armenians, Circassians, Georgians, Lesghians, Persians, Tartars, Turkomans, Kurds, Greeks and Jews, all these tribes retaining, although they are Russian subjects, their own religion and customs. Over a hundred different languages and dialects are spoken throughout the province, and even Tiflis, the capital, is a fair imitation of the Tower of Babel.

This territory, which is about the size of France, may be roughly divided into two parts which are divided by the Caucasus range, over 300 miles in length : Circassia and Daghestán on the northern, and

---

[1] Via Persia and Baluchistan. See *A Ride to India*, by the author. Messrs. Chapman & Hall, London.

Georgia and Mingrelia on the southern side—these four provinces being again subdivided into smaller states or districts. It is essentially an alpine country, although most of its ranges rise to no great height, and are of easy gradients, culminating in vast plateaux four or five thousand feet above sea level. On the other hand, isolated peaks like the Kasbek, Elburz and one or two others, attain a height of 15,000 feet and the regions of eternal snow; indeed, the highest summits of the Caucasus exceed in positive elevation the most lofty of the Alps, and its glaciers excel those of Switzerland in size and grandeur. Mount Elburz, for instance, is over 18,000 feet high and is visible for a distance of 200 miles, while Mount Kasbek, although much lower, is considerably higher than Mont Blanc. The valleys and plains possess magnificent pastures, with luxuriant wild flowers, and there are dense and as yet unexplored forests of valuable timber. This is, indeed, one of Russia's most important possessions, with boundless natural resources which, when properly exploited, will render it one of the richest countries in the world.

Vladikavkaz [1] is a picturesque little place, not unlike some large Swiss village, with its gabled houses, rich meadows and clear, rushing streams. It is a few miles north of the Caucasus range; and there are two ways of reaching Tiflis, the capital—one by rail, a circuitous journey via Petrovsk and Baku, and the other by driving over the Dariel Pass,[2] for the military protection of which Vladikavkaz was originally founded. It is well, however, to note that in late autumn and early spring the Dariel is often blocked by avalanches, and communication is sometimes interrupted for days.

The natives around Vladikavkaz, although once rebellious, are now peaceful and law-abiding people, called the Ossetes,[3] many of whom have become Christians, and are even employed in the Russian Government service. Some have, however, remained pagans, and the burial of the latter is attended with strange and

[1] Meaning literally, "Ruler of the Caucasus."
[2] "Daryol" is a Turkish word signifying "a narrow path."
[3] Some say they are descendants of a party of Crusaders who came north in returning from the Holy Land and settled in the Caucasus.

rather repulsive rites, one of which is to cut off a widow's right ear and bury it with her husband in order that the latter may claim his wife in the next world. Their marriage customs are also quaint, a newly wedded couple being ostracized for some days after the ceremony, for even an authorized union is regarded as shameful for that space of time; while a girl, when she has reached her teens, is tightly sewn into a pair of stays, which are only removed, on the wedding night, by her husband. But these practices are gradually dying out under Russian rule and the influence of civilization.

There was a public motor-car service across the mountains, but the vehicle was so dirty and crowded that I hired a comfortable "tarantass," and set out from Vladikavkaz one bright May morning to travel to Tiflis by the highest carriage road in the world. The distance is about 170 miles, and the posting so well organized that the journey can be accomplished, if necessary, in a little over twenty-four hours. My friend Kellogg would, no doubt, have done it in less, but I preferred to take it easy and sleep a couple of nights on the road !

On leaving Vladikavkaz we soon reached the " Gate of the Caucasus," a gloomy corridor composed of slate and limestone rocks, so close together that there was barely room to skirt the waters of a foaming torrent. The summit of the Pass is over 8000 feet high, and the construction of a coach road here was certainly a marvellous feat of engineering. But it is only on reaching the Dariel Gorge, about twenty miles from Vladikavkaz, that the magnitude of the task is fully apparent, for at this point the road, although blasted and hewn, at a dizzy height, out of solid rock, is as broad and safe as Piccadilly. Upon entering the famous gorge we drove between towering walls of granite and porphyry, leaning forward from either side at such an angle that, here and there, they almost met overhead, blocking out the sky and sunshine. It was almost a relief to emerge from this dark and chilly defile even into a region of valleys and slopes of shale, strewn with huge granite boulders and stones which, roughly heaped together, formed, at intervals, a road-mender's shanty, where the workmen employed are sometimes imprisoned, in winter, for days together by gale and avalanche. Nothing that I have seen in the Swiss and Italian Alps can compare with this scenery, which was almost appalling in its solitude and grandeur.

The only signs of life I saw that day were a score of camels which, with tinkling bells, padded softly past the carriage, while shortly afterwards there appeared, far down in the valley, a modern fort, with towers, loopholes, and Cossack sentries lounging outside a guard-house. This was Fort Dariel, which commands both entrances to the Caucasian Khyber, and which, in olden days, witnessed many a desperate struggle between the Ossetes and their Muscovite foes. And again above us, perched like an eagle on the edge of a cliff, was the ruined castle of Darghalan, 2000 years old, which was once inhabited by Darya, a Georgian Messalina famed for her beauty, who lured legions of lovers to her desolate fastness, only to have each one hurled, when tired of his embraces, into the swiftly-flowing river thousands of feet below.

About an hour's drive from here brought me to the little post-house of Kasbek, whence, being a fine day, there was a glorious view of the mountain of that name, with its snowy peak sparkling in the sunshine, and looking, in that rarefied atmosphere, yards instead of miles away. Here I procured a saddle-horse and rode to inspect a picturesque little church some distance away, where the Greek priest in charge informed me that the Kasbek is venerated as a sacred mountain, the cradle of Our Saviour having been brought there from the Holy Land and deposited in a certain cave, where it still remains. But the veracity of this statement was somewhat shaken when my informant proceeded to point due east to what looked like a white cloud on the horizon, and declare that it was Mount Elburz, although the latter, from this point, lies about due west !

The post-houses on this road were the best I have ever seen in Russia as regards decent food and comfortable accommodation, one even containing beds with sheets and a " buffet " for " zakouski." Kasbek post-house was, indeed, occasionally used as an hotel, for I met there an Englishman from Tiflis, who frequently made it his headquarters while stalking wild goat. And at dinner that night a portion of his bag convinced me that the animal in question is excellent eating!

Mount Kasbek was first ascended by Mr. Douglas Freshfield and two English companions in 1868, and the trail then broken by these adventurous pioneers has since been followed by many mountaineers, for the climb, except towards the summit, is comparatively easy, and guides may be procured at Tiflis or Vladikavkaz for the ascent. But Elburz is another matter, being more difficult and perilous, although Mr. Freshfield also succeeded in reaching the summit during the same year.

I passed the second night at the post-house of Mleti, where, as at every other post-house on this road, pretty specimens of crystal pyrites and various ores, found in the neighbourhood, were offered for sale. From Mleti the road gradually descends through a volcanic-looking wilderness without a sign of human habitation or trace of greenery, the only object we passed in this desolate region being a huge vulture, sitting, gorged and sullen, on a crag by the roadside. The drive now became rather tiresome, for the Dariel Pass is the only interesting spot between Vladikavkaz and Tiflis, although the former amply atones for subsequent monotony not only by its beauty, but as showing the triumph of man over the titanic forces of nature. Yet, notwithstanding the apparently perilous places over which we passed, there was nothing throughout the entire journey to inspire the most nervous person with fear or apprehension.[1]

At last we reached the plains, and vegetation consisting first of clumps of fir trees and then more extensive patches of pine forest, while the road passed through stretches of meadowland, with flocks and herds, tended by swarthy, scowling shepherds armed to the teeth, for sheep-stealing is still a favourite pastime in the rural districts. Some of the villages consisted of mere caves, hollowed out of hills by the roadside, and I learnt that sanguinary encounters often occur between the occu-

[1] Its construction cost about four millions sterling, and at least £30,000 a year are spent in keeping it in repair.

pants of these lonely hamlets, generally arising from disputes connected with the loss of cattle or misappropriation of land, while in some parts of Daghestán the " vendetta " is practised with Corsican tenacity and ruthlessness. While driving past these hovels we were often attacked by large, fierce dogs, which flew at, and even bit, the horses, while their owners looked on with amused unconcern.

Towards evening we rattled over the cobbled streets of Mtsket, now a commonplace market-town, but once the capital of Georgia, and remained here awhile to visit the quaint old church to which Christ's seamless robe is said to have been brought by a Jew from Golgotha.[1] Ancient chronicles aver that Mtsket is the oldest town in the world, but this is probably doubtful, although it was certainly the residence of the Georgian kings until A.D. 499, when the capital was removed to its present site. And here, oddly enough, it was colder than on the summit of the Dariel, for the Caucasian climate is varied and erratic, being largely influenced by snow-bearing mountains, winds, and the situation of the country between two seas. The conditions may almost be said to range from arctic cold north of the mountains, to sub-tropical warmth on the southern slopes.

Tiflis,[2] the capital of the Caucasus, is about midway between Batoum on the Black Sea and Baku on the Caspian, and is, commercially speaking, a favourite meeting-place of Western and Asiatic races. There is probably no other city in creation where European and Oriental life are so closely intermingled, or where both races, being united by mutual interests, live in such perfect peace and harmony. Nor is there any town in the world, that I know of, where the streets present such an array of fantastic costumes or where you can hear forty different languages and dialects spoken during the course of a short stroll. The town is, therefore, attractive by reason of its originality, but is situated in a sterile, sun-baked valley, formed by steep

---

[1] It is now in the Cathedral of the Assumption at Moscow.
[2] So called from the hot mineral springs which abound in the vicinity, and derived from the Russian word " teplo," warm.

hills, which in summer intercept every breeze and render the place unbearably hot and oppressive, although in winter they form a shelter which, combined with a dry, bracing climate, render this a favourite resort of invalids. Tiflis was built in this hollow, instead of on the lofty plateau above it, on account of hot mineral springs, which from time immemorial have been famed for their curative powers.

The river Kur, which falls into the Caspian, bisects the city, its precipitous banks displaying tier upon tier of old and picturesque Eastern buildings with gay façades, brightly-coloured roofs and carved wooden balconies, the whole forming a medley of incongruous architecture, where no two dwellings are alike, and where the rich man's palace is often elbowed by the squalid mud hovel. This is known as the Asiatic quarter.

The modern and European portion of Tiflis is in imposing contrast to the dirt and squalor of the latter, although costly goods and valuable art treasures from all parts of the East are stored in its bazaars, where days may be spent, profitably or otherwise, by the bargain-hunter. When last here I was entertained at the Governor-General's palace, from which radiate the principal streets, well paved and spacious, tree-lined avenues, one of which, the "Galavinsky Prospekt," would be considered a handsome thoroughfare in any European capital, while several iron bridges span the river, connecting Europe with Asia in the native quarter. Near the "Galavinsky" are the cathedral, law courts, opera and several excellent hotels, of which the Hôtel de Londres (kept by a Frenchman) is perhaps the most comfortable and by no means dear. The tram-cars here are better than those in Petrograd, and the public vehicles were almost as good as those in Bukarest, which used to be the best in Europe. The only drawback to Tiflis, so far as I could see, was a lack of pure water, but this deficiency has now, I believe, been remedied.

The Europeans here comprise Russians, Poles, Italians, French, Rumanians, Levantines, Serbians and (before the war) many Germans, of every class, who not only settled in the town, but swarmed into the villages on its outskirts, which have now been cleared of their unwelcome and unsavoury presence. And I also met many of my countrymen here who had been attracted by recent and important discoveries of oil in the Maikop district.

Society was chiefly commercial, although the Caucasian capital is, or was, like Malta, "a little military hot-house," and its streets were crowded with uniforms, many of which, worn by officers of crack cavalry or Cossack regiments, were unusually brilliant and becoming.

When I was last there, Tiflis had, as regards morals, a rather shady reputation, and this was, perhaps, partly due to the military element, and partly to the fact that the lax and cosmopolitan habits adopted by male members of the mercantile community were freely shared by their wives and daughters. Thus, I was invited by a Prince, (nearly every one here is a Prince !), to attend a ball which, although a society function, was towards its close more suggestive of a rowdy party in Montmartre than a decorous family entertainment. Yet my host, a grey-bearded, sad-looking Greek merchant, seemed quite unmoved by the *risqué* antics of his youthful wife and female guests, and even gravely joined in them himself ! The evening certainly opened with due propriety, and such refined and graceful measures as the valse, mazurka and "Lesginka" (a Lesghian dance), but it concluded, towards the small hours, with a "cancan," which recalled the wildest nights at the old "Moulin-Rouge ! "

I was also taken to a fashionable club called the "Krujok" (a kind of Murray's), where ladies were admitted at any time, even Georgian women in their pretty national dress, which contrasted quaintly with modern French and Italian "toilettes." And the native costume was generally more attractive than its wearer, for the beauty of Georgian and Circassian women has been greatly exaggerated. Most of them grow stout and look elderly before they are thirty, and even the youngest have a vacant, animal type of face, which to European eyes is almost revolting.

Ball-room "etiquette" here was rather puzzling at first, for you might not dance more than once during the evening with the same lady, whom, on concluding a short turn, you had to leave standing alone to be claimed by some one else, while you sought another partner. "Roulette" was played between the dances, sometimes for very high stakes, especially by wealthy Armenians. I must confess I have never been favourably impressed with this race, who appeared to me to have all the vices of Jews and none of their virtues, and who seemed to be cordially disliked by both Europeans and natives.

On other nights I went to the theatre, a pretty little house decorated in the Moorish style, where I attended, on the same occasion, a performance of *Hamlet* in Russian, and *Pagliacci* well rendered by Italians. The evenings were therefore never dull, the more so that Tiflis people appeared to commence the day after dark. Even business men seldom rose until eleven a.m., took a light meal and strolled down to the office until about two o'clock, when they returned home to dine. A *siesta* followed until four p.m., when work for another couple of hours left them free for the night's amusement, which, commencing with supper about nine p.m., did not generally terminate until three or four in the morning. This mode of life, however, only applies to winter and spring, for all who can afford it pass the summer months in the country, either in a "datcha" or at the seaside, for Tiflis is at this season a dusty and sweltering desert.

However immoral this city may be, there is no outward display of vice, which, however, undoubtedly exists on a scale only equalled in some Continental capitals. The mineral baths here, for instance, were largely patronized by wealthy clients, who paid prices that would certainly not have been charged for the simple treatment of rheumatic and other complaints. For a bathing establishment, run on scientific lines, does not generally provide its patrons with *cabinets particuliers* and champagne suppers, yet this was the case here, just as it used to be before the late Emperor's bogus moral crusade in Buda-Pest. Moreover, scandals have occasionally occurred in connection with the Tiflis establishment which have brought it under the notice of the authorities, especially when, some years ago, a young cavalry officer drew his revolver and shot a " droshky " driver for insulting two young and well-connected ladies whom the former was driving, at midnight, to the baths, from a ball at the Governor's palace.   The tragedy was, of course, hushed up, although not entirely, by reason of certain divorce proceedings which followed its occurrence.

A stranger may walk about the streets of Tiflis all night, unarmed and in perfect safety, so long as he keeps to the European quarter, which is beautifully lit by electricity, although certain streets and alleys on the Asiatic side are best avoided after sunset   Some parts of the country, notably those near the Turkish frontier, are still dangerous on account of highway robberies, but elsewhere you can travel quite as safely as in the remoter parts of Greece or Sicily.   I was never once molested, although I have ridden alone through some of the wildest and loneliest parts of Georgia.   Nor have I ever heard of any serious case of brigandage having occurred within the past decade throughout the Caucasus.

The latter has, of late years, increased in popularity, amongst Englishmen intent on sport or mountaineering, and I met in Tiflis a well-known Indian " Shikari " who had been there for two successive seasons for the purpose of shooting bear and ibex, numbers of which he had killed.   March, he told me, is the best time for chamois and wild boar, and pheasants, quail and wood-cock abound early in April and within easy reach of the capital, while leopards and tigers are obtainable, but only near the Persian frontier.   My informant added, however, that sport here is deteriorating, as few land-owners now preserve, and natives possessed of a gun-licence can shoot all the year round if they choose. Red-deer, for instance, which were formerly numerous only thirty miles from Tiflis, are now almost extinct. But there are plenty of wild-fowl on the shores of the Caspian, and, in the steppe country, good fun can be had coursing hares or stalking antelope, which latter, my friend told me, he had once hunted in the depth of winter, with some Tartars, by the following quaint method.   Each man was mounted, with a rifle slung over his back, and holding a greyhound balanced on his

WALRUS-HIDE HUT IN WHICH THE AUTHOR LIVED AT WHALEN (EARLY SPRING-TIME)

horse's withers. Having sighted and broken up a herd, each member of the party selected a single antelope, which he persistently followed, never pressing or losing sight of his quarry, perhaps for a whole day, until the latter, harassed and worn out by labouring with balled hoofs through deep snow-drifts, fell to the ground exhausted, and unable to move further. The Tartar then released his dog, which soon seized and despatched its prey.

The streams throughout this country abound in salmon, trout, and many other kinds of fish, which are seldom interfered with, for neither Russians nor natives ever throw a fly, and the latter, save those who live by the sea-shore, rarely use a net. Circassia is the best district for trout during the months of April, May and June, but it is well to add that a fisherman must come here provided with everything needful in the way of tackle, which, even in Tiflis, is not procurable.

CHAPTER XX

THE CAUCASUS (2)

YOU may leave the bright and busy *boulevards* of modern Tiflis, with their stately public and private buildings, luxurious hotels, attractive shops, and other signs of European civilization, and walk within a few minutes to the Asiatic Quarter—to realize that you are in another world, as essentially Eastern, in every respect, as the most secluded portions of Stamboul or Tehérán. The change is as complete as when one picture on a lantern-screen has been suddenly replaced by another.

There are here not one, but many, Bazaars, running in all directions under one rambling roof like burrows in a rabbit-warren. A guide is therefore needed to conduct you through this intricate maze, which is entered from a broad but squalid thoroughfare, running at right-angles to the River Kur. From here I walked, for nearly an hour, through a succession of dark and crowded streets and alleys before emerging again into the pure air and sunshine, which were a pleasant contrast to the stifling atmosphere and subtle odours of that human bee-hive. Yet every inch of the way was interesting, if only by reason of the strange and varied races the place contained. For here were baggy-breeched Greeks, red-fezzed, frock-coated Turks, sombrely clad Persians, and even turbaned merchants from Bokhára mingling with Armenians, Georgians, Tartars and fierce-looking " Tcherkess," bristling with daggers and silver cartridge-belts. Here an Arab water-seller, in snowy white, noisily jungled his cymbals, while next him a squatting, green-robed pilgrim from Mecca chanted nasal verses from the " Korán " and held out a skinny hand for alms, also aggressively demanded by relays of blind, and crippled beggars. There were few

222

women about, but occasionally a Turkish lady, in voluminous black gown and white " yashmak," would hurry modestly by; while her brightly clad Greek and Georgian sisters, bedizened with jewellery and rouged to the eyes, lingered on their errands, and seemed to invite the attention of casual admirers. But they, like every one else, were often scattered in all directions when a string of camels, staggering under bales of merchandise, parted, with stolid unconcern, this seething mass of humanity.

A considerable portion of the Tiflis bazaar was occupied by vendors of Manchester goods, cheap furniture, iron-ware, and the miscellaneous collection of utter rubbish formerly " made in Germany," and commonplace stores were scattered about promiscuously, special streets only being assigned to each native trade, product or manu-facture. Even the cookshops and bakers had their own street, where one could watch the frizzling of savoury " kabobs," and the baking of " tchurkebi," a pale sodden-looking pancake much relished by Armenians. Adjoining this was a passage entirely occupied by hatters, and stored with all kinds of head-wear from the local " papak," of black or grey lambskin, to the tower-ing Persian head-dress, shaped like the mouthpiece of a clarionet. And between these were wine-shops, dis-pensing red and white " Kaketi," a Caucasian vintage which is purchased in a buffalo or sheep skin according to the quantity needed. But the Caucasus wines are very inferior to those of the Crimea, for, in addition to being rough and heady, they often retain a faint but unpleasant flavour of the leather in which they have been kept. " Kaketi " is also sold in bottles for export, but will probably never be as popular in Russia as the vintages of Aloushta and the southern coast.

I found traders of every nationality here fairly honest and less rapacious than many I have known in the East, and it is therefore sometimes possible to bargain success-fully, always assuming that the purchaser is more or less of an expert in the article he needs—whether it be carpets and embroideries, or antique jewellery and silver. And hours may be spent (to say nothing of a considerable amount of money) amongst the armourers' stalls. Here I saw every sort of weapon, not only for sale, but in course of construction, and workmen busily polishing sword and dagger-hilts in silver, ivory or bone, fitting scabbards to scimitars, and stocks to clumsy barrels of the old blunderbuss type, for there was not a modern gun or rifle in the place. But there were gold-hilted poniards from Daghestán, Lesghian pistols encrusted with uncut gems, and murderous-looking knives from Mingrelia, to say nothing of ancient coats of mail and shields, one of which latter, beautifully enamelled in delicate colours, had come all the way from Chinese Tartary. And there were yet greater treasures kept under lock and key and only extracted from layers of cotton wool for the benefit of wealthy customers; one, an exquisite dagger, with a hilt of fossilized ivory, and verses of the " Korán," in pure gold sunk into its blade of blue-steel, which bore the rippled watermark of Damascus. It was said to be 400 years old, and was valued at £85.

A loftier, lighter gallery than any other was that of the jewellers and silversmiths in their quaint little stalls with glass fronts—dingy little dens whose more valuable contents are never exposed (for obvious reasons) to the public gaze, but kept in a small inner room. I only entered one of the latter, where the brilliant display of diamonds and rubies, emeralds and pearls would have staggered Monsieur Cartier of the Rue de la Paix, and where I bought an unset turquoise for which I have since been offered twice the price I paid for it. Outside every shop was a large wooden tray littered with a miscellaneous collection, varying from modern European rubbish suggestive of the pawnshop, to really old Russian and Oriental chains, brooches, cigarette cases, rings, and other articles of use or adornment in gold and silver. And here a " connoisseur," able to sift the grain from the chaff, might make many a lucrative bargain, for the dealers, although cunning enough with regard to the sale of precious stones, often underestimate the value of antique and artistic workmanship.

The fur-shops were disappointing, the more so that I had been informed that sable, sea-otter, blue-fox, and other valuable skins were to be cheaply purchased, whereas I found only bear, lynx, wolf, and astrakhan of an inferior quality, yet their prices were higher than those of Petrograd or Moscow. Only the lower orders in Russia wear astrakhan, and even this was unusually expensive. I purchased, however, a garment peculiar to the country, which is called a "bourka," a long, sleeveless mantle of coarse black or grey felt, which is fastened round the neck to fall to the feet, and which I have since found invaluable when riding in cold, wet weather. For the "bourka" is waterproof as well as very warm, and protects not only the rider but his horse's quarters. It has therefore since been my inseparable companion when travelling in the wilds.

You can get almost any kind of carpet here, from those of Bokhára, as fine as silk, with their rich crimson, brown, and ivory tints, to rugs from Broussa and Beyrout of less delicate texture and cruder colouring. The most valuable Persian carpets seldom leave Tehérán, except for London or Paris, where, being the best and costliest in the world, they fetch enormous prices. I once saw a small green prayer-rug in the Persian capital which was over five centuries old, and for which an American traveller had paid £1000.

A business engagement took me to Baku, for this is a town no one in their senses would ever visit unless compelled. For this district, although so wealthy, is the flattest and dreariest in the Caucasus, and soon after leaving the capital we entered a sandy, barren waste, with only an occasional hovel, pool of stagnant water, or flock of wild-fowl to break the monotony; while on the day I left Tiflis, the dull, grey heavens, crossed by dense black clouds, were well in keeping with the dismal landscape. The train crawled like a tortoise across the lonely plain, and towards evening every station, with its air of utter stagnation, one gold-laced official, and group of Tartar porters shivering in the rain, was more desolate and depressing than the last. The journey had seemed one of days more than hours, before a thin streak of silver, illumined by a fitful gleam of sunshine, appeared on the horizon between that drab, arid desert and lowering sky. This was the Caspian Sea, and a few minutes later we steamed into a new and imposing

Q

railway station which, like everything else here, savoured of commercial enterprise and boundless wealth.

Baku is rather suggestive of some prosperous American mining city dumped down in the neighbourhood of Port Said, for this Caspian port is white, new, and surrounded by sand and sea, while the oil-steeped soil, save in the shape of some stunted, dusty-looking trees and shrubs artificially scattered about the town, precludes all vegetation. But there was a business-like air about the crowded streets and handsome quay, where steamers were continually leaving or arriving from Russian or Persian ports, many being luxurious vessels with all the comforts of a modern liner. The hotels are good, electric light blazes everywhere at night, and there is also every modern convenience in the shape of telephones, tram-cars and the like. This is residential or what is known as " White Baku," while away across the salt-marshes and sand dunes is " Black Baku," so called because night and day its oil refineries never cease to belch forth their noxious fumes. Here the atmosphere must indeed be unbearable, for, even miles away, in White Baku, you are pursued wherever you go by the pungent smell of naphtha, which clings even to the sheets on your bed, and serviette at meal-times. The sea itself had, on calm days, a greasy appearance, and an English resident here informed me that when on one occasion he bathed off the beach, his skin absorbed so much oil that for days after he was avoided by his friends! The tainted air is, however, presumably not unhealthy, for the inhabitants seemed to thrive on it!

This permeating odour is scarcely to be wondered at, for you cannot walk a couple of miles here in any direction without encountering one of the lofty timber erections which are called " fountains," and from which naphtha sometimes spouts in such quantities and with such force that it soars 200 feet into the air, destroying both the well and wooden structure designed for its control; a serious matter, for the sinking of the latter sometimes costs £5000 or £6000. And numerous wells are bored, sometimes to a depth of over 1000 feet, without result; although, on the other hand, a lucky find may occur within a few feet of the surface, from which the precious liquid will gush freely of itself without the labour or expense of pumping. The "Russian Petroleum Company" once tapped such a "fountain" which in two months yielded 40,000,000 poods of oil.[1]

There seemed to be plenty of gaiety in Baku, in the shape of clubs, theatres and dancing-halls, also less reputable nocturnal establishments frequented by the fair sex for the exploitation of those who had literally "struck oil," fortunes here being as rapidly and easily amassed as they are sometimes lost, for speculation in this product is almost as much of a gamble as prospecting for gold. Thus I met one or two young Englishmen employed in business houses who had made considerable sums of money by investing their spare cash in promising oil concerns, but they admitted that, even when "in the know," it was all a question of luck.[2] This is partly proved by the fact that, when I was last in Baku, everybody was rushing to the "Maikop" district, which, it was then predicted, would entirely eclipse the former as a prolific oil centre, although this prophecy has never been fulfilled.

But, after all, this matters little in the Caucasus, where petroleum is constantly bubbling up in the most unexpected places, and where districts as yet unexplored may, and probably will, yield greater quantities of this essential commodity than any of the oil-fields now in operation. Moreover, petroleum is only one of the valuable natural resources of this part of Russia, which provides two-thirds of the whole country's output of manganese, of which, by the way, as the latter is used for steel, the Germans purchased enormous quantities before the war.[3] And not only manganese, but nearly every other ore is found here : gold, silver, lead, copper, zinc, iron, and mercury, besides sulphur, graphite, marble, and asbestos; all of which, although practically untouched, have been proved by scientists and engineers to exist in large quantities. Yet, as a matter of fact,

[1] A "pood" is thirty-six English pounds.
[2] The total output for the Baku district in 1899 was 2,167,801,130 gallons.
[3] The Russian output of manganese in 1913 was 1,725,000 metric tons, to which the Caucasus contributed 970,000.

*

only oil, manganese, and coal have, up till now, been
seriously and profitably worked. And one great aid
to the future development of this incalculable wealth
is the fact that there is no point throughout the Caucasus
situated more than 120 miles from either the Black or
Caspian Seas, the former of which has excellent harbours
at Novorossisk, Poti and Batoum, and the latter, ports
at Baku and Derbent.

And not only mineral wealth is here lying idle, for,
although Caucasia possesses enormous tracts of country
thickly covered with valuable trees, Baku is still supplied
with timber from the Baltic coast, while Batoum imports
it from Italy, or used to do so before the war. But the
latter has now devastated the Baltic provinces, where
numberless forests have been destroyed; and when,
therefore, peace has been declared, British capital might
well be invested in less profitable ventures than the
exploitation, (for local use), of Caucasian timber.

It is satisfactory to note that although the Caucasus
is still, from a mining point of view, in its infancy, the
Kuban district, in the north-west, is already a prosperous
agricultural centre. The Russians here cultivate wheat,
rye, barley and oats, the native tribes maize and millet,
and their abundance has resulted in the establishment
of numerous flour-mills, some of which have a turnover
of 1,000,000 roubles. The cultivation of sunflower
seed has also been tried here in connection with the
extraction of oil, and with such good results that in 1915
over 15,000,000 poods of this seed were collected
and utilized by oil-producing works, the refuse being
made into briquettes and sold as fuel. Tobacco is
also grown in the Kuban district; and of recent years
special attention has been turned to the growing of
vegetables, and a special plant erected for their preservation for export. The Kuban is well provided with out-
lets to the sea, having the ports of Novorossisk and
Anapa in the west, and Rostov on the north, which
latter is the most important, for it is connected by rail
with Central Russia. The Terek district, (which comprises Vladikavkaz), is, next to the Kuban, agriculturally
the most productive, and in 1912 furnished 6,000,000
quarters of corn and about 2,000,000 poods of maize,

which latter forms not only the staple food of the population, but also provides material for the production of spirit and starch.[1]

Since I commenced to write this book, now nearly six months ago, stupendous changes have taken place in Russia, where, as the reader may have gleaned, I have formed friends and acquaintances in nearly every walk of life, from distinguished Government officials, down to the humblest moujik. It is always easy to say, "*I told you so,*" after the occurrence of any important and unforeseen event, but I may here state, with all due modesty, that I had been informed, through certain reliable channels in Petrograd, that the recent *coup d'état* was in active preparation fully a month before it took place. It was therefore entertaining, while awaiting the cataclysm, to hear the London arm-chair critics (whose presence and advice are apparently so urgently needed at the front) sapiently declare that one result of this titanic conflict would be to establish the Romanoff dynasty on an infinitely firmer basis than it had ever known before the war! For reasons above stated, therefore, the Emperor's abdication caused me no surprise, although it naturally came as a shock to one who has now for some years been indirectly associated with the empire under the old autocratic *régime*. Moreover, I have reason to be grateful to the late Imperial Government for many favours, notably for the selection, by its penal authorities, of my humble self (at a comparatively early age) to examine, and report upon, the Siberian exile system; a task which I performed to the best of my ability, notwithstanding the vague, but unpleasant, insinuations which my favourable verdict on Russian prison treatment elicited from a portion of the British Press. Again, more recently, the success of my expedition from France to America by land was chiefly due to the friendly assistance of the ex-Premier, M. Trépoff, who (as Minister of Communications) provided me with the numberless horses, reindeer, and dogs without which I could never have accomplished the Asiatic portion of that arduous journey. And last, but

[1] I am indebted to the "Russo-British Society" for these agricultural statistics.

not least, his late Majesty personally accepted a copy of my work *Siberia as It is*, and graciously expressed his cordial approval thereof, on my third return to Petrograd from his then much-traduced land of exile.

I do not, however, for a moment underrate the inestimable benefits which every class, (but one), in Russia is now likely to enjoy, under the newly established democratic Government.   Yet, at the same time, I am convinced that had it not been for the ex-Tsar's lamentable lack of firmness, and inability to control a neurotic wife of pronounced German sympathies, he would have remained the idol of his people until the day of his death.   But fate has willed it otherwise, and perhaps, all things considered, fate has acted for the best.   For indomitable will is an essential quality in the ruler of any great empire, and there can unfortunately be little doubt that the Grand Duke Nicholas, in his famous letter of protest to the Emperor, summed up the latter's character with fatal accuracy.

" Your first impulse and decision," he wrote, " are always remarkably true and to the point, but as soon as other influences supervene, you begin to waver, and your ultimate conclusions are not the same.   If you could remove the persistent interference of dark forces in all matters, the regeneration of Russia would instantly be advanced and you would regain the confidence of your subjects."

But this decisive mode of action, although it would undoubtedly have been adopted, at the first sign of treachery, by his illustrious namesake and predecessor, was beyond the power of Nicholas II.

Yet no throne was ever graced by a monarch more universally beloved or one more solicitous of the happiness and welfare of his subjects.   " There is no one to aid and protect me ! " was a remark once made to the writer by an unjustly convicted Siberian exile; " for God is in his Heaven, and my ' Little Father ' is far away ! "

Nevertheless whatever may be the ultimate effect of this happily bloodless revolution, Russia has, at any rate, been delivered of the malignant cancer which was eating its way into her very heart in the shape of Germany's growing influence and power. I have had many opportunities, during my long connection with the country, of observing the Kaiser's methods of " peaceful penetration," which have at length aroused the pent-up rage and resentment of a long-suffering people, and called forth their summary vengeance not only upon the accursed Hun, but his even more perfidious Russian colleagues. And I have often wondered that this has not occurred before. For it was pitiable, during recent years, to witness this great empire helplessly writhing in the tentacles of the unclean octopus which cajoled and fooled the Court, corrupted the army and navy, had its agents in the Duma, dominated nearly every branch of trade and commerce, and even, by dint of usury, bribery, and other nefarious devices, sought to undermine the patriotism of the staunch and loyal moujik. I have met these miserable German parasites everywhere, managing palatial banks in Petrograd, or running squalid grog-shops in the remotest parts of Siberia, and marvelled at the tolerance and even kindness displayed, in both cases, by generous and warm-hearted Russians towards these crafty spies and emissaries, deputed to encompass the downfall and destruction of the people whose friendship and hospitality they enjoyed. And no one was more startled and amazed than these contemptible creatures when the storm broke, like a crash of thunder from a summer sky, and Teutonic intrigue and oppression became a nightmare of the past.

May it never be forgotten that although his pro-German consort has been the guiding spirit of the " dark forces " alluded to by the Grand Duke Nicholas, and the prime mover in the despicable conspiracy which would have crippled the Russian Army and concluded a shameful peace, the Tsar has always endeavoured to fulfil his sacred duties towards his people, and his pledged word to the Allies. Now the " dark forces " have been scattered to the four winds, and Holy Russia, ever true to her glorious traditions and faithful to her friends, stands forth, once more free and unfettered, to accomplish her great destiny.

The change from a " paternal " to a " democratic "

Government is no doubt a drastic one, yet if the " zemst-vos " (or rural councils) have already shown that even the moujiks are capable of ruling themselves, the more educated middle classes may surely be trusted with a voice in the government of the country. Russia has been called " an overgrown baby," probably because her people have always been treated as children; whom, however, the war has inspired with a greater sense of responsibility, and a more matured and experienced outlook on life. Wider political and international knowledge, unrestricted education, the liberty of the Press, and absolute freedom of the subject, are republican reforms which must, in due time, produce beneficial results amongst the lower classes, especially in the agricultural and industrial world. Moreover, the im-pending doom of Germany will serve as an imperishable warning that the welfare of a nation lies rather in peaceful and profitable relations with neighbouring states than in a policy of military power, and the lust of war and conquest.

And whatever may happen, in the future, in other countries, the Russian people are now firmly resolved that neither Germans nor their adherents, of whatever nationality, shall again dwell in their midst. Moreover, it is to be hoped that their beloved country's narrow escape from the deadly peril by which she was recently menaced may impel our Russian Allies to enter the approaching struggle for final and decisive victory with even greater zest and gallantry than before the day of their deliverance.

And so, with this fervent wish, I close these random notes and recollections of European Russia and Siberia, wherein, if I have on occasion been compelled to undergo the sufferings inseparable from Arctic travel, I have also, in their less remote regions, formed the closest friendships, and passed some of the happiest years of my life.

THE END

Printed in Great Britain by Richard Clay & Sons, Limited,
Brunswick St., Stamford St., S.E., and Bungay, Suffolk.

Lightning Source UK Ltd.
Milton Keynes UK
UKOW02f2218070114

224182UK00007B/468/P